# WISE UTILIZATION OF TROPICAL RAIN FOREST LANDS



TROPENBOS

MAB

TROPENBOS SCIENTIFIC SERIES 1

# WISE UTILIZATION OF TROPICAL RAIN FOREST LANDS

edited by C. F. van Beusekom, C. P. van Goor, P. Schmidt

THE TROPENBOS PROGRAMME
EDE, 1987

This book contains the full proceedings of the Netherlands MAB-UNESCO Symposium 'Tropisch regenwoud: verantwoord gebruik?' held from 10 - 12 December 1984 in Amsterdam, the Netherlands, and is published as Number 1 in the **Tropenbos** Scientific Series.

The publication forms part of the Dutch contribution to the MAB-Programme and is financially supported by UNESCO Paris, UNESCO the Netherlands, and the **Tropenbos** Programme.

This document contains the opinions of the authors and may not necessarily represent the official attitude of the **Tropenbos** Programme or of MAB-UNESCO.

CIP-data Koninklijke Bibliotheek, Den Haag

Wise

Wise utilization of tropical rain forest lands/eds. C. F. van Beusekom, C. P. van Goor, P. Schmidt. - Ede: Tropenbos. - Ill. - (Tropenbos Scientific Series; 1)
ISBN 90-5113-002-3
SISO 639.2 UDC [630*1 + (=/*4] (213.5)
Subject headings: tropical rain forests; environmental management

Cover design: Voorthuis & Mallander, Amsterdam

Photograph cover: P. J. M. Maas



Print: De Boer-Cuperus/Utrecht

# Foreword

Historically, the high population density and small land base characteristic of The Netherlands have demanded the development of judicious, and in many cases multi-purpose, land management. In developing environmentally sound land-use systems, we have learned that the natural landscape cannot be maintained without the whole-hearted support and participation of the local populations. Today analogous conditions of high population pressure in many of the tropical developing countries continue to threaten that landscape, especially the tropical moist forests, with degradation and destruction. The Netherlands' experience in developing intensive, people-oriented land-use systems plus its long tradition in silvicultural and biological research in tropical forestry have provided this study on the management of moist tropical forests as a contribution to international co-operation.

Such co-operation serves one of the main goals of the UNESCO Programme on Man and the Biosphere (MAB), to wit the international exchange of information and knowledge, especially with regard to socially acceptable and environmentally sound management of natural resources. Throughout the tropical region there are thousands of individuals with responsibilities for land-use planning and management who earnestly desire to use the best techniques available in the management of tropical forest lands. Accordingly, the decision was made to prepare a text focussing on the primary principles of tropical forest management. To provide instructive examples of the theoretical points developed in the text, a number of case studies from various geographical areas have been included. Subsequently, a seminar was held in which a variety of experts corrected and amended the original draft. The objective of the authors and the editorial committee was to develop as far as possible a document with broad relevance throughout the tropics despite the wide range of ecological, demographical, economic and political conditions existing in these regions.

It is appropriate that this document be produced within the **Tropenbos** Scientific Series as the ideas expressed herein have formed an essential part of the philosophical basis upon which the **Tropenbos** Programme is developing. Moreover, one of the main goals of the **Tropenbos** Programme is also to promote and assist in the exchange and dissemination of information, which could contribute to the improved conservation and management of tropical moist forest resources.

The MAB/SCOPE Committee of The Netherlands would like to express its thanks to the authors and their assistants for the preparation of the various chapters and case studies and to the editing committee for its efforts in transforming these contributions into an integrated whole. We are also grateful to UNESCO headquarters in Paris, to the UNESCO Committee of The Netherlands, to the Ministry of Education and Science of The Netherlands, to the World Wild Life Fund, The Netherlands and to the **Tropenbos** Programme for substantial moral and financial support. We hope that this study will prove to be not only helpful but instrumental in making many tropical moist forest regions flourish once again.

G.J. Vervelde — 20th December 1986
President
MAB/SCOPE Committee - The Netherlands

# Contents

# I. General contributions

# Introduction

by C.F. van Beusekom

Tropical rain forests (Fig. 1) are the world's richest ecosystems and are a source of sustenance for millions of people. Destruction and devastation of these forests is growing to alarming proportions due to intense pressure by populations seeking food, energy, wood, shelter and economic reward. This large-scale deforestation is not only of local or national, but even of world-wide detriment, and is gradually being recognized as one of the world's main problems. The direct and indirect effects of this process have far-reaching socio-economic, environmental and ecological consequences, such as:

- serious reduction of the availability of wood and of a wide variety of other forest products;
- elimination of unique habitats and of plant and animal species;
- 'desertification' of deforested land;
- disruption of the water regime of watershed areas, resulting in, among other things, erosion, flooding and siltation;
- possible changes in local and regional climate;
- possible changes of climate on a global scale.

Of course these consequences, though harmful to mankind as a whole, most directly affect the national interests of the tropical countries concerned. For these countries deforestation leads to a loss of vital natural resources, not only as revenue source for national economies, but also as primary living habitats for vast populations. Gradually the secondary ecological and economic problems associated with forest losses will affect national economies and social well-being so seriously, that the need for remedial actions will be compelling. In some countries this stage has, in fact, been reached.

The problem must be considered even more seriously since regeneration of devastated tropical forest land is not an easy task, at best only to be achieved at a low level, and even then at high cost and immense efforts. If destruction of tropical rain forest due to non-sustainable use would serve any sensible purpose, it would still be a serious problem but less shameful for the human race. However, apart from some short-term profits, it does not serve such purpose. Tropical forest destruction is the more to be deplored since there is good evidence that such

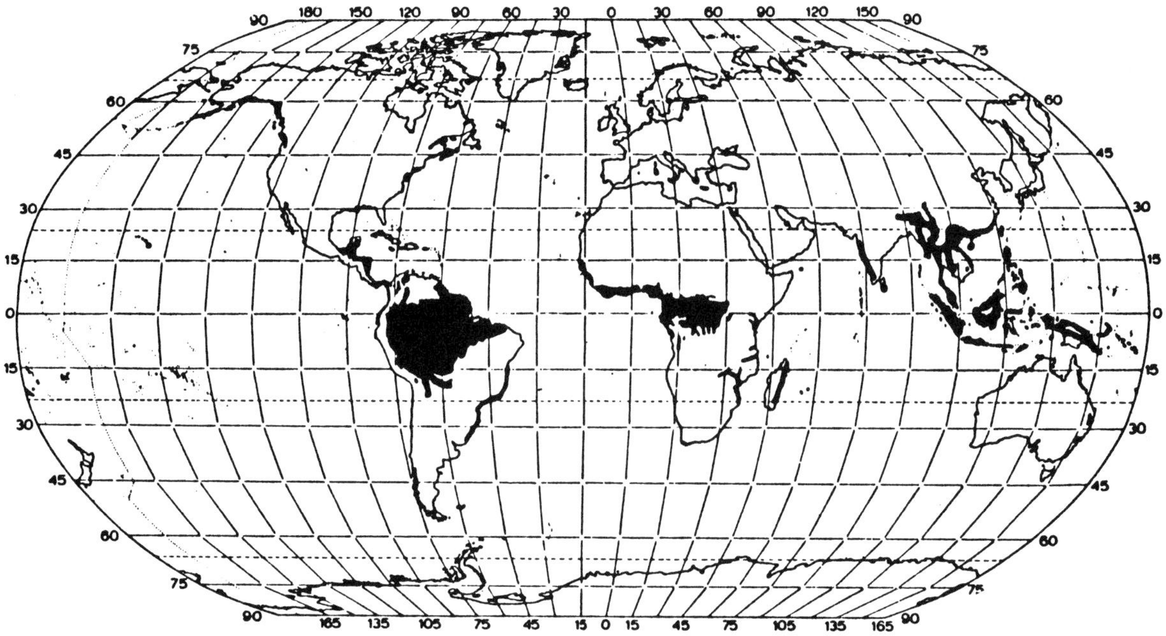


Fig. 1 Distribution of tropical rain forests (source: Golley, F.B., ed. (1983). *Ecosystems of the World* XIVA, Tropical rain forest ecosystems: structure and function. Amsterdam: Elsevier).

forest, under proper management, could be a permanent, renewable natural resource, with various great benefits for mankind. Such wise, i.e. sustainable utilization and conservation of tropical rain forests is profitable from a social, an economic as well as an ecological point of view, first of all for the tropical countries themselves, but also for mankind as a whole.

In those countries where much forest already has been destroyed, wise utilization of still existing forests will not be sufficient. In such cases there simply may not be enough forest left to meet present and future needs for fuel and timber, hence the pressure on what remains of the forests can only be relieved by offering a substitute supply. Here a wise use of remaining forests cannot be achieved if not complemented by rehabilitation of devastated forest land by means of reafforestation and by the establishment of agro-forestry plantations. It is encouraging to note an increasing awareness of the necessity of such a combined strategy in a growing number of tropical countries.

In some tropical forest development projects this two-track approach has in fact been adopted. Nevertheless it must be admitted that examples of successful projects are as yet scarce, if not wanting almost completely.

What are the causes of such overwhelming failure of mankind in this particular field? Too often it appears that failure of tropical forest projects has fundamental social, economic and political backgrounds, e.g.:

- weak financial and economic positions of many tropical countries;
- structural subordination of rural to urban interests;
- structural subordination of long-term to short-term interests;
- weak governmental infrastructure and lack of institutions;
- social and/or political instability;
- high population pressure.

It is clear that under such major constraints proper management of tropical forests can hardly be achieved. They certainly go beyond the reach of scientific and technical experts.

On the other hand, mere technical shortcomings causing failure of tropical forest projects can also be recognized, such as:

- inadequate analysis of socio-cultural and socio-economic conditions, on different levels, especially on the local one;
- inadequate knowledge of tropical forest ecosystems and their sustainability, as well as insufficient practical experience with sustainable use techniques in such ecosystems.

Moreover, many failures are probably due to communication gaps. This is not a minor aspect, since tropical rain forest development programmes are essentially multidisciplinary and thus 'stand or fall' with good co-ordination and co-operation, also communication, between the governmental, executive and scientific sectors. Not only does this sectoral triangle itself often not operate as smoothly as it should do, but also within sectors, there may be insufficient communication and co-operation; single government departments, and even scientific specialists often act quite in isolation. Project failure resulting from technical or communicative shortcomings can, unlike the more fundamental causes, in principle be avoided on the technical expert level, however, only so far as these experts are prepared to listen to and to learn from and to work with each other.

In the present book a basic approach is outlined and recommended for management of tropical rain forest land, which is essentially simple, but poorly observed or even neglected in most current tropical rain forest projects. Most of the minor constraints and perhaps even some of the major constraints could be solved when this approach is followed.

In the first place it must be realized that tropical rain forest is different from other kinds of forest. Therefore, also the problems of tropical rain forest are different, due to both its specific ecology and, equally important, to general and specific conditions in tropical human societies. Any tropical rain forest management programme that does not take these specific characteristics and conditions into account, will certainly not succeed in attaining long-term sustainable use, and probably not succeed at all.

Consequently, every management programme for tropical rain forest must be based on:

- proper analysis of socio-economic and socio-cultural needs and requirements on different levels, but especially on the local level. This is the *demand* side;
- proper knowledge of tropical rain forest ecosystems and their suitability and sustainability for relevant use. This is the *supply* side of the matter.

Demand and supply must be combined into a realistic concept for lasting, sustainable use of the forest. Land-use planning should be based on such a concept.

Successful implementation of such a forest-use concept cannot be achieved without:

- adequate legal and financial instruments;
- proper management by governmental and non-governmental institutions;
- education, training and research.

Fulfilment of these conditions does not yet guarantee positive results. As noted before, in many countries fundamental social, economic or political constraints occur, which may inhibit any successful approach towards the establishment of good forest management. On the other hand, there are other tropical countries where conditions seem to be more favourable. Anyhow, every successful tropical rain forest project is a gain, compared to the present situation.

Fortunately there is a fast-growing awareness in both tropical and non-tropical countries that adequate action is now very urgent. Several valuable initiatives (see Otto, this volume) have been taken the last few years, among others the Tropical Forestry Action Plan. The present contribution is an attempt to link up with these initiatives. The MAB-UNESCO Committee of The Netherlands considered it worthwile to bring together a wide variety of professional knowledge concerning tropical countries and tropical rain forests in order to elaborate the above general approach for tropical rain forest land-use planning.

This was effectuated during a MAB-UNESCO meeting held in Amsterdam, December 1984, assembling expert representatives of forestry, ecology, economics, sociology, commerce and industry, government and politics. The results of this multi-disciplinary seminar is found in the present book. It is composed of:
I General contributions
II Case studies.

The General contributions deal with the following themes: the *demand* aspect is treated in theme 1 'The need for tropical rain forests and their products' (Luning) and theme 2 'Land use in tropical rain forest areas' (Boerboom and Jonkers). The *supply* aspect is dealt with in theme 3 'Tropical forest: the ecosystems' (Oldeman) and in theme 4 'Spatial variability of tropical rain forests and forest lands' (Van IJssel and Sombroek). In theme 5 'Suitability of tropical forests or relevant use' (Van Goor) the outline of a land-use planning system for tropical rain forest is given, based on analysis of demand and supply as well as an analysis of legal and financial instruments, organizing and management capacity, available and required. Theme 6 'Forestry and agriculture: an alliance for survival' (Otto) presents a survey of various constraints resulting from political, social and economic structures as well as from insufficiently developed organization and information level in tropical countries. Furthermore, priorities are recommended to tackle these constraints. Thus the themes 1 to 6 together comprise the essential elements that ought to form part of every sensible planning of tropical rain forest development or management projects.

The second part of this book deals with case studies of tropical rain forest development and management projects in South America (Brazil, Suriname), Africa (Ivory Coast) and Asia (Java), illustrative for the issues discussed in the thematic chapters. Comparison of these case studies to the general principles given in themes 1-6 reveals their shortcomings and merits, often decisive for ultimate failure or success.

On the basis of the evidence presented in the themes and case studies, in the summary a rough outline is drawn of the essentials of a planning model for proper management of tropical rain forest lands on a sustainable basis. Moreover, since positive results of such tropical rain forest development projects can never be possible without regard for certain basic rules, an attempt has been made to derive such rules from the foregoing chapters.

Author's address: Dr. C.F. van Beusekom, State Forest Service, P.O. Box 20020, 3502 LA Utrecht, The Netherlands.

# The need for tropical rain forests and their products

by H.A. Luning*

## 1. Introduction

In the context of the planning for and the decision making regarding the use of tropical forests, a primary question concerns the need for such forests, as expressed directly or indirectly by society. This theme has been dealt with as follows:

- in paragraph 2, a broad classification is made of the tropical forest resource base, followed by a brief analysis of factors which appear relevant in arriving at a typology of tropical countries;
- in paragraph 3, society's needs for tropical forests and their products are analysed. Attention is drawn to the major factors, determining utilization from different angles (national, private-economic viewpoints);
- in paragraph 4, the human pressure on tropical forests is discussed and major factors responsible for increasing pressure are elaborated;
- in paragraph 5, an attempt is made firstly to come to a clustering of countries with substantial tropical rain forests, based on the man/land ratio and infrastructural developments, i.e. the opening-up of areas. Secondly, needs and requirements are set against groups sharing the same interest. This classification can be a helpful tool in the development of planning and policy-making in tropical forest management, as has been set out by Otto (this volume).

## 2. Tropical rain forests in developing countries

Table 1 presents an overview of the world's tropical forests, compiled by FAO (1982). It should be borne in mind that these aggregate figures are estimates at best. This is due to two factors. Firstly, definitions are not uniformly applied by member countries, secondly FAO feels obliged to accept official figures from national governments which usually contain an upward bias in the total area under forest cover. In a number of cases the selected use of satellite imagery has certainly been instrumental in arriving at more accurate and up-to-date information.

A further breakdown can be made which separates the tropical rain forests from other types, such as monsoonal forests. From a global point of view the area under tropical rain forest is unevenly distributed with more than half of it in Amazonia, about a quarter in Asia and the remainder in tropical Africa. Forest statistics of countries which encompass several distinct agro-climatological zones (e.g. India, Thailand) often do not single out sufficiently these types of tropical forests.

Table 1 The tropical forest resource base (in million hectares). Source: FAO, 1982.

| Region | Closed forest | Open forest | Forest fallow, scrub land | Total |
|---|---|---|---|---|
| Tropical America | 679 | 217 | 316 | 1,212 |
| Tropical Africa | 217 | 486 | 609 | 1,312 |
| Tropical Asia | 305 | 31 | 109 | 445 |
| Total tropical regions | 1,201 | 734 | 1,034 | 2,969 |

* I wish to thank R.C. van der Giessen, H. Nooteboom, F.G.M.N. Poelhekke, P. Schmidt, and K.F. Wiersum for their constructive criticisms and useful suggestions.

Relating tropical rain forests to particular countries it should be emphasized that developing countries have greatly varying natural resources and have different positions on a transformation continuum as regards the rates of change in socio-economic conditions. The diversity and complexity of these conditions can be expressed (among others) in *per capita* incomes and their regional and population distribution patterns, the degree of urbanization, man/land ratios and farm size patterns for major agro-ecological zones, the distribution of the labour force per economic sector (agriculture, mining, industry, services), the existence of oil and other sources of energy. An overriding factor is the political economy as it affects the development of both natural and human resources. Each country and the regions in these countries are in a sense unique and are characterized by location-specific factors.

Relationships are complex, for instance, the regionalized patterns of the country's local agricultural production and the position of its tropical rain forests. Where the land is suitable for the sustained production of foodcrops, forest clearing generally appears inevitable, ultimately. Depending on population pressure this applies in many instances also to forested areas which are less suitable or wholly unsuitable for agriculture (crops, livestock) on a permanent basis.

## 3. The needs

Coming now to the need for tropical rain forests, the question must be posed whether this need is linked to the forest *per se* or merely to the land on which the forest is presently found. This leads to the following distinction of needs in relation to the forest and its products:

a. *needs which are unconditionally linked to the ecosystem of natural rain forest* (a system which is sustainable in itself, in which drastic changes are irreversible):
   - certain wood species and other animal/plant material, including diverse genetic materials;
   - specific forms/activities of scientific study;
   - maintenance of the ethnic integrity of indigenous forest tribes;
   - recreation and tourism;
   - resource maintenance.

b. *needs which are conditionally linked to the ecosystem of natural rain forest but can be replaced locally by other forest and land utilization types* (see van Goor, this volume, for definition) depending on land qualities and management practices:
   - sustained production of wood and agricultural products (crops, livestock, fish);
   - watershed protection (anti-erosion, protecting the hydrological regime).

c. *needs which are not linked to rain forest land in particular.* These needs could be satisfied by shifting these activities to other parts of the country. For example, the use of tropical forest as a factor of production or as an object of speculation (Brazil). Why open up new areas when the intensification of the use on existing farm land is still feasible? (Of course the answer to this question is not so simple. Consider the land tenure situation in the 'old' areas which does not give access to land for small farmers/the landless. See also Poelhekke, 1984).

d. *needs which are location-bound but not tied to a certain ecosystem*:
   - mining, infrastructure development;
   - geo-political factors.

Another way to look at needs is to take two complementary points of view: the sociological or economic view-point and the private one. The government typically represents the national interests and this is reflected in its macro-economic objectives, for instance, increased production; higher productivity, employment and income; an improved income distribution; more foreign exchange, etc. The private entrepreneur, for instance a farmer, has a micro-economic orientation; the farm household sets priorities for self-sufficiency in food, risk avoidance, continuity, and maximizing money income only once food security is achieved.

The needs mentioned under a and b are clearly linked to the socio-economic view-point, but they are also manifest in c and d.

Needs which are conditionally linked to the ecosystem are also expressed by individual households and are often conflicting with the governments, objectives, as on the issues of sustained production and watershed protection. In many cases property rights are not well-defined (or laws to protect forest land are not enforced) and thus tropical forest land is considered common property with no particular incentive to refrain from excessive use. Within the private economic sphere there may be conflicts of interest as well; for example, the land-use conflicts in a rain forest area between the indigenous population and immigrants, be they (multi-)national companies or small farmers.

From a macro-economic view it must be pointed out that conventional economic analyses often do not give sufficient weight to future scarcities (see also the subparagraph on the need for conservation), hence valuation of forest products against existing market prices leads to undervaluation. Without going into details it is suggested that in practice an adjustment of the discount rate and a scrutiny of future benefits by taking account of future scarcity conditions can help in alleviating these problems.

As regards geo-political factors, this may also mean different things to different categories of people. For a defence minister, undisturbed tropical rain forests may represent a protective shield against the neighbouring country; for insurgents the forest provides a relatively safe harbour against the present political regime. This brings us to a further delineation of interest groups in relation to the need for the tropical forest and its products, as follows:

*Private sector, economic interests:*
- landless people, tenants, squatters;
- small (marginal) farmers, indigenous people, settlers*;
- large-scale (commercialized) farmers*;
- large enterprises, estates, plantations, (inter-) nationally based;
- (external) speculators;
- urban groups;
- others (guerillas, etc.).

*Public sector, economic interests:*
- government (at various ministries and levels, often with opposing views!).

Winding up this section, we observe that there is a large measure of diversity and dynamics in patterns of rain forest land use. This is connected with the following factors (not necessarily in order of importance) of which each factor usually acts in combination with one or more other factors:
- agro-ecological factors, e.g. rainfall (distribution), topography, land capabilities;
- population pressure/growth, including migration and the role of urbanization;
- income distribution/growth, food preferences and other socio-cultural factors;
- the decision-making process at farm level: how much and what to produce (intensity, choice of activities), how (choice of techniques), often determined by risk-avoidance attitudes;
- regional presence of other natural resources, which leads to particular patterns of basic needs (food, shelter, fuel, drinking water, etc.);
- macro-socio-economic and political framework;
- role of infrastructure (access) and institutions, serving rural people: research, extension, education and training, credit, co-operatives, marketing and input distribution, land-management systems;
- existence of international markets;
- indigenous land tenure and land-use systems and national public administrative and judicial systems, as these relate to forest;
- role of technology and the indigenous knowledge about ecosystems;
- the occurrence of externalities: whereas one group experiences the damage, hence costs

* Groups are positioned on a continuum, covering the near landless and the 'big' farmers and everything in between.

(silting up and deterioration of the water regime of valuable lowland agriculture), the other has the benefits (the income from timber harvesting, on steep slopes leading to soil erosion).

After the foregoing it should be evident, that the need for tropical rain forest exists also without the need for its products. The functions of tropical rain forest *per se*, as an ecosystem, become more manifest now that so much of it has been destroyed recently. They can be arranged roughly into three groups:

- species richness;
- watershed protection;
- cultural function.

*Species richness*

The species richness of and the diversity in the tropical rain forest is unsurpassed in the entire world. The estimates of the total number of species, including insects, amounts to tens of millions. Many of those are not or insufficiently known and most of them are due to disappear when tropical rain forest is destroyed. Among the tropical rain forest species there are an uncounted number of relatives of many food crops and otherwise economically important plants and animals. For many if not most cultivated species an influx of wild genes can be necessary to survive. For instance, pest resistance is frequently lost during breeding and has to be build up again by hybridizing with wild relatives. This can only be done if these wild relatives are still alive. Furthermore, there are countless plants and animals in tropical rain forest that could become useful to man as food crops, medicines, etc., but are not yet detected as such (although many were or are used by forest dwellers).

*Watershed protection*

Regions where large tracts of tropical rain forest or other forests have disappeared are now facing problems like erosion and disruption of water balances. The former causes loss of fertility upstream and silting of water basins downstream with many unfavourable consequences. The latter is caused through a loss of water absorption capacity upstream, which leads to flooding and drying up of rivers downstream. Moreover, indications exist, that through a reduction of the evapo-transpiration and a rise in the albedo, deforestation affects the climate. It seems that deforestation leads not only to a drier climate but also to climatic instability with an accentuation of the dry periods and mass rainfall in the wet periods. These effects are cumulative with the reduction in water absorption capacity upstream, resulting in more rigorous drought as well as more extensive floods downstream. Intact tropical rain forest performs this protective function very well. It must be said, however, that if and only if in the course of a land evaluation survey the soils upstream are found suitable for forest plantations and if and only if a very cautious management of these plantations is guaranteed, this protection function can be fulfilled nearly equally well by forest plantations.

*Cultural function*

Under cultural function of tropical rain forest a number of functions are collected, among those:

- maintenance of the ethnic integrity of indigenous forest tribes;
- maintenance of the cultural roots of many people now living outside the forest, whose ancestors lived in the forest;
- specific forms of scientific research on the many stil unknown processes in tropical rain forest directed at the development of non-destructive and better yielding land utilization types;
- recreation in various forms.

The need for the fulfilment of these functions exists, already, among present generations, as is demonstrated by the many problems in regions where large tracts of tropical rain forest have been destroyed, and surely will exist among future generations. The fact that it is nearly impossible to translate these functions into socio-economic terms and figures makes them not less real.

## 4. Pressure on the tropical rain forest

Pressure can be analysed in a particular local situation according to the following framework:

*Pressure due to opening up forest* for the extraction of timber and/or minerals, for infra-structural developments (reservoirs, roads, settlements) or geo-political/military actions.

*Pressure due to the need for land* as factor of production, caused bij migration, related to opening up new areas, government policies (transmigration, resettlement) and lack of access to other areas (power and land-owning elite) due to land hunger; owing to stagnant technology in agriculture as a capital factor (investment, speculation).

Looking at this pressure on a world-wide scale three major factors contributing to forest destruction can be singled out:

- needs for farming/livestock raising;
- need for firewood;
- the consequences of the need for timber, meeting consumers' demand at national and international level.

FAO attributes 45 per cent of all tropical forest clearing to shifting cultivation. The problem varies by region, being the principal cause of 70 per cent of the closed forest clearings in Africa, nearly 50 per cent in tropical Asia, and 35 per cent in tropical America, where it is primarily related to road construction.

Populations in countries with tropical forests have been growing (since about 1945 with the breakthrough of antibiotics) at the rate of 2 to 4 per cent per year. Whereas before World War II doubling of population in these countries took place in between 75 and 100 years, this now happens in 35, 24 and 18 years at annual population growth rates of 2, 3 and 4 per cent, respectively. Effective demand for food and other agricultural products increases at a rate of 3 to 4 per cent per year, which is even higher in fast-developing, medium-level income countries (with per capita annual income between US $ 400 and US $ 1,000). This demand cannot be met by the agricultural sector without substantial investments in the sector itself, or through the alternative of food imports; in addition one must hope for a substantial contribution through technological developments, leading to increased production and higher productivity on existing farm land (intensification) rather than

Table 2 Average annual growth rates of production, area harvested and output per hectare of major food crops in selected groups of countries, 1961-70 and 1971-80.

| Country group | Period | Average annual growth rate | | | Output per hectare growth rate as percentage of production growth rate |
|---|---|---|---|---|---|
| | | Production of major food crops | Area harvested (percent) | Output per hectare | |
| Asia* | 1961-70 | 2.7 | 0.8 | 1.9 | 70 |
| | 1971-80 | 3.3 | 1.0 | 2.3 | 70 |
| Sub-Saharan Africa | 1961-70 | 2.3 | 2.5 | -0.2 | -9 |
| | 1971-80 | 1.2 | 1.1 | 0.1 | 8 |
| EC | 1961-70 | 2.5 | -0.5 | 2.9 | 116 |
| | 1971-80 | 1.3 | -0.4 | 1.7 | 131 |

* Excluding China

Source: Mellor and Johnston, 1984.

development through extension of present farm land, at least in a number of countries with high man/land ratio's.

In India, for example, a 66 per cent increase in the number of farm households between 1953-54 and 1971-72 was accompanied by an increase in the cultivated area of only 2 per cent. Subsequently, the number of landless or nearly landless households (less than one acre) increased from 15.4 to 35.6 million (which will be in the order of 60 million in 1984) and the average size of a farm holding declined from 6.3 to 3.8 acres in that period (Mellor and Johnston, 1984). Employment absorption capacity is only modest in industry and services, particularly in the capital-intensive parts of these sectors. Hence in many cases the agricultural sector remains as the residual sector, receiving new generations, together with the 'informal', low-capital industrial and service sectors in the urban centres.

Although very aggregate, Table 2 clearly illuminates conditions in Asia, Sub-Saharan Africa and the European Community regarding the factors contributing to growth of agricultural production. The annual increase in output per hectare has been impressive in Asia and in the EC; this contrasts greatly with the poor performance in Sub-Saharan Africa. Whereas there have been substantial breakthroughs in Asia (particularly in the irrigated areas) in rice, wheat and sometimes maize production thanks to the new high-yielding varieties, hardly any such technological changes have occurred in Africa. The pressure on the farm land is evidently off in Europe (and also North America), but is increasingly felt in many parts of Africa and Asia, where population densities are very high and agricultural technologies not sustainable. Family planning programmes do have an impact in the developing countries with relatively high incomes and high income growth (such as Taiwan and South-Korea), but one should realize that the labour force of the year 2005 has already been born. With population pressure there is also the growing need for firewood, charcoal and timber (for instance in the Kali Konto Project area, this volume), but this is a far more serious problem in the tropical and subtropical areas having monsoon climates and semi-arid and arid conditions.

The need to cut tropical timber to earn foreign exchange is a pressure felt in many tropical countries, but there are exceptions in case these countries have substantial sources of energy (e.g. Brunei, Gabon, and to a lesser extent Venezuela).

## 5. Towards a typology of tropical countries/regions with tropical rain forests*

In Table 3 tropical countries have been included (per continent) with an area of closed (moist) tropical forest of at least 3 million hectares. A further classification is made: from 7 million hectares up we talk about a large-sized tropical rain forest asset, between 3 and 7 million of medium size. For each country a number of important variables and ratios have been collated. The major use of tropical rain forest has been indicated, the present and expected state, etc. Based on this overview it appears possible to arrive at clusters of countries (regions) with a number of common characteristics:

*Tropical Africa*

- group of countries in Central Africa: Zaire, Gabon, Congo, Central African Republic (parts) with reasonable to high tropical rain forest acreage per head of population, little or limited threats to tropical rain forest connected with low population pressure and poorly developed infrastructure in the interior. Rural incomes are low;
- two countries (Ivory Coast, Nigeria) with low tropical rain forest acreage per head, high income growth, related to economic policies in the period 1960 to the present (Ivory Coast), or to oil (Nigeria), and large population growth, partly due to migration from neighbouring poor West African countries. Infrastructure is reasonably well-developed, forests are disappearing rapidly (for Ivory Coast, see Vooren, this volume);
- intermediate position is taken by countries such as Cameroon and Liberia.

* Myers (1980) has given useful guidance in preparing this paragraph.

*Tropical America*

- group of countries with parts in the Amazon Basin: Brazil, French Guyana, Suriname, Guyana, Venezuela, Colombia, Ecuador, Peru, Bolivia, Paraguay (small part) (for Suriname: see Boxman et al., this volume). With the exception of Bolivia and Guyana it concerns countries with a large degree of urbanization and from a global view these developing countries have an average per capita income which is in the medium range; population pressure on the land is low. The tropical rain forest is particularly little disturbed in French Guyana, Suriname, Guyana and Venezuela; the population is settled for the largest part along the coast, is urbanized or is occupied with agriculture in the coastal plains. In the Latin American countries the population growth is high. The limited infrastructure is the most important reason why the Amazon Basin has so far remained relatively untouched. Brazil and Peru consider their part of the basin as an avenue for alleviating their food and population problems;
- group of countries in Central America: higher population growth, the pressure on tropical rain forest is greater, smaller per capita area under tropical rain forest, lower average per capita income levels than the earlier mentioned Tropical America Group. Extensive ranching areas in Central America, doubled between 1961 and 1978 because of the large demand for lean meat in the USA (Myers, 1981). The same situation is found in parts of Brazil (multinationals). The threat to deforestation is real and large (with the exception of parts of Panama).

*Tropical Asia*

- group of countries (regions) with large areas under tropical rain forest, low population pressure, reasonable conditions for good forest management, provided the political intention exists: Papua New Guinea, parts of Indonesia (Irian Jaja, parts of Kalimantan, Sulawesi and Sumatra), East Malaysia, parts of Burma*. In this group more than half of Asia's tropical rain forest is situated. Infrastructure is lacking or limited;
- group of countries (regions) with quickly disappearing tropical rain forest threatened by high population pressure and high population growth: Philippines, Thailand, West Malaysia, parts of Indonesia (e.g., Java, parts of Sumatra). Reasonable to good infrastructure (see Thalen, this volume).

*Finally*

A further cluster-grouping is possible, taking the global view. Leaving out Brazil, the country with by far the greatest area under tropical rain forest, which is a category by its own (see also Groeneveld, this volume), the following grouping emerges:

I. Countries with a medium to large tropical rain forest area per head of population, little deforestation, also linked with limited infrastructure. Tropical rain forest little or not disturbed and not apparently threatened in near future; parts of: Zaire, Congo, Central African Republic, Venezuela, Bolivia, Guyana, Suriname, French Guiana, Panama, West Irian, Sabah, Burma.

II. Group of countries/regions with small tropical rain forest area per head, considerable amount of deforestation caused by population pressure, or opening up for external markets of tropical rain forest products (Japan, USA, Western Europe). Infrastructure is more developed compared with situation in Group I: Cameroon, Liberia, Ecuador, Colombia, Guatemala, Honduras, Nicaragua, Panama (part), Thailand (part), West Malaysia (part), Sarawak, Indonesia (Sulawesi, Sumatra, Kalimantan), Philippines (Mindanao).

III. Group of countries/regions with small tropical rain forest area per head, deforestation reaches limits because of population pressure, demand for food, commercial timber, firewood. Infrastructure is reasonably well developed: Ivory Coast, Nigeria, Java, Thailand (part), West Malaysia (part), Philippines.

* Insecurity is large because of local guerilla activities.

Table 3 Some socio-economic indicators regarding forest and society for countries with a sizeable area under tropical rain forest.

| Country | Closed forest area | Closed forest area per capita<br>ha | Estimated annual rate of deforestation 1981-85<br>% | Annual population growth rate 1970-80<br>% | Per capita income (G.N.P.) 1981<br>US $ | Population density<br>capita $km^{-2}$ |
|---|---|---|---|---|---|---|
| *Tropical Africa* | | | | | | |
| Cameroon | large: between 10 and 80 million ha | 2.0 | 0.4 | 2.2 | 880 | 12 |
| Congo | ,, | 12.6 | 0.1 | 2.9 | 1,100 | 3 |
| Gabon | ,, | 29.3 | 0.1 | 1.2 | 3,810 | 2 |
| Zaire | ,, | 3.4 | 0.2 | 3.0 | 210 | 10 |
| Ivory Coast | medium: between 2 and 6 million ha | 0.5 | 6.5 | 5.1 | 1,200 | 14 |
| Nigeria | ,, | 0.7 | 5.0 | 2.5 | 870 | 90 |
| Liberia | ,, | 1.0 | 2.3 | 3.5 | 520 | 17 |
| Central African Republic | ,, | 1.4 | 0.1 | 2.3 | 320 | 3 |

| Urban population % | Major use of tropical rain forest | State of tropical rain forest | Remarks |
|---|---|---|---|
| 30 | Timber harvesting | Little knowledge available | – |
| 45 | Timber | No disturbance | Not much infrastructure |
| 32 | Little timber exploitation | No disturbance | Population concentration near mines along coast. Little inland infrastructure |
| 34 | Some shifting cultivation | Not much disruptive pressures foreseen in near future | Hardly any infrastructure |
| 40 | Timber exploitation and agricultural expansion | Primary forest will disappear before 1990 | Large influx of migrants from Sahelian countries, start farming in forests. Good infrastructure |
| 20 | Shifting cultivation, limited logging; exports banned after 1976 | No more commercial timber by 1990 at the latest | With present plantation programme Nigeria becomes timber importer in near future |
| 33 | Shifting cultivation and commercial logging | Primary forests gone within 5-10 years | Shifting cultivation is dominant form of agri-culture |
| 41 | Timber | Little disturbance | – |

Table 3 (*Cont.*)

| Country | Closed forest area | Closed forest area per capita ha | Estimated annual rate of deforestation 1981-85 % | Annual population growth rate 1970-80 % | Per capita income (G.N.P.) 1981 US $ | Population density capita km$^{-2}$ |
|---|---|---|---|---|---|---|
| *Tropical America* | | | | | | |
| Ecuador | large: between 9 and 360 million ha | 1.6 | 2.4 | 3.4 | 1,180 | 23 |
| Colombia | ” | 1.7 | 1.8 | 1.9 | 1,380 | 20 |
| Venezuela | ” | 1.8 | 0.4 | 3.4 | 4,220 | 12 |
| Peru | ” | 3.6 | 0.4 | 2.6 | 1,170 | 11 |
| Brazil | ” | 2.7 | 0.4 | 2.1 | 2,220 | 11 |
| Bolivia | ” | 7.5 | 0.2 | 2.6 | 600 | 5 |
| Suriname | ” | 37.1 | neg. | -0.6 | 3,030 | 3 |
| Guyana | ” | 23.1 | neg. | 1.1 | 720 | 4 |
| French Guiana | ” | 129.1 | neg. | 2.2 | 3,430 | 1 |
| Guatamala | medium: between 3.8 and 4.5 million ha | 0.6 | 2.0 | 3.1 | 1,140 | 65 |

| Urban population % | Major use of tropical rain forest | State of tropical rain forest | Remarks |
|---|---|---|---|
| 45 | Settlement of people due to high population growth | Amazonian forests largely undisturbed, coastal forests rapidly disappearing | Rainforests extraordinarily diverse and species-rich |
| 70 | Settlement agriculture and cattle raising; timber harvesting | Exhaustion varies per region (accessibility) | Steady decrease of tropical moist forest |
| 83 | Logging, crop growing, livestock | Most people live in urban areas, pressure low in most forest areas | Exhaustion is only very local |
| 67 | Agricultural settlement | Growing spread of agriculture in Amazonia | Government inclined to regard parts of forests as potential salvation for food and population problems |
| 68 | Agricultural settlements, cattle raising, timber exploitation | About one-tenth of the forest cover has been eliminated | Much activity from multinationals in cattle raising |
| 33 | Some shifting cultivation | Virtually undisturbed | Very poor country |
| 50 | Some timber | Primary forests are safeguarded | Population in coastal zone |
| 30 | Some timber | Virtually undisturbed | ” |
| 80 | Negligible | None | ” |
| 39 | Agricultural settlement and cattle raising | Little known about deforestation | – |

Table 3 (*Cont.*)

| Country | Closed forest area | Closed forest area per capita ha | Estimated annual rate of deforestation 1981-85 % | Annual population growth rate 1970-80 % | Per capita income (G.N.P.) 1981 US $ | Population density capita $km^{-2}$ |
|---|---|---|---|---|---|---|
| Paraguay | ,, | 1.2 | 4.7 | 2.6 | 1,630 | 8 |
| Honduras | ,, | 0.9 | 2.4 | 3.4 | 600 | 34 |
| Nicaragua | ,, | 1.6 | 2.7 | 3.9 | 860 | 19 |
| Panama | ,, | 2.0 | 0.9 | 2.3 | 1,910 | 25 |
| *Tropical Asia* | | | | | | |
| Papua New Guinea | large: between 7.5 and 114 million ha | 11.0 | 0.1 | 2.2 | 840 | 7 |
| Thailand | ,, | 0.2 | 2.7 | 2.6 | 770 | 71 |
| Malaysia | ,, | 1.4 | 1.2 | 2.5 | 1.840 | 32 |
| Philippines | ,, | 0.2 | 1.0 | 2.7 | 790 | 130 |
| Indonesia | ,, | 0.7 | 0.5 | 2.4 | 530 | 64 |
| Burma | ,, | 0.8 | 0.3 | 2.1 | 190 | 19 |

Source: Myers (1980).

| Urban population % | Major use of tropical rain forest | State of tropical rain forest | Remarks |
|---|---|---|---|
| 39 | – | Rapid deforestation | – |
| 36 | – | Cattle raising | – |
| 53 | Shifting cultivation, cattle raising, timber exploitation | Rapid deforestation | – |
| 54 | Shifting cultivation | – | – |

| | | | |
|---|---|---|---|
| 18 | Shifting cultivation | Quite rapid change through shifting cultivation in some areas | Still considerable potential for protection |
| 14 | Shifting cultivation and agricultural settlement | Remaining forest stocks will be exhausted within 10 years (in theory) | Country is importing logs from Malaysia and Indonesia |
| 29 West<br>16 East | Timber harvesting,<br>Agricultural settlements | Prevailing exploitation patterns for West Malaysia will exhaust available forest in 5-10 years | Forest development is not responsibility of federal government but rests with states |
| 36 | Agricultural encroachment | Forests will disappear (theoretically) within 15 years | Much degradation of major watersheds |
| 20 | Transmigration, shifting cultivation, logging | Deforestation varies greatly by location | Half of Asia's tropical rain forest in Indonesia |
| 27 | Shifting cultivation, logging | Disturbances much localized | Burma has 75% of world's teak; lack of infrastructure |

IV. Group of countries/regions where tropical rain forest has been present but has practically disappeared: Ghana, Kenya, Nigeria, Sierra Leone, etc.

The above classification is only a broad one and must be considered a first step. In making further refinements one must bear in mind that these should be relevant for planning and decision making. For the latter purpose this classification is still too rough.

It appears appropriate to combine the needs specified in paragraph 3 with the various interest groups analysed in the same paragraph. It is evident from this matrix (Table 4) that the largest number of interest groups both at the private-economic and the national-economic level are interested in the use of the land (rather than the forest) for crop and livestock enterprises.

Such (non)material needs as those expressed by scientists, particularly researchers, conservationists, such as recreation, must be defended, otherwise all land suitable for agriculture (even for a short period) will ultimately be taken as long as returns exceed the variable costs involved in forest clearing and cultivation/grazing, which is a serious problem of countries in group II and III mentioned above.

Table 4 Matrix linking various types of interest groups with needs

| | Private sector economic interest groups | | | | | | | National economic interest groups |
|---|---|---|---|---|---|---|---|---|
| Needs | landless tenants squatters | small farmers | big farmers | estates & plantations | speculation | urban groups | others | (government) |
| **Needs unconditionally linked to ecosystem:** | | | | | | | | |
| ■ species, plants/animals gene material | | | | * | | * | | researchers national (international) |
| ■ scientific study | | | | | | | * | researchers (national) |
| ■ protection forest | | | | | | | | |
| ■ recreation | | | | | | * | | government |
| **Needs conditionally linked to ecosystem:** | | | | | | | | |
| ■ sustained production of agricultural products | * | * | | * | future | | loggers | * |
| wood | * | * | * | * | future | * | insurgents | * |
| **Needs not linked to particular area of forest land:** | | | | | | | | |
| ■ factor of production | * | * | * | * | * | * | | * |
| ■ speculation | | | | * | * | | | |
| **Location-bound but not tied to ecosystem:** | | | | | | | | |
| ■ mining | | | | * | | | mining companies | * |
| ■ infrastructure | | | | | | | insurgents | * |
| ■ geopolitical factors | | | | | | | | politicians military establishment |

Note: For further explanation, see paragraph 3.

Source: H. A. Luning, 1987.

## REFERENCES


FAO (1982). Tropical forest resources. *Forestry Paper* 30. Rome.

Mellor, J.W. and Johnston, B.F. (1984). The world food equation: interrelations among development, employment and food consumption. *Journal of Economic Literature* 22, 531-574.

Myers, N. (1980). *Conservation of tropical moist forests.* Washington D.C.: National Academy of Sciences.

Myers, N. (1981). The hamburger connection: how Central America's forests become North America's hamburgers. *Ambio* 10, 3-8.

Poelhekke, F.G.M.N. (1984). Prikkeldraad in het oerwoud. De veeteelt in het proces van economische en sociale integratie van het Amazonegebied in Brazilië. *Nijmeegse Geografische Cahiers* 25. Nijmegen: Katholieke Universiteit.

Postel, S. (1984). Protecting forests. In *State of the world: a world watch institute report on progress toward a sustainable society,* ed. L.R. Brown et al. New York: Norton & Co. Pp. 74-94.

World Bank (1984). *World development report.* Oxford: Oxford University Press.



Author's address: Prof. Dr. H.A. Luning, International Institute for Aerospace Survey and Earth Sciences, P.O. Box 6, 7500 AA Enschede, The Netherlands.

# Land use in tropical rain forest areas

by J.H.A. Boerboom
W.B.J. Jonkers

## 1. Introduction

A wide variety of land-use types exists in tropical rain forest areas. Some make use of the intrinsic characteristics of the forest ecosystem (soil conservation, water regulation, climate stabilization, possibilities for scientific research, nature conservation and tourism); others exploit forest produce or use the forest for crop production. In the first case, economic benefits are indirect and cannot be estimated accurately. Users form a large group of people, which is often hard to delimit, such as farming communities in the lower parts of a forested river catchment which are dependent on irrigation water. In the second case, produce is tangible and benefits become available to a comparatively well-defined group of users, i.e. people and companies involved in exploitation, or the government.

Which land-use types are applied depends on the nature of the ecosystem (vegetation, fauna, physical setting) and on the user's aims and means. Users vary from isolated small tribal communities to large multinational companies. A very important point is that each form of land use limits possibilities for other types of land utilization and for future use:

- harvesting one forest component affects development and viability of other components;
- eliminating or damaging forest cover affects land-use possibilities elsewhere (externalities, see Luning, this volume);
- presence of two types of users can be incompatible and may lead to the extinction of one of these groups (e.g. social incompatibility between rubber collectors and Amerindians in Amazonia).

In other words, combining different forms of land use is often impossible or puts restrictions on one or both uses. This means that choices have to be made and limitations have to be imposed. This contribution is to describe and analyse current forms of forest land use. Four broad categories can be distinguished:

- utilization types which leave the original ecosystem virtually untouched;
- utilization types which damage or modify the forest ecosystem and result in altered ecosystems comparable in structure and functioning to the original one;
- utilization types which imply elimination of the original vegetation. The forest is replaced by an artificial plant cover and the physical setting (soil, climate) is used for agriculture or forest plantations. What remains of the original flora and fauna is usually considered a nuisance and is seldom appreciated;
- utilization types which imply a virtually complete destruction of the ecosystem. These non-agricultural uses (urban and industrial development, mining etc.) are outside the scope of the discussion.

Individual forest land-use types are discussed below. Some important characteristics of each type are summarized in Table 5.

Table 5 Characteristics of various land utilization types in tropical rain forest areas.

| | Land utilization type | Nature of produce | Type of eco-system | Long-term prospects |
|---|---|---|---|---|
| 1. | Nature conservation | n | o | s |
| 2. | Protection of environment | n | o/d | s |
| 3. | Recreation and tourism | n | o/d | s |
| 4. | Gene pool conservation | e | o | s |
| 5. | Gathering and hunting | e | o/m | s |
| 6. | Selective commercial exploitation of natural forest | e | m | s/i/t |
| 7. | Wood production from managed natural forest | e | m | s |
| 8. | Shifting cultivation, aboriginal | e | o/m | s |
| | Shifting cultivation, established | e | d | s |
| | Shifting cultivation, guided | e | d | s |
| | Shifting cultivation, deteriorated | e | d | i |
| | Shifting cultivation, transmigratory | e | d | t |
| 9. | Gardening | e | d/m | s |
| 10. | Non-wood production from ligneous species in plantations | e | d | s |
| 11. | Wood production from plantations | e | d | s/i |
| 12. | Pasture | e | d | s/i |
| 13. | Permanent cropping (no trees), rain fed | e | d | s/i |
| 14. | Permanent cropping (no trees), irrigated | e | d | s |
| 15. | Clear cutting for integral harvesting of wood | e | d | t |
| 16. | Zero use | nil | n.a. | n.a. |

d = derived ecosystem, i.e., artificial system not resembling original ecosystem in species composition and structure
e = produce by extractive exploitation
i = production not substained (decreasing)
m = modified ecosystem, resembling original ecosystems in structure and species composition
n = produce not tangible
n.a. = not applicable
nil = no produce
o = original ecosystem, eventually imperceptibly modified
s = sustained production
t = transitory production system.

Source: Boerboom et al., 1987

## 2. Nature conservation *(sensu stricto)*

Objectives: to conserve forests for purposes of non-material nature, e.g. to preserve flora, fauna and landscape; as a medium for research, education and training.

Forest types and scale: all forest types. Minimum size of a reserve is the smallest area in which the whole forest ecosystem can perpetuate itself. In some cases, a strict reserve of limited size is adequate if surrounded by a partially protected sanctuary for species which require a large area, e.g. some big mammals.

Produce: benefits are of non-material nature. In some cases payments may be received for allowing research or scientific training.

Impact on forest ecosystem: none.

Remark: can be combined with other forms of land use with negligible impact on the forest ecosystem.

## 3. Protection of environment

Objectives: to maintain or establish forest for protection of the environment *in situ* and/or elsewhere (soil conservation, regulation of climate and water).

Forest types: all forest types, but mainly on hilly or mountainous terrain and along the coast (mangrove).

Produce: most benefits are indirect but nevertheless of considerable economic importance. Forests on slopes protect lower-lying areas against floods (rainy season) and water shortage (dry season) and other undesirable effects of erosion. Forest plantations on degraded soils improve soil fertility and may yield forest products in the future.

Impact on forest ecosystem: forest is fully protected. Ecosystem remains intact or is allowed to recover from previous disturbances.

Remark: can be combined with other forms of land use which protect forest cover adequately. Limited yields of forest products are acceptable in some cases, provided that strict regulations can be enforced.

Beach forest nature reserve. Fishermen use shore for boats (Java-Indonesia; source: Boerboom and Jonkers, 1987).

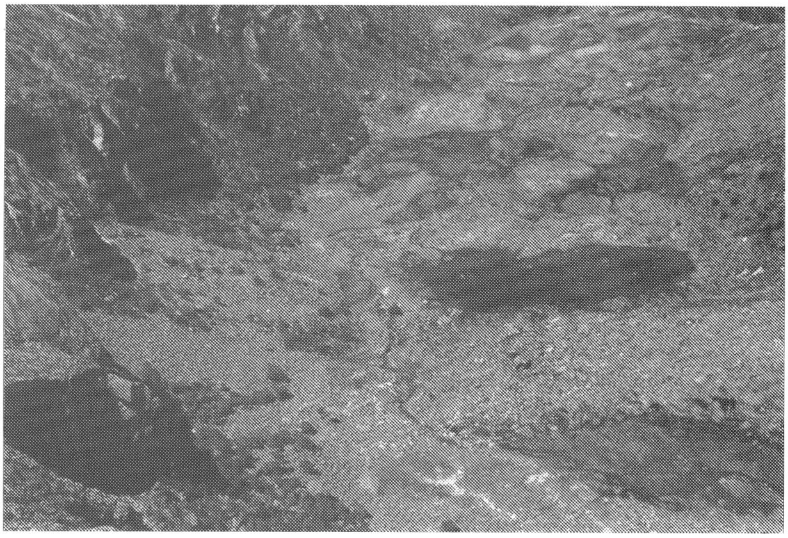

*Polylepis*-forest near timberline (Pico Espejo, altitude 4,000 m, in National Park Simon Bolivar, Venezuela; source: Boerboom and Jonkers, 1987).

## 4. Recreation and tourism

Objectives: to conserve natural or semi-natural forest for recreation and tourism.

Forest types: mainly 'attractive' forests, i.e. with beautiful scenery and/or other attractive features (fauna).

Produce: of non-material nature if not exploited commercially. Commercial exploitation may be profitable, especially if aimed at international tourism.

Impact on forest ecosystem: recreation and tourism cause some damage to the ecosystem. Under proper management, such damage remains within acceptable limits.

Remark: can be combined with forest land-use types 'nature conservation' (see Boxman et al., this volume), 'protection of environment' and gene pool conservation.

## 5. Gene pool conservation

Objectives: to conserve forests as gene banks, in particular for species of economic importance or economic potential.

Forest types: virtually all forest types contain species of current or potential agricultural or pharmaceutical importance. Each reserve should contain a large number of mature individuals of the species concerned (for plant species: 1,000 to 25,000 individuals).

Produce: biological material (genes) either for improvement of agricultural and horticultural crops or domesticated animals or for development of new, yet unknown crops. Also for identification of natural substances which may prove of pharmaceutical importance.

Impact on forest ecosystem: forest is fully protected. Quantities of produce extracted are negligible and have no ecological consequences.

Remark: so far, applied only in combination with nature conservation, protection of the environment or recreation and tourism. Formalization by law of reserves is most urgent where forests occur on comparatively rich soils.

## 6. Gathering and hunting

Objectives: to harvest a wide range of products from natural forest for domestic consumption.

Forest types: mainly in mesophytic tropical rain forest, also in swamp forests, riparian forests and savannas. To supplement other forms of forest land use.

Produce: a wide variety of vegetable products, game and fish. Extraction by (semi-)nomadic tribal groups is dispersed and intermittent. Extraction by sedentary groups is more concentrated and continuous.

Technology: ranging from primitive (bow and arrow, blow pipe) to modern (rifle).

Product utilization: products are consumed within the tribal group. Sometimes barter trade.

Population density: very low for (semi-)nomadic tribal groups, which depend solely on gathering and hunting (0.005-0.12 persons per $km^2$). Production capacity of the ecosystem is not necessarily the limiting factor. Individual groups tend to maintain buffer zones between their territories to avoid hostile contacts or out of fear for supernatural influences (shamanism). Population densities are higher when sedentary groups are involved. If gathering and hunting contributes substantially to the food supply of such a group, production capacity of the forest ecosystem may be a limiting factor for population density.

Impact on forest ecosystem: nomadic groups can be considered part of the ecosystem rather than a disturbing factor. Disturbance by sedentary groups varies from negligible disturbance to local extinction of species harvested.

Long-term prospects: sustained production if population pressure and intensity of use remain low.

## 7. Selective commercial exploitation of natural forest

Objectives: to harvest natural forest produce for industrial or trading purposes, often for export.

Forest types: virtually all forest types.

Produce: exploitation is aimed at one product or one group of products, usually high-quality timber. Also selective exploitation of minor forest products (rattan, nuts, orchids, latex, etc.).

Technology: sometimes primitive or intermediate (harvest of minor forest products), but mostly modern (timber exploitation).

Product utilization: industrial, often for export. Exploitation usually by private or state-owned companies.

Population density: no direct relation with this form of land use. Commercial forest exploitation takes place mainly in sparsely populated areas. It may jeopardize culture and subsistence of the indigenous population. Labour may be recruited from the local population but is often imported from other regions.

Impact on forest ecosystem: virtually complete absence of long-term management objectives and lack of care for the forest ecosystem are characteristics for this form of commercial ex-

Timber exploitation in lowland rain forest in Suriname (source: Boerboom and Jonkers, 1987).

ploitation. Simple yield regulations exist in most countries but they are usually hard to enforce and therefore ineffective. Over-exploitation may occur and selective exploitation may cause damage to other components of the ecosystem than those extracted (logging damage).

Long-term prospects: in most cases, the resource will deteriorate due to lack of effective long-term management and the selective nature of the exploitation.

## 8. Wood production from managed natural forest

Objectives: to manage (modified) natural forest for sustained wood production.

Forest types: all forest types containing wood of commercial value, ranging from mangrove forest to mountain forest.

Structure of production forest: managed stands are different from natural forest. If the original forest is uneven-aged and rich in species, silvicultural management may result in less botanical variation and greater uniformity in tree size. Differences in forest structure and botanical composition between managed and natural forest may be smaller where the original stand is more or less even-aged and poor in species (e.g. some mangrove forests).

Management of mangrove forest (*Rhizophora*) by clear-cutting of strips and natural regeneration (Venezuela; source: Boerboom and Jonkers, 1987).

Produce: wood, in species-rich forest mostly high quality timber.

Technology: predominantly modern. Equipment and techniques used should be such that damage to the residual stand and soil is minimized.

Product utilization: usually industrial, often for export, sometimes for local consumption.

Population density: has no direct relation with this land-use type. Increasing population pressure may result in conversion of production forest to allow more intensive forms of land use.

Impact on forest ecosystem: depends on the management system applied. Forestry in semi-natural forest (selective logging followed by a natural regeneration treatment) may conserve the original ecosystem rather well. However, most of these systems lead to important shifts in flora and fauna and alter forest structure, especially in the regeneration phase.

Long-term prospects: depend on methods used. Logging techniques should be adapted to allow future utilization and yields should not exceed certain threshold values. Silvicultural treatment should not result in undesirable shifts in species composition or forest structure.

Remark: see also Boxman et al. (this volume).

## 9. Shifting cultivation (swidden agriculture)

Objectives: to use forest land temporarily or intermittently for cultivation of short-living agricultural crops.

Forest types: mostly in mesophytic tropical rain forest, also in thin-stemmed xerophytic forest and riparian forest.

Methods: small tracts of forest are cleared and planted. Mixed cropping is applied. Annual crops are often combined with perennial species.

Produce: mostly staple food for own consumption (maize, rice, manioc, various tuber crops, bananas, etc.).
Technology: primitive to intermediate. Chain-saws may be used to clear the forest.
Product utilization: for domestic consumption, sometimes also for the local market.

Five subtypes can be distinguished:

*Aboriginal shifting cultivation*
Characteristic: fields are used for one growing season to a few years and are abandoned forever after the crops have been harvested. This form of land use is applied by small groups of forest dwellers, i.e. either nomadic groups which make a living out of gathering and hunting during most of the year and grow annual crops (maize, rice, gourd) during one season; or semi-sedentary groups which subsist on swidden agriculture, use fields around their settlements only once and move their villages every five to ten years.
Population density: very low, usually less than one person per km$^2$.
Impact on forest ecosystem: abandoned fields are colonized by pioneer species and later occupied again by species from primary forest. No lasting effect on the forest ecosystem, although late-secondary species may mark old fields for centuries.
Long-term prospects: increasing population density may lead to other forms of shifting cultivation and eventually jeopardize sustained production.

*Established shifting cultivation*
Characteristic: fields are used one to several years, followed by a relatively long fallow period (15-25 years) before the next occupation. Applied by sedentary groups and often combined with other agricultural systems (gardening, in some cases permanent cropping).
Population density: usually 10-50 persons per km$^2$.
Impact on forest ecosystem: original vegetation disappears, rain forest species with edible parts may be spared. Secondary species colonize abandoned fields and fauna changes drastically. Some soil deterioration may occur, especially on yellow kaolinitic soils (xanthic ferralsols, ferric acrisols). Nutrient status stabilizes at lower level.
Long-term prospects: a long fallow period is needed for sustained production. Required length of fallow period depends on climate and soil. Increasing population density and one-sided

Cassave-crop, underneath regeneration of tree species, preceding the secondary forest (Suriname; source: Boerboom and Jonkers, 1987).

demand for cash crops may destabilize the system and lead to deteriorated shifting cultivation. This trend prevails in many parts of the humid tropics.

*Guided shifting cultivation*

Characteristic: as established shifting cultivation, except that the fallow vegetation is (partly) artificial. Ligneous species are introduced or favoured before the field is abandoned to increase the proportion of useful species in the fallow vegetation or to speed up soil recovery.

Population density: may reach high values (Chimbu region, Papua-New Guinea: 225 persons per km$^2$, S.E. Nigeria: 300 persons per km$^2$).

Long-term prospects: this form of land use has proven to be ecologically stable in regions where it is based on a long tradition. However, increasing population pressure and demand for cash crops tend to destabilize traditional systems. In some cases, further intensification seems possible (e.g. alley cropping).

*Deteriorated shifting cultivation*

Characteristic: as established shifting cultivation, but fallow period is shorter and/or fields are used for longer periods leading to soil deterioration and erosion. Is often applied on terrain unsuitable for shifting cultivation. Usually, just a few crops are grown which are capable of producing acceptable yields on poor soils (manioc, sweet potato).

Population density: variable. Sometimes fairly high, especially when other economic activities provide additional income. May decrease sharply in seriously affected areas but is always too high for sustained production.

Impact on forest ecosystem: endemic vegetation has been destroyed completely and is unlikely to recover. Fallow vegetation consists predominantly of pan-tropical weeds originating from drier regions. Original fauna has disappeared almost completely and the soil is degraded seriously or decapitated by erosion.

Long-term prospects: no sustained production. Leads to further decline of productivity.

*Transmigratory shifting cultivation*

Characteristic: fields are used during a period of several years and then abandoned for ever. Applied mostly by farmers who originate from other regions, often from another ecological zone (colonists). Often applied in recently opened-up forest with little previous disturbance other than selective logging. After abandoning his field, the farmer moves further into the forest and the process is repeated. Abandoned fields are often used for another form of land use: pasture, in some cases cultivation of perennial crops (banana, coffee).

Grazing cattle in *Acacia*-woodland (Kenya; source: Boerboom and Jonkers, 1987).

Population density: not relevant. Farmers are progressing into the forest as a front. Population stabilizes at a low level when this front has passed.

Impact on forest ecosystem: biocoenose as such is destroyed. Some species may be spared intentionally (palms, commercial timber species and species which are difficult to cut, e.g. strangler figs). Soil deterioration is common due to the colonist's lack of knowledge about the ecosystem and their short-term interests ('mining mentality').

Long-term prospects: a short transition phase by definition.

## 10. Gardening

Objective: mixed cropping of a wide variety of crops, including tree species. Very old traditional form of agro-forestry.

Original vegetation: various forest types, mostly oncomparatively rich soils, often in or near settlements.

Structure of production 'forest': vegetation is layered and includes various tree, shrub and herbaceous species, sometimes also climbers. Wild species may be grown besides cultivated species of native or exotic origin. Grazing is integrated in some of these small-scale land-use systems.

Produce: many products: fruits, seeds, vegetables, tubers, wood, meat, etc.

Technology: low or intermediate.

Product utilization: mainly for own consumption, often also for the local market.

Population density: often applied in combination with another land-use type (shifting cultivation, permanent agriculture), which determines population density. In central Java in combination with irrigated paddy cultivation: up to 2,000 persons per km$^2$. 'Home gardens' in this region occupy about 25 per cent of the agricultural land.

Impact on forest ecosystem: where gardening has developed from favouring useful species in the original vegetation, such species may be important elements in the system (e.g. sago gardens in New Guinea were developed out of the original sago swamp forest). Presence of human settlements nearby may result in gradual improvement in soil fertility.

Long-term prospects: traditional systems have shown a great stability. Gardening has been applied in the Philippines for at least 2,000 years. Newly developed systems may require artificial fertilization if insufficient natural dung is available.

Homegardens in villages in area of rice-cultivation near Yogyakarta (Indonesia; source: Boerboom and Jonkers, 1987).

## 11. Non-wood production from ligneous species in plantations

Objectives: to grow ligneous species (trees or shrubs) for products other than wood (fruits, latex, balm, leaves, etc.).

Original forest: rain forests in lowlands, hills and mountains.

Structure of production 'forest': mostly one layer, consisting of trees or shrubs of one species. In some cases, more layers, e.g. shade tree layers in coffee and cacao plantations (agroforestry), pineapples growing under coco, cover crops under rubber trees, etc.

Produce: many cash crops: coffee, tea, rubber, cacao, palm oil, spices. Also resin. Wood is sometimes used as well (rubber plantations in Malaysia).

Technology: intermediate, often with modern elements (fertilizing, plant improvement;

Conversion of dipterocarp rain forest into oil-palm plantations (Malaysia; source: Boerboom and Jonkers, 1987).

Rubber plantation (Malaysia; source: Boerboom and Jonkers, 1987).

mainly in large estates).

Product utilization: mainly for the international market.

Population density: production may require a substantial labour force as most work is done manually.

Impact on forest ecosystem: virtually nothing is left of the original biocoenose as a rule. In some cases, understorey trees from the original forest are used as shade trees (S. America: *Inga* spp. in coffee plantations).

Long-term prospects: in existing plantations, soil qualities are usually kept at an adequate level (fertilization, nitrogen-fixing cover crops or shade trees). Methods applied in establishing new plantations should be such that soil degradation is avoided and nutrients present in the original ecosystem remain available for plant growth (see 12. Wood production from plantations). Pests and diseases render certain regions unfit for some crops (e.g. rubber in Amazonia).

## 12. Wood production from plantations

Objectives: to grow trees in plantations for wood production.

Original forest: many forest types, often on moderately well to somewhat excessively drained, rather poor soils.

Structure of production forest: usually even-aged, uniform, monocultural stands, mostly of fast growing species in short rotation (pines, eucalypts, *Gmelina*, Albizia). Sometimes combined with agricultural crops during the first years (taungya, e.g. rice cultivation in young teak stands). Some silvicultural systems result in characteristic forest structures (e.g. coppice stands, plantations of teak and *Leucaena*).

Produce: wood, mainly for industrial purposes (pulp, sawn timber, veneer), firewood.

Technology: predominantly modern, often intermediate in communal forests and small holdings.

Product utilization: locally (e.g. firewood) or for domestic or export market.

Population density: usually in sparsely to fairly densely populated areas. Production in more densely populated regions mostly for local consumption (exception: teak cultivation in central Java).

Impact on forest ecosystem: during the first rotation, part of the original forest may be spared initially (line plantations in natural forest). More often, the original forest is cleared before planting (artificial regeneration after clear felling). In line plantations, the original forest is eliminated gradually to favour planted trees. Some rain-forest species may establish themselves in the undergrowth of tree plantations.

Long-term prospects: may lead to soil degradation, especially on shallow yellow sandy soils, imperfectly drained soils and soils liable to surface sealing and compaction (xanthic fer-

Coffee plantation, without shade trees (Costa Rica; source: Boerboom and Jonkers, 1987).

Harvesting in teak plantation (Indonesia; source: Boerboom and Jonkers, 1987).

ralsols, ferralic arenosols, podsols, plinthic and orthic acrisols). Loss of nutrients may be critical, especially where the climate is hot and humid and cation exchange capacity (CEC) of the soil is low. Risks are greatest when clear felling, tillage and short rotation are applied. Soil conservation measures (mulching, cover crops, sparing the litter layer during clearing) reduce soil degradation and leaching.

## 13. Pasture

Characteristics: the forest is cleared and burned and the terrain is turned into pasture. Some trees may be spared. Farms are large with a low production per hectare (1 head of cattle per 1-2 ha).

Forest type: mostly mesophytic forest on residual soils, also on alluvial soils.

Produce: meat, sometimes also dairy products, during the first year some timber.

Technology: intermediate.

Product utilization: meat for national and export markets. Dairy products for national market.

Population density: low, especially in recently cleared areas.

Impact on forest ecosystem: biocoenose is eliminated, except for some trees which are difficult to fell and/or some useful species. In some cases, efforts are made to maintain the tree component (silvo-pastoral systems, e.g. pasture with *Cordia alliodora* in Costa Rica). Soil fertility may remain at an acceptable level through proper management if pasture is established directly after burning (i.e. no shifting cultivation phase). Degradation of soil structure is common.

Long-term prospects: failing management leads to degradation of pasture and proliferation of unpalatable species. Many farms are abandoned within one decade, giving way to secondary shrub vegetation or poorly developed forest. Sustained production may be achieved under favourable conditions and good management, e.g. in regions with a seasonal climate on deep red soils with highly stable soil structure (rhodic ferralsols and rhodic nitosols).

Mountain slopes submitted to heavy grazing, Andes, altitude 2,100 m (Venezuela; source: Boerboom and Jonkers, 1987).

Grazing in recently deforested rain forest area (Ecuador; source: Boerboom and Jonkers, 1987).

## 14. Permanent cropping (no trees), rain fed

Objectives: permanent cultivation of crops other than trees. Usually a variety of annual crops, grown together or in sequence without irrigation.

Forest types: various, on fertile soils.

Produce: annual crops like rice, maize, pulse, pepper and vegetables; sugar.

Technology: intermediate, in some cases modern.

Product utilization: mainly for own consumption or local market. Sometimes for export (pepper, sugar).

Population density: fairly high, e.g. on volcanic soils in Mexico (Vera Cruz, Chiapas): 40 persons per $km^2$. Higher densities may be possible if a higher input level is applied. Sugar plantations also in regions with lower population densities.

Terraced slopes, irrigated, for rainfed crops near Dieng plateau (Indonesia; source: Boerboom and Jonkers, 1987)

Impact on forest ecosystem: forest disappears, except on steep slopes and other less suitable sites.

Long-term prospects: it proved possible to apply permanent cultivation of annual crops for several decades on comparatively rich volcanic soils in regions with seasonal climates and 1,500-2,000 mm of annual precipitation. Experiments on poor soils (acrisols, ferralsols) have been unsuccessful so far. Comparatively promising attempts (e.g. Yurimaguas, Peru, acrisols with high CEC) require advanced technology, high nutrient input, frequent tillage and year-round pest and weed control. Sugar plantations can be sustained if properly managed.

## 15. Permanent cropping (no trees), irrigated

Objective: permanent cultivation of irrigated annual crops (rice).

Forest types: swamp forest, tropical rain forest.

Technology: intermediate (small holdings) to modern (mechanized cultivation).

Product utilization: for own consumption, local, domestic or export market.

Population density: Variable; very high in some regions with volcanic fertile soils (Java, Philippines: up to 2,000 persons per km$^2$, see also 10. Gardening).

Impact on forest ecosystem: original ecosystem disappears. In Java and densely populated parts of the Philippines, forest remnants are mainly at high altitudes and at sacred places.

Long-term prospects: traditional wet rice culture in S.E. Asia has been applied for many centuries. Mechanized rice cultivation can probably be sustained under good management.

## 16. Clear cutting for integral harvesting of wood

Objectives: to harvest virtually all stem wood for industrial purposes (cellulose pulp, charcoal, energy). Usually by private or state-owned companies.

Forest types: predominantly in tropical rain forest (*terra firma*).

Produce: mainly charcoal and cellulose pulp. Timber species may be extracted first in a selective logging operation. Virtually all stems beyond a specified (low) diameter limit are harvested. Large branches may be used too (charcoal exploitation).

Terraced slopes, irrigated, for rice cultivation (Indonesia; source: Boerboom and Jonkers, 1987).

Technology: predominantly modern. Charcoal is produced *in situ*, using kilns (traditional method) or retorts.

Population density: not relevant. Usually a transitory form of land use, which may be followed by other forms of land use which determine population density.

Impact on forest ecosystems: biocoenose is virtually destroyed. Just a few trees survive exploitation and fauna is disturbed severely. The soil is exposed and the use of crawler tractors and wheeled skidders results in serious compaction. Erosion (in hilly terrain) and deteriorated physical soil characteristics hamper regrowth of pioneer and other tree species. Absence of seed trees impedes establishment of primary species, unless wide strips of forest are spared for this purpose.

Long-term prospects: natural regrowth of a new, secondary forest is possible in theory, consisting mainly of species of inferior quality for pulp or charcoal production. In practice, the forest is seldomly allowed to recover (transitory form of land use). In some concessions (e.g. Jari, Brazil), reforestation is applied, using a limited range of (exotic) species planted in monoculture.

## 17. Zero use (waste land)

Forest land without any function useful for mankind exists only where misuse in the past has lead to excessive degeneration of soil and vegetation (waste lands). Such land may be counter-productive and may affect land qualities of ecologically dependent areas. For instance, waste lands on hills and mountains have a negative impact on water supply to land downstream and may result in floods after heavy storms and water shortage in dry seasons. Reforestation aiming at improvement of land qualities is often technically possible, but requires considerable capital input for land reclamation and special planting techniques. Costs involved are very high and often prohibitive.

Clear-cutting of rain forest for charcoal production (Suriname; source: Boerboom and Jonkers, 1987).

## REFERENCES


Anonymous (1978). *Proceedings of the Eighth World Forestry Congress.* Jakarta.

Andreas, B. (1972). *Landwirtschaftliche Betriebsformen in den Tropen.* Hamburg: Paul Parey.

Boerboom, J.H.A. and Wiersum, K.F. (1983). Human impact on tropical moist forests. In *Man's impact on vegetation,* ed. W. Holzner, M.J.A. Werger and I. Ikusima. The Hague: Junk Publishers. Pp. 83-107.

Chadwick, A.C. and Sutton, S.L. (in press). *Tropical rain forest: ecology and management.* Oxford: Blackwell Scientific Publications.

Furtado, F.I., ed. (1980). *Tropical ecology and management. Proceedings of the Fifth International Symposium on Tropical Ecology.* Kuala Lumpur: The International Society of Tropical Ecology.

Mergen, F., ed. (1981). *International Symposium on Tropical Forest Utilization and Conservation, Ecological, Socio-political and Economic Problems and Potentials.* New Haven: Yale University.

Myers, N. (1980). *Conversion of tropical moist forests.* Washington D.C.: U.S. National Research Council.

Ruthenberg, H. (1976). *Farming systems in the tropics.* 2nd ed. Oxford: Clarendon Press.

Sutton, S.L., Whitmore, T.C. and Chadwick, A.C., ed. (1983). *Tropical rain forest: ecology and management.* Oxford: Blackwell Scientific Publications.

Unesco/ UNEP/ FAO (1978). *Tropical forest ecosystems. A state of knowledge report.* Paris: Unesco.



Author's address: Dr. J.H.A. Boerboom and W.B.J. Jonkers, Agricultural University, Department of Silviculture and Forest Ecology, P.O. Box 342, 6700 AH Wageningen, The Netherlands.

# Tropical forest: the ecosystems

by R.A.A. Oldeman*

## 1. Introduction

Without tropical forests, there would be no tropical forest problems. Therefore it is of the utmost importance to know and understand tropical forest ecosystems, before making statements on patterns and processes occurring in situations called 'deforestation', 'forest degradation' or 'soil degradation'. Tropical forest ecology has made spectacular progress during the last fifty years (Jacobs, 1981). Although a huge stream of information has come, and continues to come, it is still very difficult to link it together and all but impossible to give a short and comprehensible image of tropical ecosystems as a result. Still, it is necessary to present some sort of general picture in these pages, as well as can be done now.

The presentation chosen hence is centred upon diagrams and other visual documents, which will be explained in the text. The first three diagrams will outline the three main aspects of tropical forest ecosystems: architecture, energy and nutrient budgets, and species composition (Figs 3, 5 and 8). The next three diagrams will concern the patterns and processes induced by man, at the level of one forest unit, of a whole forest mosaic, and of a formerly deforested terrain under reforestation (Figs 9, 10 and 11).

## 2. Man is in

In a strict ecological sense, there is no reason to separate the human species from other potentially or actually deforesting species. Cherret (in: Sutton et al., 1983) shows that neotropical leaf cutting ants (Fig. 2) are potentially deforesting organisms with a resource-conserving strategy. Kortlandt (in press), in his 'bulldozer herbivore' theory, presents tropical rain forests as *overforested* landscapes, due to a lack of 'natural' pressure from large herbivores. This reasoning can easily be extended to human activities, explaining tropical rain forests by an 'unnaturally' low human pressure. This thought may seem rather absurd, however, it would be more absurd still not to compare influences by man and those of other forest components on an objective basis.

Except for its taxonomical properties, the human component is the only forest component which is able to *dose* its influence and to conceive *alternative* ways of exercising it. Whatever the dosage and whatever the method, such human influences *always* have some non-human equivalent. Westhoff (1976) stated this for temperate forests and it is also true for tropical ones. Clearcutting or nomadic agriculture find their equivalent in the effects of forest fires, earthquakes or storms. Selective cutting corresponds to the influence of factors such as elephants or squalls. The use of chemicals is paralleled by allelopathic effects, so much so that Brünig (1983) speaks of 'natural chemical warfare in natural tropical forests'.

Undesirable effects are caused by human exaggeration, always in dosage and sometimes in means. Chain-saws and man-made chemicals are new means of interaction, even if their effects may be compared to abiotic or biotic ones. Clearcutting in most cases is like an overdose of fire, such as very rarely occurs spontaneously. Chemicals have been used in ridiculously large doses to begin with (pesticides, arboricides) and only recently the use of 'medical' doses has been practised (Boxman et al., this volume; Brünig, 1983). The results have been surprisingly 'natural'.

In this paper, human and other influences in and on tropical forests will not be separated as fundamentally different phenomena, for the reasons given above. The locus of impact and the degree of in-

* I wish to thank L. A. Bruynzeel, A. M. Cleef and P. Schmidt for their constructive criticims and useful suggestions

teraction between human activities and other processes in the forest ecosystem will be assessed as precisely as possible, and in the same way as for other, non-human, biotic and abiotic factors.

## 3. The choice of criteria

Three main aspects have interested forest ecologists up to now. They are:

*Species and populations*
Forest ecology has its roots in plant sociology. Species are identified and counted in a vegetation area, and individuals of each species are also counted. Population analysis is a science of numbers. Results, most often, are given in terms of *species distributions*, floristic and faunistic richness, and *species diversity* per hectare.

*Structure and architecture*
Centuries ago, the species concept has been founded on the description and analysis of *forms*. These are measured and drawn. Differences and correspondences between sizes and proportions are studied. Visualization of results makes structural analysis into a science of *geometry*, like mapping. Most often, the results are given in terms of *scale drawings*, more or less *abstract* or *schematical* and explained by means of *graphical codes*: colours, hatchings and the like.

*Ecophysiology, biogeochemical and energy flows*
In physiology, organic functions have been analysed for a long time in terms of the nature, dosage and movement of molecules in plants and animals. Functions and their regulation are assessed, measured and calculated. This makes

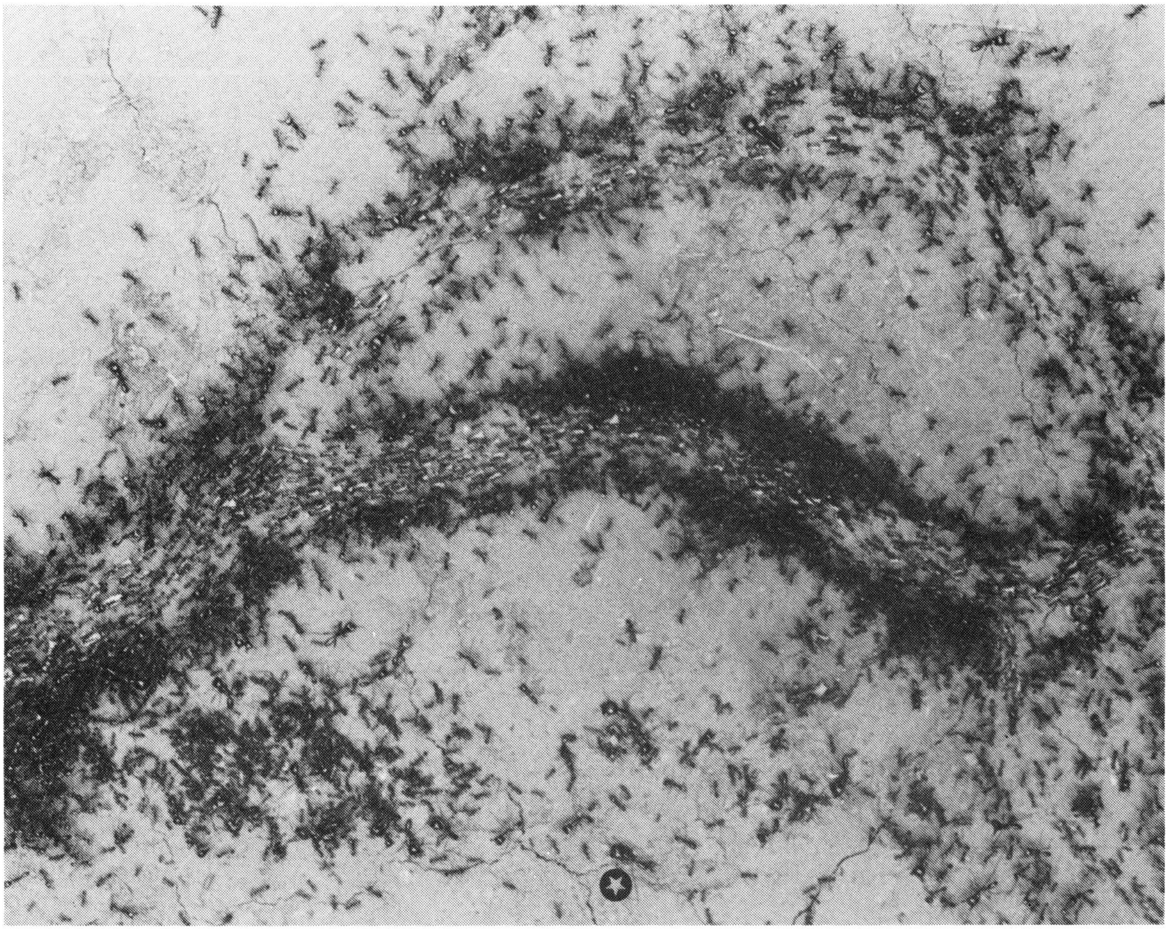

Fig. 2 Army ants (Gabon, 1980), note large-headed warriors (star). Life-strategy comparable to humans, with resource-conserving behaviour (see Sutton et al., 1983).

ecophysiology into a science of *chemistry* and *physics*. Results, most often, are given in terms of *flows*, *reservoirs*, and *feedback loops* of *matter (including water)* and *energy* in living systems.

These aspects should be and are considered on various scales or abstraction levels. For rain forest studies four scales are the most important as a first approximation:

| *Scale* | | *Individual* | *Examples* |
|---|---|---|---|
| organs | | one organ | a feather, a leaf, a liver, a stem |
| organisms | | one organism | an ant, a tree, a bacterium, a man |
| eco-units | eco-systems | one eco-unit | a cornfield, a chablis (Fig. 3) a plantation |
| forest mosaics | | one forest mosaic | rain forest on red clay (Fig. 3), various plantations combined in one forest |

This arrangement of criteria allows a *basic conclusion*, important for the rest of this paper, that is *an individual system is a system which is born, grows up and dies.* This has always been considered at the levels of organs (leaves, nails) and organisms (plants, animals). But ecosystems have never been considered in this way, most of all because no individual limits have been sought. Whereas some sort of skin delimits an organ or an organism, ecosystems have *no skin* which defines their individuality. Still, if ecosystems are considered limitless and measured per hectare, which is *not* a natural limit, many of their properties cannot be understood correctly. Therefore the two following definitions are proposed and used consistently throughout the text:

- Eco-unit: any forest surface (or volume with a basic surface) on which forest development and growth starts, or has started, at the same moment (Fig. 3.B).
- Forest mosaic: a forest surface on one site (soil, climate as defining criteria) containing all different eco-units possible on that site, at all ages (Fig. 3.A).

## 4. Forest architecture and the gene pool (Fig. 3)

Architecture can now be defined as the complex of forms which determine an individual *at a certain scale.* Therefore Figure 3 represents both the architecture at the scale of an individual eco-unit (Fig. 3.B) and at the scale of a forest mosaic (Fig. 3.A). Once the 'ground truth' about the mosaic is known, it can be recognized on aerial photographs and other remote-sensing images.

Architecture is linked to growth and development, because it concerns living systems. The apparent constancy of rain forest mosaics is not a static situation. In a balanced rain forest mosaic, the different eco-units die in the same numbers as they are born and hence are always present in the same average numbers. The character of the mosaic changes only with the site (other climate, soil, slope, and relief) or with impacts from environmental factors which, passingly or over a long time, favour one kind of eco-unit at the cost of another. If the chablis (Fig. 3.A, right hand) causes a new eco-unit to be born, as may be frequent in regions with high thunderstorm frequencies, small eco-units are favoured. In earthquake regions, large eco-units are predominant. A bibliography of recent studies is to be found in Brokaw (in: Leigh et al., 1983) or in Florence (1981).

Looking more precisely at a forest mosaic, there are several kinds of eco-units. They correspond with classic 'seral stages' in the succession theory: large

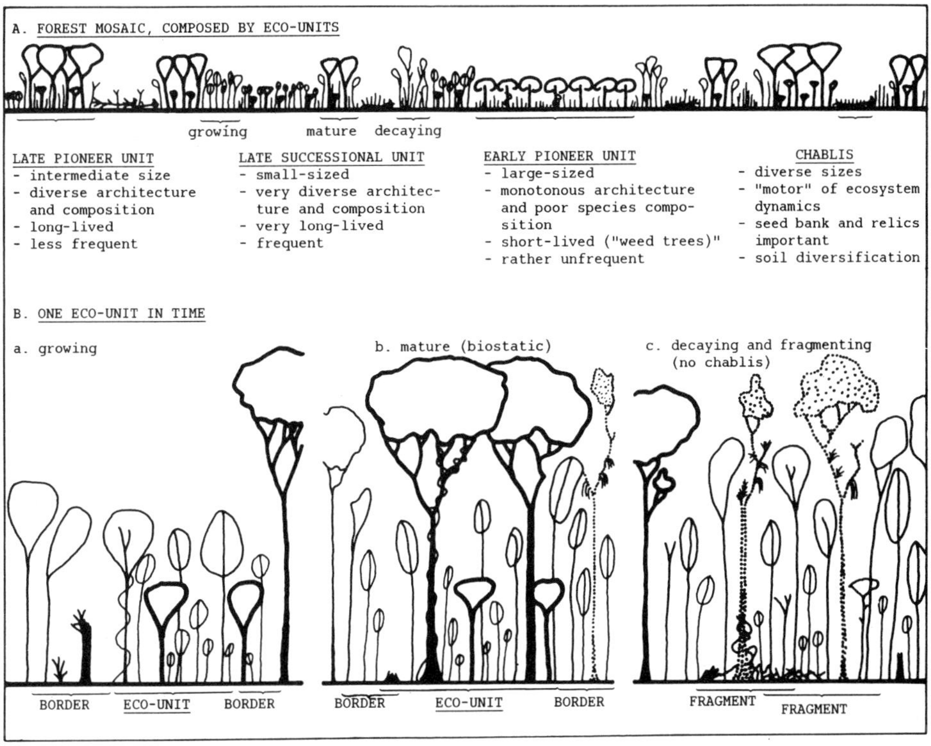


Fig. 3 Architectural analysis of rain forests. Schematic drawings after scale drawings for Ecuadorian and Guyanese rain forests, which differ in several respects from those in Asia and Africa.

A. Forest mosaic, showing different kinds of eco-units which compose it. The mosaic is not complete: note for instance the absence of growing or decaying pioneer eco-units. Proportion of dead, uprooted trees ('chablis' and normal for many tropical American forests. The chablis is the 'motor' of forest genesis ('succession'), because it creates the place where a new eco-unit is 'born'.

B. Three development stages of the same eco-unit, of a late pioneer character. Note difficulty in delimiting eco-units, because no individual 'skin' exists: transitions from 'in' to 'out' are gradual and the limits are border zones of interaction with other eco-units. When the eco-unit dies (c) its place is taken by two smaller young ones. In this case, death is caused by dying of trees on stem, which is a gradual process, not a chablis.

Legend:

- thick-lined: trees of the present, having reached maximum dimensions (small species also);
- thin-lined: potential trees, still having expansion capacity given the occasion, or expanding;
- dotted-lined: trees of the past, decaying or dead.

This code allows to evaluate forest dynamics (see Hallé et al., 1978). Note appearance and disappearance of niches for herbs, lianes, epiphytes with forest development; this also is valid for animals (e.g. decaying wood fauna). On the mosaic level, each different eco-unit provides niches for different species; some species can live in several units. For analytic purposes these transects should be accompanied by maps on level (A) or (B). For other systems of architectural analysis see Vooren (this volume), Boxman et al. (this volume), Kahn (1982, 1983), Guillaumet et al. (1984), Torquebiau (1981).

eco-units are 'pioneer forest', medium-sized units resemble 'late pioneer forest' and small eco-units are similar to 'climax forest'. In real forests, only rarely is there a 'succession' leading from pioneers to late pioneers and from late pioneers to climax. Sooner or later, rain or wind or parasitic fungi interfere, and climax can be succeeded by either pioneer, late pioneer, or other climax eco-units. This leads to a dynamic structural diversification; in each case of death and replacement of an eco-unit, the mutual relations with other eco-units change abruptly.

The richness of these relations co-determines the nature and diversity of plants, animals and micro-organisms which are participating; generally, pioneer eco-units are not very species-rich, late pioneer units are richer, and in the 'climax' eco-units there is an enormous variety in eco-unit architecture which also leads to an enormous diversi-

Fig. 4 Apparent chaos at a gradient between two eco-units, a chablis (foreground) and a fully grown intermediate eco-unit. Upper Approuague River, French Guiana, 1968 (source: Oldeman).

ty in species. Moreover, the smaller the eco-units, the more important the transition zones between eco-units which yield living space to yet other organisms (Fig. 4). The composition of the forest mosaic in terms of different eco-units hence largely determines the species richness of the whole mosaic. Deforestation, which heavily favours pioneer eco-units, also called 'secondary forest', therefore, impoverishes the forest flora and fauna. There are less species, each in larger numbers of individuals.

Within eco-units, relations change with age. As illustrated symbolically on Figure 3.B, young growing eco-units have places where ground herbs can grow, and these herbs are associated with animals. When the canopy closes (Fig. 3.B.b), these organisms have no more living space in that eco-unit and are replaced by others, such as epiphytes (e.g. orchids, bromeliads, ferns) with their associated faunas, whereas the abundant fruiting of the large trees attracts monkeys and birds. At each age, flora and fauna are different. Harvesting large trees causes a shift to eco-units being larger or smaller, but always younger on the average, and so has an impact on species composition of the whole forest mosaic.

In the article of Boerboom and Jonkers (this volume), the use of the forest as a gene pool is mentioned. It is shown here, that every impact on the forest mosaic changes its architecture. This architecture determines the diversity of 'niches' for plants and animals. If the rain forest is to be used for gene production, i.e. as a source for new or improved crops, utmost care should be taken not to perturb its architecture.

Figure 3 finally shows, that rain forests are not 'layered'. Layering is not a property of forest mosaics, but occurs in mature stages of eco-unit development. Young eco-units (Fig. 3.B.a) are not yet layered, old ones (Fig. 3.B.c) are not layered any more. Layering, and 'storeys', occur in parts of the rain forest, but the forest as a whole is not layered. Moreover, layering is not determined by *all* trees in mature eco-units (Fig. 3.B.b), but by the 'trees of the present' only. All other organisms are submitted to the layers (storeys) formed by some few trees. The terms 'herb layer', 'shrub layer', 'small tree layer', 'high tree layer' are average concepts for whole forest mosaics, in which they have only statistical value and no structural significance.

## 5. Ecophysiology and forest productivity (Fig. 5)

The term 'tropical rain forest' refers to site properties, in other terms to 'attributes' of 'land mapping units' as considered by Van Goor (this volume). 'Tropical' here denotes regions without a winter, it is commonly accepted that in this context it does not refer exactly to the regions between the Tropics of Cancer and Capricorn, but to tropical climates. 'Rain' is added because these forests only occur where water is never lacking. There is no 'dry winter' just as there is no 'cold winter'. In these pages, however, no precise definition of rain forests will be given, because is is thought more important to consider the variety of such forests than to establish a watertight definition.

The origin of the name is to be found in Schimper's 'Plant Geography on a Physiological Basis' (1903). Indeed, the name 'tropical rain forest' concerns the *inputs* of heat, light and water into the forest ecosystem and its plants. These inputs are considered illimited in this forest, for all practical purposes. Now, what happens to these inputs in the forest? Figure 5.B shows the calculated or evaluated amounts of energy passing through and being processed by forest components in a rain forest (Fig. 6). It can be read from this figure, for instance, that the 'cost' of the breakdown of dead wood, leaves, flowers and fruits on the forest floor ('litter decomposition') is 13.3 Kcal $m^2$ $day^{-1}$, taken out of the budget of incoming sunlight of 3,830 Kcal $m^2$ $day^{-1}$ on the average. The interaction between these energy flows and the processing of water can be found at the lower left corner of Figure 5.B; 'transpiration work', outlined in another figure not reproduced here.

The same principle can be followed for every quantity of energy and every dose of chemical substances which enters, passes through and remains in or exits from a forest. Boxman et al. (this volume) illustrate this for nutrient turnovers.

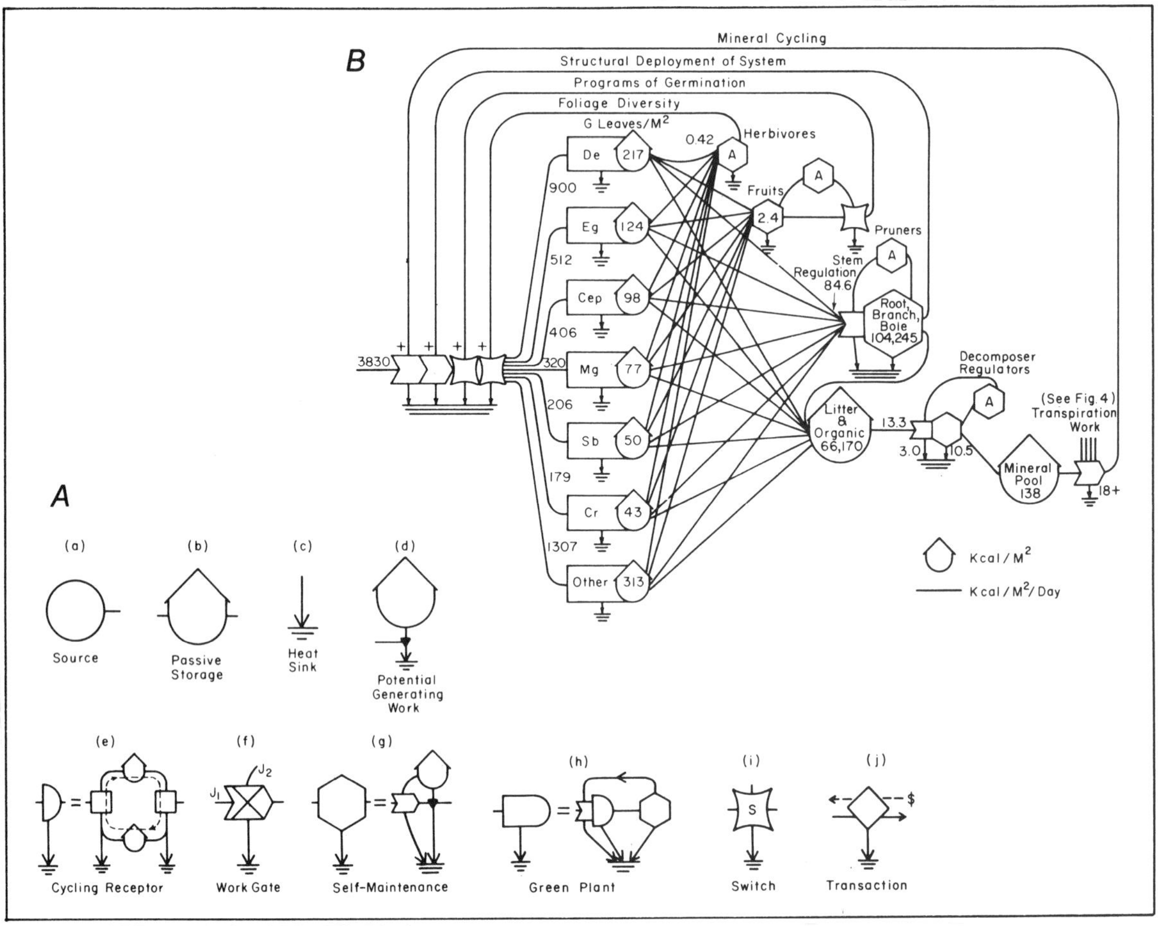


Fig. 5 Ecophysiological image of a rain forest at El Verde (Puerto Rico), after H.T. Odum (in: Odum and Pigeon, 1970). Symbols are explained in: (A) note simplified symbols for more complex loops (Ae, Ag and Ah). Energy network diagram (B) shows some species compartments (symbols De, Eg, etc), estimated according to basal areas ($m^2$ $ha^{-1}$ occupied by tree foots of that species). Some estimated storages of energy, mean rates of energy flow, and some principal known energy flows. Not shown are the details of the auxiliary energies and special repair mechanisms that operate from the storages shown, when activated by stress.

Note: values are averages for arbitrary forest volumes: in this model, populations and energy flows are taken into account, but without individualizing ecosystems as is done on Figure 3. The model may be considered representing average values for an incomplete forest mosaic. For a comparable model, integrated in a MAB-UNESCO project site, see Boxman et al. (this volume), also Brünig (1982).

These figures, when given for forests, are measured, calculated and checked on arbitrary forest surfaces or volumes. No ecophysiological model of one eco-unit (Fig. 3.B) exists as yet, with the exception of man-made forests in which each 'stand' is an artificial eco-unit. Hence such figures are to be used only to characterize *average values for whole forest mosaics*, *if* the description of the forest studied is sufficiently representative for the mosaic. Biomass measurements are related to ecophysiological diagrams because biomass is an important reservoir for energy or nutrients (e.g. root/branch/bole on Figure 5.B).

With these reserves in mind, which are given here to avoid wrong conclusions, such figures are eminent-

Fig. 6 Very steep light gradients between canopy and forest floor play an important role in the energy and nutrient budget of a rain forest. Photo Wide-Lux with sweeping objective over 135° vertically, Crique Grégoire, French Guiana, 1971 (from Oldeman, 1974, p.100; profile diagram and map p. 93 and 95).

ly useful. They illustrate, for instance, the importance of energy bound in living biomass and even in litter, as compared with the energy bound in the mineral soils; in the forest patch of Figure 5, both organic compartments bind more than 1,200 times the energy present in the mineral pool. The figures are less extreme for nutrients; some two-thirds of the total average nutrient content of a rain forest is locked into the living biomass, and one-third in the soil and organic litter. Such facts allow the diagnosis of the effects of *tree cutting, which shifts energy and nutrients* from a living compartment to a dead one, and *harvesting, which is energy and nutrient removal* from the system. This is the basis for the impact evaluations in Figures 9 and 10, later in this paper.

*In fact, ecophysiological diagrams show the balance of gains and losses in a living forest ecosystem or part of it.* They teach us the lesson that there is no free way to obtain biomass, such as wood, fruits, resins or fibres. Every loss will have to be compensated by a gain, if forests are to sustain their natural productivity, not taking into account their diversity. If there are 'natural' gains, such as mineral inputs dissolved in rainwater (not 'acid rain'!), forest productivity recuperates from losses. The mineral reservoir in the soil rather often is poor as a resource for rain forest recuperation, but it allows for some compensation of losses. The rate of reversal of degradation trends is determined by the richness and availability of these resources: some forests may obtain 'easy loans' enabling them to revert to previous productivity levels, other rain forests have trouble finding 'credit'. Ricklefs (1976) quite rightly writes on the 'economy of nature'.

Tropical rain forest soils often are poor to rather poor (see also van IJssel and Sombroek, this volume). This has lead to the evolution of a soil flora and fauna specialized in recuperation of minerals, before these are leached out of reach of the roots. A particular spectacular case are mycorrhiza, associations of tree roots and fungi, which take up nutrients immediately from the litter, i.e. the minerals do not return to the soil, but go directly back to the organisms (Mikola, 1980; Smits, 1982).

As long as mechanical factors, such as storms, squalls, thunderstorm frequency and impact, or soil cohesion are not taken into account in ecophysiological diagrams, no direct link with the architecture of the forest mosaic can be established.

However, the available diagrams of energy, nutrient and water flows do establish a firm connection between the site, as mapped on soil and climatological maps, and the productivity of the forest. In its turn, this productivity is linked to the age of each eco-unit. Young eco-units produce much, mature eco-units produce little or nothing because losses equal gains, and decaying eco-units have a negative production rate (Fig. 3.B).

This build-up of the forest mosaic has much to do with the much-discussed role of tropical forests as 'oxygen producers'. In a balanced forest mosaic, the age distribution of all eco-units is in equilibrium. Because decaying eco-units consume the oxygen produced by the growing ones, and mature eco-units consume what they produce, a forest region has no net oxygen production. Carbon dioxide is as important as oxygen. This gas is bound in living matter. Mean values of biomass volume per hectare hence are a measure for $CO_2$-fixation, and heavy wood harvesting (cf. Fig. 10) hence is a source of carbon dioxide mobilisation, especially when wood is burned as in shifting cultivation.

The fact that the major part of minerals and energy is locked away in forest biomass, explains that there are many tropical rain forest types, depending on the abiotic site resources (see also van IJssel and Sombroek, this volume), which do or do not allow the 'cost' of particular plant, animal or eco-unit strategies in terms of energy and nutrients. Land evaluation methods, as developed in agriculture (van Goor, this volume) hence cannot be applied to rain forest regions without being adapted to this state of affairs. The same data indicate why deforestation often has such enormous impacts, that the absence of forest has much more spectacular consequences than its presence. As soon as the stabilizing forest disappears, whole landscapes can easily become the victim of heavy erosion, rapid leaching, freshets or mud streams (see Otto, this volume).

Finally, it is suggested that no real forest economics are possible if they are not based on the energy and mineral budget of a forest type as a measure for its sustained productivity. Oil-barrel equivalents (energy) and sack-of-fertilizer equivalents (nutrients) would be a more appropriate basis for such economics than dollars or ECUs.

*Nutritional aspects of rain forest ecology, expressed as averages per hectare in a mosaic, lead to relevant conclusions**

The classical conception of a tropical rain forest is that of a lush forest growing on often very poor soils (Richards, 1952). In such a situation most of the nutrient capital of the entire ecosystem (soil plus vegetation) will be found in the living biomass rather than in the soil (Rodin and Basilevich, 1967). These forests maintain themselves through an efficient use of nutrients supplied from the atmosphere or from weathering of the substrate, continuously recirculating these nutrients and allowing very few of them to be lost through leaching out of the soil (Fig. 7, and Boxman et al., this volume).

A very good example of the above is provided by the Evergreen Seasonal Forest on never flooded terrain ('terra firma') near Manaus in the Amazon Territory of Brazil. Figure 7 summarizes the organic matter, calcium, and magnesium budgets for this forest type. Clearly this forest is capable of maintaining its living biomass at the high level of 473 t $ha^{-1}$ despite the small amount of calcium in the soil and of potassium below 30 cm depth. Such a lack of correlation between soil fertility status and biomass of old forests is to be expected as long as there has been enough time for them to build up their nutrient capital from nutrients brought into the system via rainfall. Indeed, some of the highest biomass figures for tropical forests have been reported for forests growing on exceedingly nutrient-poor soils in Sarawak (Proctor et al., 1983).

Rather than on site fertility alone one would expect forest biomass to be dependent on the interactive effects of a number of climatic and topographic factors, such as length of dry season, prevailing temperatures, cloud incidence, occurrence of hurricanes, slope stability and drainage situation (Grubb, 1977; Odum, in: Odum and Pigeon, 1970;

* Sub-paragraph by L. A. Bruynzeel.

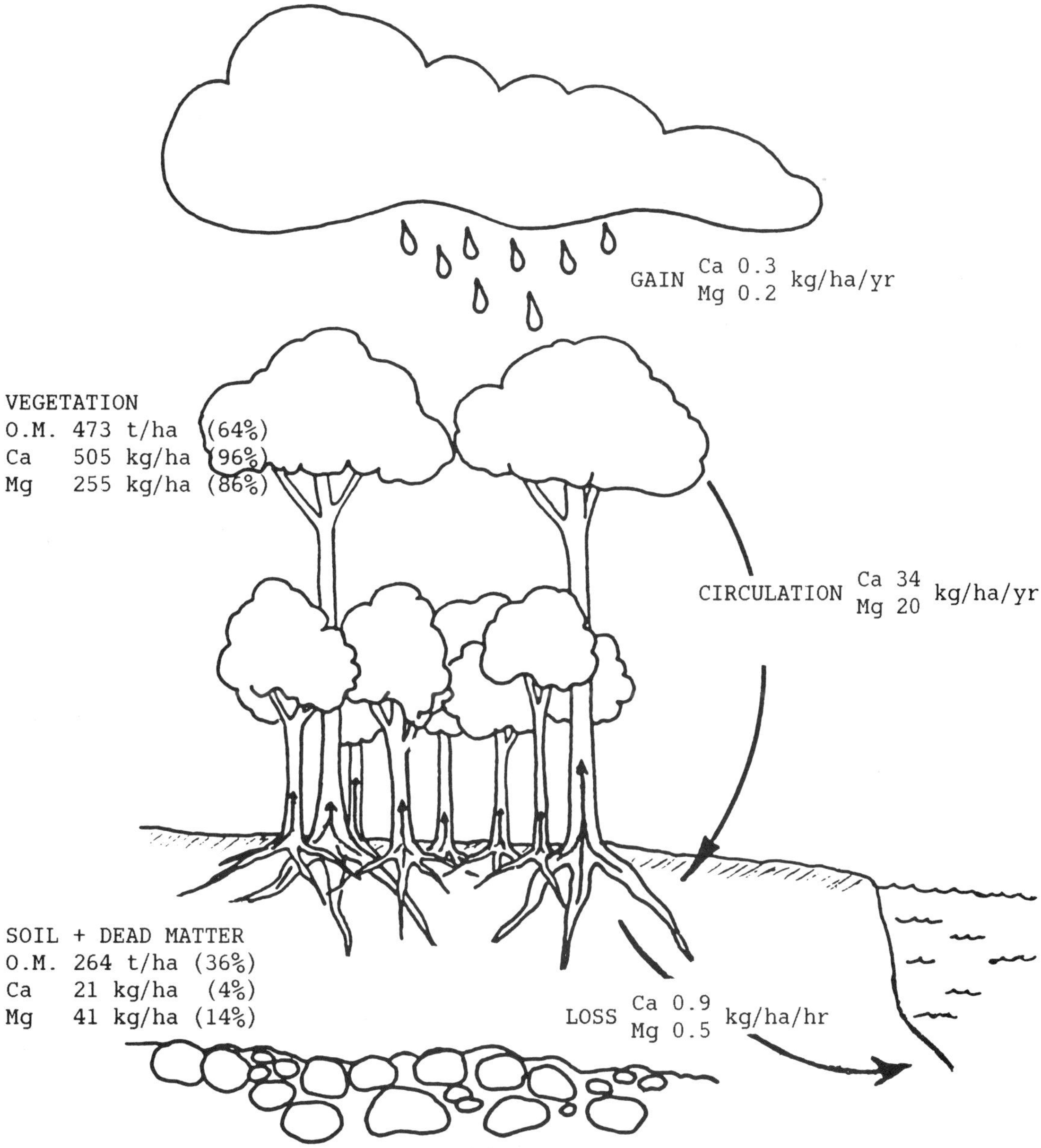


Fig. 7 Organic matter (O.M.) and selected nutrient budgets for an evergreen seasonal forest in Central Amazonia; data from Klinge (1976) and Brinkmann (1983), put together by Bruynzeel. This figure shows the average condition of an Amazonian forest mosaic as imagined by the designer: it does not represent an architectural analysis of its mosaic.

Fölster et al., 1976; Proctor et al., 1983). However, despite great differences in rainfall regime, cloud occurrence, soil fertility and drainage condition, very similar biomass figures have been obtained for two montane forests in Venezuela (Steinhardt, 1979) and Papua New Guinea (Edwards and Grubb, 1977, 1982), both growing at an altitude of 2,500 m above sea level.

The 'tightness' of the nutrient cycle in the Amazon forest of Figure 7 becomes evident when one compares the amounts of calcium and magnesium transferred to the forest floor by crownwash and litterfall ('circulation') with those leached out of the soil profile (see also Boxman et al., this volume).

In their paper on structure and functioning of Amazon ecosystems Herrera et al. (1978) have suggested a number of nutrient-conserving mechanisms through which forests are able to maintain themselves. The most important of these mechanisms are the development of a thick root mat composed by roots and mycorrhiza hyphae which filters out most of the nutrients passing through as well as the occurrence of production-efficient thick leathery leaves to reduce insect damage and leaching of nutrients out of the leaves. Another major strategy is believed to be the withdrawal of nutrients from leaves before they fall.

Forests growing on nutrient-poor substrates thus appear to be highly adapted to their environment and therefore are very vulnerable to disturbance. Disruption of the nutrient-conserving mechanisms - especially the root mat and the humus layer - will certainly cause a deterioration of the environment (Brinkmann and Nascimento, 1973) and a diminishing production capacity.

## 6. Species, populations and diversity of organisms (Fig. 8)

Organisms are easily seen to be either different or similar. As much as two centuries ago, tropical rain forests hence were already studied as if they were collections of species, for instance by Von Humboldt (see Botting, 1973). Much has been written on species compositions of rain forests. It cannot be denied that one of the most ethical and powerful interactions between modern man and rain forest is the esthetical pleasure of admiring the many wonders of creation among its plants and animals (e.g. Sandved and Emsley, 1979 or Ayensu, 1980).

Describing and naming plants and animals, in order to recognize them, is a first necessity to come to grips with their teeming diversity. Generations of systematic botanists and zoologists have not yet achieved completeness. According to Myers (1979), some 85 per cent of existing species are neither known nor named, and this may well apply to tropical rain forests. Nevertheless, the most frequent and the largest rain forest species are more or less known, although this differs per rain forest region. West Africa, for instance, is rather well covered. Large parts of Amazonia, on the contrary, still yield a considerable number of 'new' plants and animals each year, among which are large forest trees.

Taxonomists sometimes stress the necessity to make a complete description of all species before rain forests can be understood (e.g. in: Fournier and Sasson, 1983). Still, the species composition of tropical rain forests has been studied, even if this meant limiting the species to be listed, for instance to 'all trees over 5 cm diameter at breast height'. Figure 8.A shows one method to do this. The number of species is counted on 10 x 10 m (one are), then the next one, and so on until there are no more species appearing. The comparison with Figure 3.A shows that in this way the number of species, belonging to a certain forest mosaic and a certain category of species, e.g. trees, can be established. It is to be noted, that *neither the eco-units, nor the age of the plants* and animals sampled are taken into account in this sort of analysis. Very often only regression curves are given, allowing to evaluate the total number of species present in the 'forest ecosystem' studied. Spectacular graphs in this sense are to be found in Rollet (1974), some being reproduced in Fournier and Sasson (1983).

More recently, but starting much longer ago, this approach has been more and more replaced by species mapping (Fig. 8.B and C). Clustering of species, or their isolated occurrence, can be established and mathematically analysed. Van Roosmalen (1980) used tree maps to analyse the home range of spider monkeys, especially with a view to pinpointing food sources for these animals (Fig. 8.B). Although these maps are much more significant for the *explanation* of the forest ecosystems, they still lack precise links with either architecture or ecophysiology of the forest mosaic. One may suppose that clustered *Trichilia* trees find their niche in special eco-units, but there is no proof of this. The explanation may also reside in soil fac-

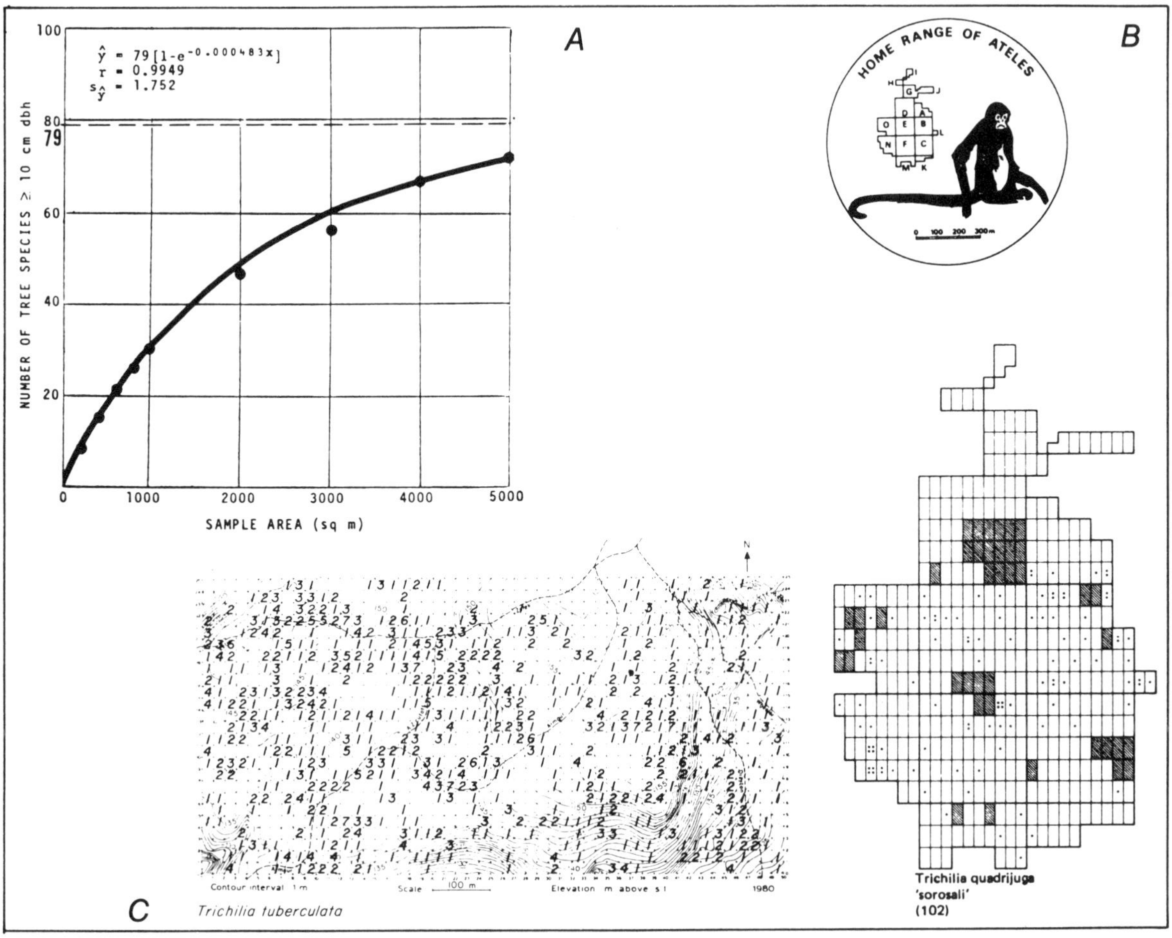


Fig. 8 Examples of population-analytical images of neotropical rain forests.

A. Species-area curve for the Los Inocentes site in Costa Rica, after Holdridge et al., 1971. The regression curve represents an average for part of the mosaic, and hence may not be used to characterize any one eco-unit.

B. Distribution of one food-tree in the home range of the Suriname spider monkeys studied by Van Roosmalen (1980). This distribution could be linked to forest architecture if transects were available, and to ecophysiological functions if turnover rates were known.

C. Distribution of a tree species on Barro Colorado Island, Panama, studied by Hubbell (in: Sutton et al., 1983).

Note: The geometrical grid is used as a reference system in (B) and (C); the rectangles are not small ecosystems, because they do not represent natural limits in nature. For other population-oriented studies there is a large literature; the most extended study, of over 3,000 km of Venezuelan rain forest is due to Rollet (1974).

tors, seed dispersal mechanisms, or still other causes.

Based on the sampling and processing methods mentioned above, many formulae have been developed to obtain 'species richness indexes' or 'diversity indexes'. Such data, and such conclusions are useful to provide insight in 'minimal areas'. Minimal areas are the minimal surfaces of rain forest in which it is judged that all species may exist and survive. Minimal areas hence are different for each forest type, i.e. for each Land Mapping Unit (van Goor, this volume). The question has been treated by Jacobs (1981).

This limited use of indexes has been felt in the first place by zoologists, like Van Roosmalen (1980), Rijksen (1978), Hladik (e.g. in: Montgomery, 1978) or Bourlire (in: Meggers et al., 1973). Figure 8.B shows how *explanations* were sought of the ecological relations between one monkey species and a large array of plant species. The figure represents one map out of hundreds. Bourlire (l.c.) rightly places such research in the context of *co-evolution.*

Co-evolution is the process of species selection under the selection pressure of other species. In this sense, the breeding of domestic animals and of crops is an example of co-evolution between *Homo sapiens* and other species. Generally, the questions relating to co-evolution are attacked by a thorough study of one species and its relations with all others in its environment. The monkeys mentioned are 'generalists', in relation with hundreds or thousands of other species. The *Atta* ants (Fig. 12) probably have a lesser number of relations with other species, and true specialists like some sloths mainly depend on interaction with one food tree. On the other hand, many plant species depend for the dispersal of their seeds largely on mammals or birds. Elimination of the latter will have a strong impact on the composition of the forest.

Now relationships between species, the pressure they may exercise one upon another, and the new species that slowly develop under this pressure, are not the fruit of hazard. As stated above, the architecture of the forest mosaic and of the eco-units composing it procures 'ecological niches' for all species, 'niches' which appear and disappear with forest development. When they disappear in one place in the mosaic, they appear again in other eco-units. It can now be understood that the relations between plants and animals are both the result and the builders of forest architecture (Charles-Dominique et al., 1981).

On the other hand, the possibilities for co-evolution largely depend on the 'budget' which is available in the form of abiotic resources. Sun radiation, water and minerals are for each plant individually available in limited amounts as described above; in the rain forest most often the minerals form the minimum factor. A minimum factor is the resource which, by its rapid exhaustion, immobilizes other resources. Individual plants and animals, or the species they belong to, can be analysed as the 'carriers' of part of the forest productivity and part of the interrelationship web. Co-evolution stands under the pressure of a limited 'budget'. *Functional shifts* from one species to one or more others are generally possible and do occur. Examples are the symbiotic relationships between fungi and trees. Between the same fungal species and the same tree species, this relationship may be mutualistic in one forest type (mycorrhiza) and parasitic in another forest type with another mineral budget.

In terms of the gene pool, this means that tropical rain forests are not only interesting because of their enormous species richness, but still more so because all the time there are new races and species being born. The genetic variability is so enormous, that within some groups (e.g. the genus *Aspidosperma*, an Apocynaceous tree group from South America) there is a continuum of trees *between* species, an ever ongoing reshuffling of the genetic cards. Tropical rain forests hence are the earth's most promising source of *innovation* for crops and domestic animals.

*Tropical forests are often said to contain the highest number of plant species in the world as compared to any other vegetation type**

* Sub-paragraph by A. M. Cleef

Indeed, zonal tropical rain forests contain a considerable number of vascular *species* for a given forest type. *Comparative* inventory has started quite recently in the tropics (Gentry, 1981; Prance, 1982). On the average, the neotropical flora seems most rich with some 90,000 vascular species. This is three times the estimate for Africa and 2.5 times that of Australasia (Raven, in: Simmonds et al., 1976; Gentry, 1982a, b). Gentry and Dodson (in press) conclude that vascular plant species richness of lowland tropical rain forests is mostly due to non-tree habit groups, such as shrub and herb species; especially epiphytes account for the richness in number and in species in wet and pluvial tropical American forests both in lowland and in the submontane reaches (Gentry and Dodson, in press).

In general, diversity in vascular plants decreases towards drier forest types (Gentry, 1982a, b) and along the altitudinal (temperature) gradient (Cleef et al., 1984) and towards the border zones of the tropics (Gentry, 1982a, b). Moreover, it is a well-known fact that diversity of species in tropical rain forests is not distributed homogeneously. Particular regions are especially rich in species, which often occur nowhere else. These so-called refugia or relic areas (see Van IJssel and Sombroek, this volume) should be taken into account in land-use evaluation and land-use planning, because of their immense value as gene reservoirs and their significance for science and nature conservation.

## 7. Dosage of influence by the human component (Figs 9 and 10)

In his contribution to this volume, Luning defines the 'requirements' of human society concerning the tropical rain forests. In our context, these requirements are part of human autecology. All requirements lead to human intervention in rain forests, so much so, that no strictly 'virgin' forests remain on this planet.

The disquieting thing is not this human influence *per se*, but its growing menace for the survival of those forests on which it depends. Whatever the philosophy at the base of human requirements (Jacobs, 1981), sooner or later the time comes when requirements are no more than dreams, for the simple reason that the real forest can only yield so much, and no more. There are several ecological rules applying to this development, when ever more human beings try to satisfy ever more requirements with ever ruder, cheaper and more powerful means. To prevent ultimate loss of the forest, these rules should be borne in mind in forest management:

*The rule of functional shifting*, which has been presented in the paragraph on species and their evolution, applies to human interventions. Shifting of a 'squall function', the making of chablis, towards a 'human function', selective cutting, also means the shifting of selection pressure on all species in the forest. Every systematic intervention hence is followed by demographic effects on both plant and animal species, so that in the end, the whole system, the human component included, has adapted to changed conditions and can function once more within a comparable energy and nutrients budget. To demonstrate this, the Figures 9 and 10 compare light and heavy human interventions, at the eco-unit and the mosaic level successively.

*The rule of reversibility* is already implicit on Figure 3.B. Once functional shifts become important, two phenomena may cause these shifts to become irreversible. One is extinction of a plant or animal species, which is forever, and which occurs when the minimum population numbers during a demographic oscillation fall below those of minimal survival requirements. In such cases, only human help may sometimes reverse the development towards disappearance of a species. The second phenomenon is the triggering of self-reinforcing degradation cycles. This is so often the case, that there are common names for such cycles: pests (Fig. 12), diseases, erosion, leaching and others. Some of them appear suddenly, others, such as the loss of minerals, develop more slowly. The right-hand columns of Figures 9 and 10 indicate reversibility on a time-scale, related to one average tree life of about 80 years. It is known that planning horizons are normally limited to four years and never exceed ten years (Wing

| Human-induced processes at the ECO-UNIT LEVEL<br><br>✪ = tree to be cut<br><br>A. "selective cutting" (by chainsaw and skidder)<br><br>B. "clearcutting", burning and agriculture (by chainsaw and burning, no skidder) | A  | * | B  | * |
|---|---|---|---|---|
| Consequences | | | | |
| 1. ARCHITECTURE | - breaking up of one eco-unit in two<br>- artificial form of new eco-unit | +<br>++ | - producing of one large eco-unit<br>- no lateral gradients left | ±<br>- |
| 2. ENERGY, WATER AND NUTRIENTS | - soil compaction, permeability<br>- leaching and erosion<br>- nutrient loss by harvest biomass | ±<br>-<br>++ | - mineralization organic matter<br>- leaching and erosion<br>- nutrient loss by cutting and burning and agricultural harvest | ±<br>--<br>- |
| 3. COMPONENT SPECIES | - richness flora & fauna (whether poorer or richer)<br>- diversity<br>- nature of participants diversity<br>- soil compation, soil life | +<br>++<br>-<br>- | - impoverishment of flora and fauna<br>- diversity<br>- nature of participants diversity<br>- soil compaction, soil life | ±<br>-<br>--<br>-- |

✱ Reversibility of effects
++ very fast + rather fast ± within 1 tree-lifespan - longer than 1 tree-lifespan -- perhaps, in centuries

Fig. 9 Examples of effects of human impacts on one eco-unit: selective cutting (A) as compared to slash-and-burn agriculture (B). The measure of the impact is the time necessary to reverse it, between very fast (less than 10 years) and irreversible in practical terms (longer than two centuries, if ever). *This evaluation is not very accurate.* As a provisional tool to establish impact and weight of human-induced processes it takes into account three categories of criteria. The precision of this evaluation should be improved and the number of criteria increased along with the development of knowledge, but today it can serve already as a diagnosis which, previous to human intervention, can make sure whether such intervention is justified in view of the aims of forest management or land management. Note that this diagnosis will *not* be the same of different sites or land mapping units (LMU, Van Goor, this volume) and will change also with different technology (e.g. selective cutting with machines; shifting agriculture by hand). Compare with Figure 3 natural development of same eco-unit.

Easton, 1976). For the human mind, events lack reality when considered over larger time-spans. Such events can just be calculated, not planned, and are perceived at most as ghostly menaces or purposes. For *planning* purposes a human-induced process hence is only reversible when reversal occurs within 4 to 10 years, whereas from the ecological view-point the natural forest makes no haste, a century is nothing.

*The rule of scale* is complex. Comparing Figures 9 and 10, it is easily seen that Figure 9.A (light intervention with heavy machines) is reproduced in several eco-units of the mosaic on Figure 10.A. On the mosaic scale, however, it represents a regularly recurring intervention, which is selectively directed not only to one wood species, but also to the eco-unit that gives its niche to that species. An example is African Ebony (*Diospyros* sp.div.), or Guyanese

Human-induced processes at FOREST MOSAIC LEVEL

| Consequences | A. SELECTIVE CUTTING (★ = to be cut) | ✱ | B. All-TIMBER CUTTING (● = to be cut) | ✱ |
|---|---|---|---|---|
| 1. ARCHITECTURE | - changed eco-unit distribution | + | - some large eco-units | - |
| | - lateral gradients eco-units | ++ | - lateral gradients eco-units | ± |
| | - form eco-units | + | - form eco-units | - |
| | - changed micro/meso climate | + | - change micro/macro climate | - |
| 2. ENERGY, NUTRIENTS, WATER | - soil compaction, permeability (localized) | ± | - soil compaction permeability (all-over) | - |
| | - erosion | + | - erosion | - |
| | - leaching (localized) | + | - leaching (generalized) | - |
| | - energy and matter flows | + | - energy and matter flows | - |
| 3. COMPONENT SPECIES | - richness flora and fauna | ++ | - richness flora and fauna | ± |
| | - diversity changes | ++ | - diversity changes | - |
| | - participants in diversity (species) | + | - participants in diversity (species) | - |
| | - soil flora and fauna | + | - soil flora and fauna | - |

PLEASE, NOTE THAT DIAGNOSIS WILL BE DIFFERENT ACCORDING TO SITE (LMU) AND TECHNOLOGY APPLIED

✱ Reversibility of effects
++ very fast + rather fast ± within 1 tree-lifespan - longer than 1 tree-lifespan -- perhaps, in centuries

Fig. 10 Examples of human impacts on a forest mosaic: selective cutting (A) compared to massive harvesting of all usable trees (B), both mechanized (compare Boxman et al., this volume). For measuring criteria see Figure 9. Heavy impact by massive harvesting on soil and hydrology: in fact, the original land maping unit (LMU) is changed in several of its attributes and hence transformed into another LMU (see Van Goor, this volume). Again, the diagnosis can not be precise enough at our present level of knowledge, but it can and does predict trends to be taken into account before starting land management operations.

Snakewood (*Piratinera* sp.; *Brosimum* sp.) which occur in rare, old, small-sized eco-units showing a particular development. The whole ecosystem as a complex hence becomes unbalanced, a large risk in 'nature-conforming' silvicultural systems which aim at enriching the forest in some marketable species at the cost of un-marketable ones. In such systems the designers nevertheless aim at reversible effects.

When heavy interventions occur, comparison between Figures 9.B and 10.B shows that a shifting cultivation field, covering some eco-units at most, differs much from a intensive wood-harvesting operation. This last intervention may cover more than one mosaic, e.g. all mosaics on hilltops, on slopes and in valleys. So whole drainage basins may become deforested with the well-known consequences. For one mosaic, which is most often bound to topography, the effects have been evaluated in the right-hand column on Figure 10.B. A drainage basin, however, is commonly covered by different mosaics, and the effects then become compound. Here, the techniques used in deforestation are determinants for the effects; remnants together with heavy machinery or fire may trigger extremely fast degradation with sheet or gully erosion, and freshets to be endured by the people downstream (see Otto, this volume). If deforestation is done by hand and forest remnants together with the organic soil layer remain largely intact, the soil may be spared to a certain extent. Spontaneous recuperation of the forest, however, will take many centuries. If in the meantime the land is put to agricultural use, still another sequence of forest reconstitution is followed. The few known examples of these processes known include the forests on the river Comt in French Guiana, which grew back on the large farms abandoned by the Jesuits in the 1770s. These forests are still very different from other forests nearby, as shown by their species composition. No architectural analysis or ecophysiological models are available for these forests, the general aspect suggesting a late-secondary character.

These rules in general apply to all forest uses enumerated by Boerboom and Jonkers (this volume), except for agriculture and tree plantations. Those will be treated in the next paragraph.

## 8. Let there be forest (Fig. 11)

Reforestation is a term often heard these days. The very and dire need of reforestation or afforestation is the result of mismanagement of forests in the past. Excessive human 'requirements' in many places have led to deforestation, followed by soil degradation. Between the disappearance of the forest and the exhaustion of the soil, most often some system of agriculture has been intercalated.

It cannot be said too often that good forest management of existing forests is economically much more interesting than the recuperation of degraded lands by means of afforestation. Prevention not only is better than healing, it is cheaper too.

Figure 11 represents the development stages of a planted forest. This is a very general outline. In fact, this development so much depends on the state of the land available and on the techniques and species to be applied, that this figure may only be used as a very global illustration of reforestation processes. Hence in the last column all kinds of variables have been listed under the title 'diagnostic features'. They refer to the many 'ifs' that one encounters when making a reforestation design for a particular site or land mapping unit (van Goor, this volume).

As in all plantation systems, agricultural crops included, the 'production-carriers' are a few species only. Most often, they are chosen because their product is not only useful for human survival, but marketable too. An exception would be pure protection forests, designed to counteract erosion or to regulate the water regime. The rule of functional shifting (see above) hence applies very strongly to such artificial eco-units. Most ecosystem functions are concentrated on a few species in a simply structured eco-unit. Such an 'agricultural field' or 'forest stand' has to possess enough components, structures and ecophysiological eco-unit processes to be able to survive (see Brünig, 1984).

In this sense, a forest plantation is an authentical ecosystem, in the same way that a cow, however artificially bred, is an authentic animal capable of survival. In forestry this means that such eco-units will have to be capable of survival during tens of years at least, after which they should be regenerated. The initial plantation design therefore is much more important than in agriculture, because interactions between components, and between the stand and the environment, should be functioning in a stable way for a long time. The necessity of reforestation already is an economic liability, caused by previous unsound economics. This liability should not, and most often cannot, be bought off by expensive measures to help plantations survive. The most elegant way to solve this dilemma is to start the plantation with as many inbuilt security factors as possible, biological factors, to be sure.

On degraded lands, nutrients always are more or less exhausted. In the humid tropics, in general, they can only be recuperated in very small amounts from the soil and from rain-water (Fig. 7). Hence the forest often has to be provided with a small nutrient capital to begin with. Degraded soils, moreover, show an impaired hydrological turnover, and notwithstanding heavy rain, irrigation may be necessary. The choice of species is of the first importance. It is to be stressed that limiting this choice to tree species only is too narrow an approach. Productivity and ecosystem rehabilitation can be much improved if certain root fungi (mycorrhiza) are added in the nursery; they cause trees to have an enhanced capacity for water uptake and mineral processing. The introduction of herbaceous plants most often takes the form of

| | | | |
|---|---|---|---|
| Human-induced processes<br>MOSAIC LEVEL<br><u>reforestation</u> | degraded land<br> | ARCHITECTURE:<br>- none, or herbaceous vegetation<br>ECOPHYSIOLOGY:<br>- barren, often water shortages<br>COMPONENT SPECIES:<br>- hardy herbs, few animals, poor microflora and -fauna | DIAGNOSTIC FEATURES:<br>- waterbalance<br>- soil structure and chemistry<br>- relief, slopes, microrelief<br>- local species<br>- local technology and land use |
| PLANTING | plantation, canopy open<br> | ARCHITECTURE:<br>- one large eco-unit, still growing<br>ECOPHYSIOLOGY:<br>- compensated by irrigation, fertilizer, ...<br>COMPONENT SPECIES:<br>- introduced by human, local relics | DIAGNOSTIC FEATURES:<br>- irrigation technology<br>- fertilizer balance; site preparation<br>- compatibility of species<br>- availability, quality land |
| TENDING | canopy closed<br> | ARCHITECTURE:<br>- large eco-unit, growing, trees competing<br>ECOPHYSIOLOGY:<br>- compensation ending, nearly self-support<br>COMPONENT SPECIES:<br>- poor in large ones, enriching microlife | DIAGNOSTIC FEATURES:<br>- de/increase water loss?<br>- chemical balance: growth?<br>- erosion?<br>- balance between populations (or imbalance: diseases?)<br>- human impact: care for trees |
| THINNING | canopy passingly opened<br> | ARCHITECTURE:<br>one eco-unit, no mature architecture<br>ECOPHYSIOLOGY:<br>self-supporting even with thinning losses<br>COMPONENT SPECIES:<br>slight enrichment, tolerant species | DIAGNOSTING FEATURES<br>as above, dosage of human impact very important here: choice products <u>or</u> ecosystem |
| (thinnings omitted)<br>at least 50 yr<br>HARVEST | canopy closed/opened<br>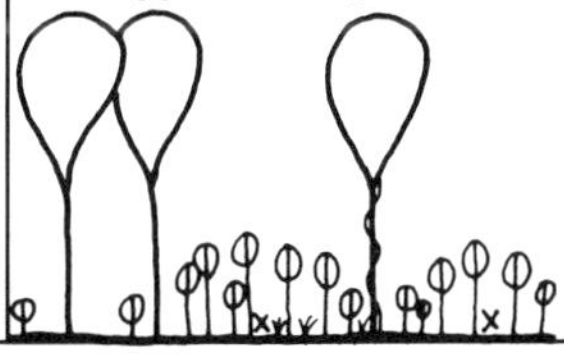 | ARCHITECTURE:<br>- large eco-unit fragmented in smaller ones<br>ECOPHYSIOLOGY:<br>- set-back in biomass by harvest<br>COMPONENT SPECIES:<br>- possibility to enhance diversification by natural immigration or introduction in diverse environment | DIAGNOSTIC FEATURES:<br>- water and soil stabilized?<br>- harvesting systems: selective cuttings? group cutting? clearcutting?<br>- selection of species and/or regulation of populations (diseases, pests)? |

Fig. 11 Reforestation, as exemplified here, is very expensive and takes a long time as compared with correct sustainable management of the original resource. Land degradation in this example has not gone very far, because it is supposed to be possible to start diversification of artificial pioneer plantation forest as soon as 50 years after planting. The line of development, as measured according to architectural, ecophysiological and population criteria, can show enormous variation, hence the list of diagnostic features to be taken into account has been added; if these factors change, other techniques and species have to be chosen for the job, and the development may take somewhat less time but most often considerably more time. In fact, deforestation and land degradation have changed Land Mapping Units (LMU) and Land Utilisation Types (LUT). Reforestation is site restoration or upgrading of spoiled forest lands. Features of the natural forest come back very slowly and depend much on the presence or absence of intact pristine forest nearby as a gene source. Complete restoration of the original ecosystem complexity is deemed impossible in time-spans that can be planned (source: Oldeman, 1987).

agricultural crops (taungya system), but for fast forest establishment the use of green manure plants, such as leguminous herbs or small climbers should be seriously considered for the reconstruction of an organic soil layer. Finally, thought should be given to the choice of insects to be introduced in the young plantation; this aspect has been little researched but soil-burrowing insects may rapidly improve soil structure and predatory insects would prevent pests. The way to further diversification can so be laid from the beginning, although it may take a long time before tree species diversification becomes possible. In this respect, Figure 11 may well be over-optimistic.

A comparison between Figures 3.B and 11 shows the impoverishment of such artificial stands as seen against 'virgin' forests. Still, it should not be accepted that in tropical forestry monospecific tree plantations are the last word. Even if the associated species are well chosen, the biological risks remain considerable. Reforestation implies large investments, and designs to lower the risk of their loss are no luxury. Work should henceforth be stimulated to lay the ecological basis for the design of mixed, low-risk plantations which should replace the actual monospecific ones gradually. If human beings fully realize their place as a forest component, i.e. a species which has to give to the forest as much as it receives from it, they cannot remain satisfied with poor, high-risk, artificial forests as more than a transitional step towards better forests. The penalty is the gradual loss of all forests, consecutive to the gradual loss of one component species after another.

## 9. There is no conclusion

The present text, as the title announces, has been rather severely limited to the ecological view-point on tropical forests. This short analysis is not in vain and allows the presentation of some facts, viewpoints, and suggestions that seem useful. *If* human beings assume their responsibility as self-regulating forest components, there is a future both for tropical forests and for those human beings. A statement beginning with 'if', however, is not a conclusion.

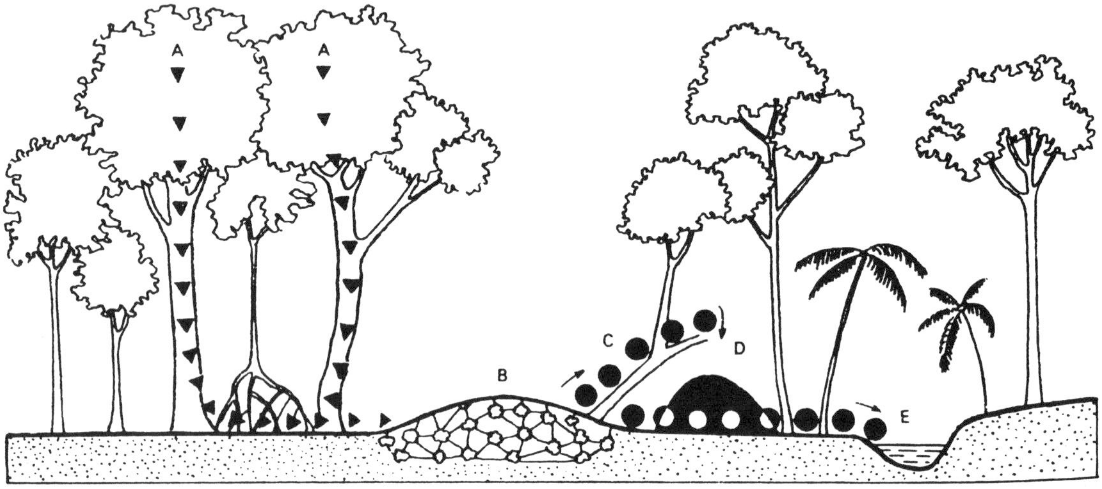


Fig. 12 Simplified example of the interaction between forest architecture, population biology and biogeochemical cycling, as linked in the way of life of the South-American leaf-cutting ant, *Atta collombica tonsipes*. Harvesting of leaf fragments along two-way mini-roads (A). Cultivation of fungi by ants on fermented leaf fragments in their city (B). Garbage disposal roads (C) leading to 'city dumps' (D) or creeks (E). Energy consumed (leaf production by trees, leaf harvesting, city building, city maintenance) is enormous, and impact on the surrounding forest is visible to the naked eye. When food plant assortment is changed, as in human agriculture, the delicate checks and balances that keep ant populations in balance with their forest resource are perturbed. The species then becomes a major agricultural pest, contributing significantly to earlier exhaustion and degradation of land, because huge amounts of energy and nutrients are channeled not to human consumption but to prolific ant life. It's not the species which is a 'pest', but its role in a denatured environment. Leaf-cutting ants in balanced amounts are healthy components of healthy forests (source: after Jeník, 1979).

An enormous amount of work awaits us. Tropical rain forests deserve this work, both as one of the wonders of creation and as a source of innumerable blessings for humanity, in the form of products and services. Tropical forest conservation and management still are in the Stone Age; there are some tools, but these are not the tools to solve the forest problems of the twenty-first century. There is only one way forward; let's go to the field, the laboratory and the drawing-table to gather the facts and make the necessary designs.

The tropical rain forest regions need forest doctors, the old-fashioned village variety who establishes his diagnosis on symptoms that are sure, who makes a prognosis of further development, and who conceives and puts into action the preventive or curative measures necessary. There can be no conclusion as long as such doctors are not there.

## REFERENCES

Ayensu, E.S. (1980). *Jungles.* London: Jonathan Cape.

Botting, D. (1973). *Humboldt and the cosmos.* London: Sphere Books.

Brinkmann, W.F.L. (1983). Nutrient balance of a Central American rain forest: a comparison of natural and man-managed system. *International Association Hydrological Science Publication* 140, 153-163.

Brinkmann, W.F.L. and Nascimento, J.C. (1973). The effect of slash burn agriculture on plant nutrients in the Tertiary region of Central Amazonia. *Turrialba* 23, 284-290.

Brünig, E.F., ed. (1982). *Transactions of the Third International MAB-IUFRO Workshop on Ecosystem Research.* Bonn: German National Committee MAB.

Brünig, E.F. (1983). Chemical warfare and the dynamics and management of tropical forest ecosystems. Paper working group 1. *International Symposium on Long-Term Ecology and Human Consequences of Chemical Warfare in Viet-Nam.* Ho Chi Min City.

Brünig, E.F. (1984). Designing ecologically stable plantations. In *Strategies and design for afforestation, reforestation and tree planting,* ed. K.F. Wiersum. Wageningen: PUDOC. Pp. 348-360.

Charles-Dominique, P., Atramentowics, M., Charles-Dominique, M., Gérard, H., Hladik, A., Hladik, C.M. and Prévost, M.F. (1981). Les mammifères frugivores arboricoles nocturnes d'une forêt Guyanaise: interactions plantes-animaux. *Terre et la Vie* 35, 341-435.

Cleef, A.M., Rangel Ch., O., Hammen, T. van der and Jaramillo M., R. (1984). The forest vegetation of the Buritaca transect. In La Sierra Nevada de Santa Marta (Colombia), transecto Buritaca-La Cumbre, ed. T. van der Hammen and P. M. Ruiz. *Studies on Tropical Andean Ecosystems* 2, 267-406.

Edwards, P.J. and Grubb, P.J. (1977). Studies of mineral cycling in a montane forest in New Guinea. I. The distribution of organic matter in the vegetation and soil. *Journal of Ecology* 65, 943-960.

Edwards, P.J. and Grubb, P.J. (1982). Studies on mineral cycling in a montane forest in New Guinea. IV. Soil characteristics and the division of mineral elements between the vegetation and soil. *Journal of Ecology* 70, 649-666.

Florence, J. (1981). Chablis et sylvigénèse dans une forêt dense humide sempervirente du Gabon (Thèse de Spécialité). Strasbourg: Université Louis Pasteur.

Fölster, H., Salas, G. de las and Khanna, P. (1976). A tropical evergreen forest site with perched water table, Magdalena Valley, Colombia. Biomass and bioelement inventory of primary and secondary vegetation. *Oecologia Plantarum* 11, 297-320.

Fournier, F. and Sasson, A., ed. (1983). Ecosystèmes forestiers tropicaux d'Afrique. *Natural Resources Research* 19.

Gentry, A.H. (1981). Inventario florístico de la Amazonia peruana: estado y perspectivas de conservación. In *Sem. Proyectos Invest. Ecol. Manejo Rec. Nat. Renov. Bosque Trop. Hum.*, ed. T. Gutièrrez G. Iquitos. Pp. 36-44.

Gentry, A.H. (1982a). Neotropical floristic diversity: phytogeographical connections between Central and South America, pleistocene c limatic fluctuations, or an accident of the Andean orogeny. *Annals Missouri Botanical Garden* 69, 557-593.

Gentry, A.H. (1982b). Patterns of neotropical plant species diversity. *Evolutionary Biology* 15, 1-84.

Gentry, A.H. and Dodson, C. (in press). Plant species richness of lowland tropical rain forests: mostly due to non-tree habit groups.

Grubb, P.J. (1977). Control of forest growth and distribution on wet tropical mountains: with special reference to mineral nutrition. *Annual Review of Ecology and Systematics* 8, 83-107.

Guillaumet, J.L., Couturier, G. and Dosso, H. (1984). Recherche et ménagement en milieu forestier tropicale humide: le projet Taï de Côte d'Ivoire. *MAB Technical Notes* 15.

Hallé, F., Oldeman, R.A.A. and Tomlinson, P.B. (1978). *Tropical trees and forests.* Heidelberg: Springer Verlag.

Herrera, R., Jordan, C.F., Klinge, H. and Medina, E. (1978). Amazon ecosystems. Their structure and functioning with particular emphasis on nutrients. *Interciencia* 3, 223-232.

Holdridge, L.W., Grenke, W.C., Hatheway, W.H., Liang, T. and Tosi, J.A., Jr. (1971). *Forest environments in tropical life zones: a pilot study.* Oxford: Pergamon Press.

Jacobs, M. (1981). *Het tropisch regenwoud, een eerste kennismaking.* Muiderberg: Coutinho.

Jeník, J. (1979). *Pictorial encyclopedia of forests.* Feltham: Hamlyn Publishing Group.

Kahn, F. (1982). La réconstitution de la forêt tropicale humide; Sud-Ouest de la Côte d'Ivoire. *Mémoires ORSTOM* 97.

Kahn, F. (1983). Architecture comparée de forêts tropicales humides et dynamiques de la rhizosphère (Thesis D. Sci.). Montpellier: Université des Sciences et Techniques de Languedoc.

Klinge, H. (1976). Bilanzierung von Hauptnährstoffen im Ökosystem tropischer Regenwald (Manaus) - vorläufige Daten. *Biogeographica* 7, 59-77.

Kortlandt, A. (in press). Vegetation research and the 'Bulldozer Herbivores' in tropical Africa. In *Tropical rain forest: ecology and management,* ed. A.C. Chadwick and S.L. Sutton (Supplementary Volume). Oxford: Blackwell Scientific Publications.

Leigh, E.G., Jr., Rand, A.S. and Windsor, D.M., ed. (1983). *The ecology of a tropical forest.* Oxford: Oxford University Press.

Meggers, B.J., Ayensu, E.S. and Duckworth, W.D., ed. (1973). *Tropical forest ecosystems in Africa and South America: a comparative review.* Washington D.C.: Smithsonian Institution.

Mikola, P., ed. (1980). *Tropical mycorrhiza research.* Oxford: Clarendon Press.

Montgomery, G.G., ed. (1978). *The ecology of arboreal folivores.* Washington D.C.: Smithsonian Institution.

Myers, N. (1979). *The sinking ark.* Oxford: Pergamon Press.

Odum, H.T. and Pigeon, R.F. (1970). *A tropical rainforest* 1, 2, 3. Springfield: US Atomic Energy Commission.

Oldeman, R.A.A. (1974). L'architecture de la Forêt Guyanaise. *Mémoires ORSTOM* 73.

Prance, G.T., ed. (1982). *Biological diversification in the tropics.* New York: Colombia University Press.

Proctor, J., Anderson, J.M., Chai, P. and Vallack, H.L. (1983). Ecological studies in four contrasting lowland rain forests in Gunung Mulu National Park, Sarawak. I. Forest environment and floristics. *Journal of Ecology* 71, 237-260.

Richards, P.W. (1952). *The tropical rain forest.* Cambridge: Cambridge University Press.

Ricklefs, R.E. (1976). *The economy of nature.* New York: Chiron Press.

Rijksen, H.D. (1978). A field study on Sumatran orang utans (*Pongo pygmaeus abelii* Lesson 1827). *Mededelingen Landbouwhogeschool* 78.

Rodin, L.E. and Basilevich, N.I. (1967). *Production and mineral cycling in terrestrial vegetation.* Edinburgh: Oliver and Boyd.

Rollet, B. (1974). *L'architecture des forêts denses humides sempervirentes de plaine.* Nogent-sur-Marne: CTFT.

Roosmalen, M.G.M. van (1980). Habitat preferences, diet, feeding strategy and social organization of the black spider monkey (*Ateles paniscus paniscus* Linneaus 1758) in Surinam (D. Sc. Thesis). Wageningen: Agricultural University.

Sandved, K.B. and Emsley, M. (1979). *Rain forests and cloud forests.* New York: Harry N. Abrams Inc.

Schimper, A.F.W. (1903). *Plant geography upon a physiological basis.* Oxford: Clarendon Press.

Simmons, J.B., Beyer, R.I. and Branchham, P.E., ed. (1976). *Conservation of threatened plants.* New York: Plenum Press.

Smits, W. (1982). *Dipterocarpaceae, vegetative propagation and mycorrhiza.* Wageningen: Agricultural University.

Steinhardt, U. (1979). Untersuchungen Über den Wasser- und Nährstoffhaushalt eines andinen Wolkenwaldes in Venezuela. *Göttinger Bodenkundliche Berichte* 56: 1-185.

Sutton, S.L., Whitmore, T.C. and Chadwick, A.C., ed. (1983). *Tropical rain forest: ecology and management.* Oxford: Blackwell Scientific Publications.

Torquebiau, E. (1981). Analyse architecturale de la forêt de los Tuxtlas (Vera Cruz), Mexique (Thèse). Montpellier: Université des Sciences et Techniques de Languedoc.

Westhoff, V. (1976). Het zichzelf handhaven van bos in de gematigde luchtstreken. *Nederlands Bosbouw Tijdschrift* 48, 58-65.

Wing Easton, N.J. (1976). *De manager en de kwaliteit van zijn organisatie.* Deventer: Kluwer.

Author's address: Prof. Dr. R.A.A. Oldeman, Agricultural University, Department of Silviculture and Forest Ecology, P.O. Box 342, 6700 AH Wageningen, The Netherlands.

# Spatial variability of tropical rain forests and forest lands

by W.J. van IJssel
W.G. Sombroek

## 1. Introduction

Although the tropical (lowland) rain forest on a global scale counts for only one formation type, with indeed striking similarities in physiognomy and functioning (see Oldeman, this volume), a closer look will show that several environmental factors may vary over a wide range. These variations not only appear to influence the natural vegetation, but affect, together with this natural vegetation, to a great extent the (forest) land-use possibilities. Therefore, whenever land-use planning is concerned, these environmental factors should be thoroughly investigated. The following text gives a general introduction in major variations occuring in climate, geomorphology, soils and related hydrological conditions, and some remarks on survey and mapping of forest lands.

## 2. Climate

Although the tropical rain forest belt is subject to different climatic systems, rainfall and temperature in general are no limiting factors to growth. Where they do become so, other vegetation types develop. Therefore the overall picture of the tropical rain forest climate is one of high and stable temperature, heavy rainfall and dense cloudiness. The mean annual temperature lies between 22° and 27°C, and the seasonal variation (< 5°C) is less than the diurnal variation (7°-11°C on a sunny day). The total amount of rainfall varies greatly within the tropical rain forest formation type from about 1,800 mm to over 10 m, but usually lies between 2,000 and 4,000 mm. An essential characteristic is that although there are nearly always seasonal changes in the amount of rainfall, there is no prolonged seasonal drought. Nevertheless annual variations in total amount can be considerable. Regional and even local variations occur, due to topography, exposure of slope or coast-line to the prevailing wind, distance to the sea, etc. These differences lead to variation in the types of rain forest (structure and physiognomy) or to more subtle variations, mainly in species composition. However, variation of the vegetation cover should never be seen apart from other environmental factors such as soil type and hydrological conditions.

Violent storms lasting for hours, as in the temperate regions, are no important ecological phenomena in the rain forest belt. Thunderstorms are, however, very common in the tropics and often preceded by squalls of strong wind. These may last for a few minutes only, but play an important role in forest dynamics, creating gaps (chablis) in which new eco-units develop, as treated by Oldeman (this volume).

In the limited areas where hurricanes and cyclones occur and where they often seem to follow more or less the same track, a type of subclimax forest, deficient in large trees, is found. Beard (quoted in Richards, 1964) studied these effects on the slopes of the Soufrière in St. Vincent (West Indies) and named it 'hurricane forest' and Whitmore (1974) found similar effects on the Solomon Islands.

In general the northern and southern climatic boundaries of the tropical rain forest formation type are in most places determined by the occurence of a distinct dry season. Here the rain forest gives way to forest types with an increasing share of species that shed their leaves in the dry season (seasonal forest, monsoon forest, deciduous forest, see Fig. 13). In the same general terms the altitudinal boundaries are determined mainly by temperature, although to what specific element of temperature - mean monthly minima, absolute minima, etc. - is still uncertain (Richards, 1964). Here the lowland rain forest gives way to submontane and montane rain forest. However, it should be noted that the boundaries are never easily determined, because they are always the result of complex interactions between several ecological factors. Drought, for example, is not only dependent on the amount of rainfall but also on edaphic conditions. Whenever one reaches the boundaries (climatic or edaphic) of the rain forest, the changes in climax vegetation generally are a shift in species composition, a decreasing number of species, a decreasing height of the canopy, and a more simple structure of the forest as a whole.

An important feature of macroclimate and vegetation cover is that together they determine the microclimate within the forest. The tropical rain forest can only sustain itself by virtue of its self-induced microclimate. Thus, when considering utilization types using not only the soil, but also the forest and its characteristics (see Boerboom and Jonkers, this volume), major attention should be paid to changes in microclimate and its effect on growth and regrowth of the different elements within the ecosystem. Another climatical aspect that should be kept in mind, when adapting (or even converting) the original ecosystem for another kind of land use, are the two effects of rain-water when falling in excessive amounts. On the one hand water as such is a source of life, and a solvent for plant nutrients. On the other, water is a potential transport medium which may carry away plant nutrients (see Oldeman, this volume), soil particles and even complete soils.

Moreover, it may be mentioned that in geological times climatic changes caused the rain forest area to expand and retreat. During Pleistocene interpluvials in America and Africa, the area has been pushed back (probably several times) to relic areas (*refugia*). This has been of great influence to species diversity and biogeography. Therefore the exact localization of these relic areas is of importance to nature conservation (Jacobs, 1981; Vanzolini, 1973).

With respect to climatological classifications, it is difficult to find one that is useful for land-use planning purposes. So far the most widely used classification is that of Köppen. But his classification only discriminates very large regions, based on pronounced differences. When available, climate diagrams according to Walter (Fig. 13) give quickly a very useful notion of the main climatological features (see Walter, 1979; Walter and Lieth, 1967). More land-use orientated approaches are the

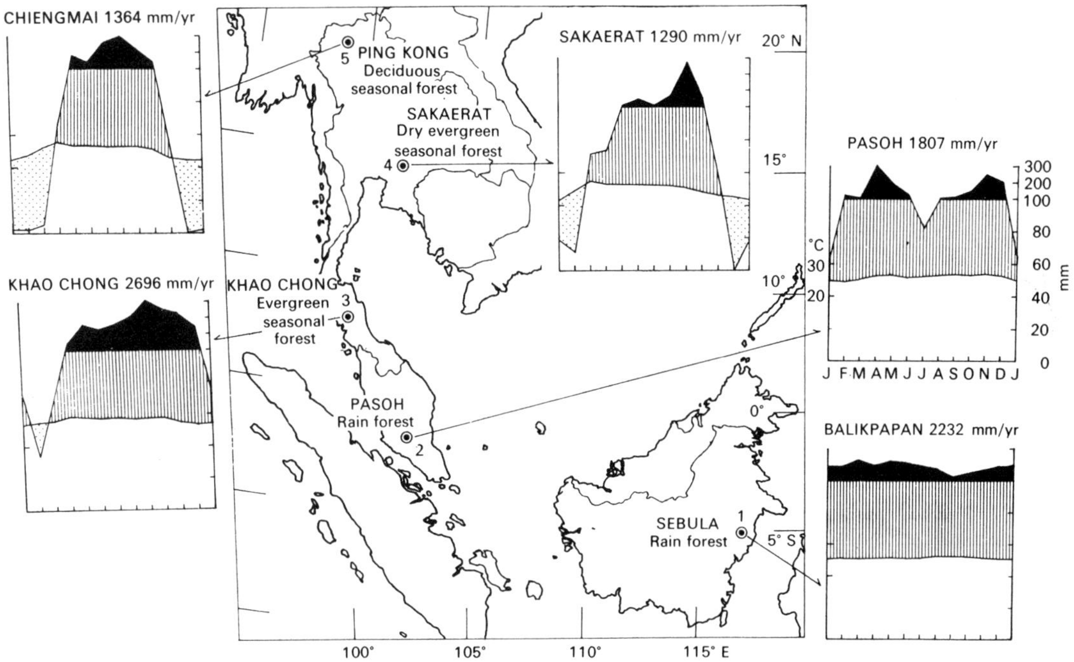


Fig. 13 Location and climate of five selected forests in Southeast Asia. Climate diagrams, drawn according to Walter's method, show annual distribution of monthly mean temperature and precipitation. Dotted areas indicate dry season. Note Khao Chong with higher total amount of rainfall than Pasoh, but yet seasonal forest type due to a distinct dry season (source: Kira, 1978).

classifications of Papadakis (1966) and of the Agro-Ecological Zones Project (FAO, 1978). The latter determines agro-ecological zones, based on the length of the growing period, i.e. days when water and temperature permit crop growth. These zones can be plotted on the Soil Map of the World. In very rainy climates, suitability for many crops declines with growing periods of over 270-300 days (too wet, too little radiation, too many pests and diseases). However, these classifications are, so far, exclusively focused on agricultural crop production, and do not account for very important microclimatological influences by trees within the various forest land uses (e.g. agro-forestry systems).

## 3. Geomorphology

Marked differences in forest types, soils and thus forest land-use possibilities are related to differences in parent material, the land form, and its geological stability. A very general and short overview will be given.

*Amazonia* consists of a low sedimentary area, the Amazon valley proper, and parts of the crystalline shields of Central Brazil and the Guyanas (Sombroek, 1966).

The landscape of the shields is characterized by level erosion surfaces (pediplains) related to several successive erosion cycles. Such landscape forms are explained by the process of pediplanation: river incision, slope retreat, and collection of erosion residues at the foot of the retreating slope; thus the pediplain grows at the expense of the initial surface. Successive uplifts of the area result in a stepped landscape. However, because the degradational processes at work proceeded at variable speed from period to period and from place to place, the landscape development was much more complex. Therefore, besides the old level land surface with a thick waste mantle in an advanced stage of weathering, areas of residual relief occur, that have a youthful dissected character (often associated with resistant rocks). A third category consists of the valley bottoms and enclosed sedimentary areas, where weathering *in situ* is insignificant and most properties of the waste mantle (alluvium) are inherited (FAO/UNESCO, 1971). Within the huge sedimentary basin three important sedimentation levels have been recognized:

- the Amazon planalto; a flat plateau land of Plio-Pleistocene age, mostly bordering the shield areas. The elevation varies between 150 and 250 metres in the west and becomes less towards the east (FAO/UNESCO, 1971). Noteworthy is the extensive occurrence of the very heavy textured 'Belterra clay' at this level (Sombroek, 1966);
- Pleistocene terraces at various levels resulting from redissection of the Amazon planalto and sedimentation of remodeled Tertiary and older deposits, after the Amazon river began its action. The topography here may be rather steep or gentle (FAO/UNESCO, 1971), depending upon the degree of dissection during successive relatively dry periods (interpluvials). In some areas, notably the Solimões-Purus area of Amazonia State, this Pleistocene dissection is completely absent and the fluviatile origin of the terraces is clearly apparent on radar images (Fig. 14);
- Holocene sediments, consisting largely of silts and clays. They cover the flood plain areas along the Amazon proper and the lower parts of its main tributaries and are found as well in the estuary region (Sombroek, 1966).

The whole *African* continent consists almost entirely of one unbroken crystalline basement complex, which is exposed over large areas. There are many undulating plateaux and plains (pediplains) at different levels corresponding again to different erosion cycles, usually separated from each other by escarps and bordered by narrow coastal plains. On the surface of the African plateau are broad shallow depressions such as the basins of the upper Niger, Lake Chad and the Congo. The West African rain forest grows in a region of extensive plateaux and plains, interrupted by some higher small plateaux and residual 'inselbergs'. The different surfaces are usually separated by escarps or narrow zones of broken country. Equatorial Africa consists of a geomorphological region including a variety of mostly dissected plateaux and some minor mountainous areas which completely surround the Congo basin. The broad and flat basin itself constitutes a slight depression of the African continental platform, with an average altitude of 400 m. It is filled with alluvial deposits partly of aeolian origin. Small remnants of larger lakes and extensive swamp areas occur. Between Angola and Cameroon a low coastal plain is mostly bordered by the mountains surrounding the Congo basin. The plain is crossed by numerous rivers bordered by mangrove forests along estuaries. Lagoons, lakes and swamps are found as well (FAO/UNESCO, 1977).

The geology and geomorphology of *Southeast Asia* are very complex. The region is dominated by its island character and its many orogenic systems. Four morpho-structural regions can be distinguished:

- the Sunda shelf comprising the Indochinese Peninsula, the greater part of Borneo and the east coast of Sumatra, together surrounding the nowadays inundated part (South China Sea);
- the Sahul shelf, the northern extension of the Australian continental mass, is partly inundated by the shallow Arafura Sea. The southern alluvial plain of Irian Jaya and the Aru Islands form part of this shelf;
- on the north this shelf is bordered by the circum-Australian orogenic system extending along the central axis of Irian Jaya through the archipelagoes east of Australia to New Zealand;
- the two shelves mentioned above are separated by the circum-Sunda orogenic system, including the Philippines and merging southwestward into the great Sunda mountain system, extending from the Banda arc in the east along the Lesser Sunda Islands, Java, Sumatra and on to Burma. Throughout its length the Sunda mountain system consists of two parallel belts of mountain ranges. The inner belt is volcanic and the outer belt non-volcanic.

For further details about geology and lithology of Southeast Asia reference is made to the overview given by FAO/UNESCO (1979). But especially in the tropical Far East a considerable part of the land is occupied by soils in which the overriding pedogenic factor is characteristic of the local rather than the regional environment (Whitmore, 1975).

On very old stable surfaces, e.g. nondissected plateaux and terraces, weathering processes have reached their final stage: very deep, leached soils with kaolinitic clay minerals and sesquioxides. In geological younger areas with relatively recent dissection and/or sedimentation of fluviatile or aeolian origin (volcanic ashes, desert sand or dust), weathering processes may be more or less at their beginning.

## 4. Soils

The following overview of major soil groups that are predominant within the tropical rain forest belt can only be general and is far from complete, due to the endless variation in local environmental conditions. The described groups range from the older soils (Ferralsols, Acrisols) to relatively younger ones (Cambisols, Nitosols, Andosols, Lithosols), and finally the soils developed under imperfectly drained conditions (plinthic Acrisols, Podsols, Fluvisols, Gleysols) and poorly drained conditions (Gleysols, Histosols). The classification used in this text is of the FAO/UNESCO Soil Map of the World. Other widely used classifications are the US Soil Survey Staff (1975) 'Soil Taxonomy' and the classifications by Aubert et al. (1967) and D'Hoore (1964). Information is derived mainly from the following publications: FAO/UNESCO (1971, 1977 and 1979), Buringh (1979) and Sombroek (1984). Figure 15 shows the geology-landforms-soils relationship for the Amazon region.

The most common soils in the tropical rain forest belts of South America and Africa are the *Ferralsols*. They occur mainly on flat to undulating terrain in areas which are unaltered over a very long period. They are deep, porous, acid, red or yellow, well-drained soils with a homogeneous clay content to a considerable depth and without weatherable minerals. The soil profile looks uniform and may be some metres thick. Intensive and continuous weathering over a long period has resulted in leaching of bases and silica and relative accumulation of sesquioxides (iron and aluminium oxides) and in formation of kaolinitic (low-activity) clays.

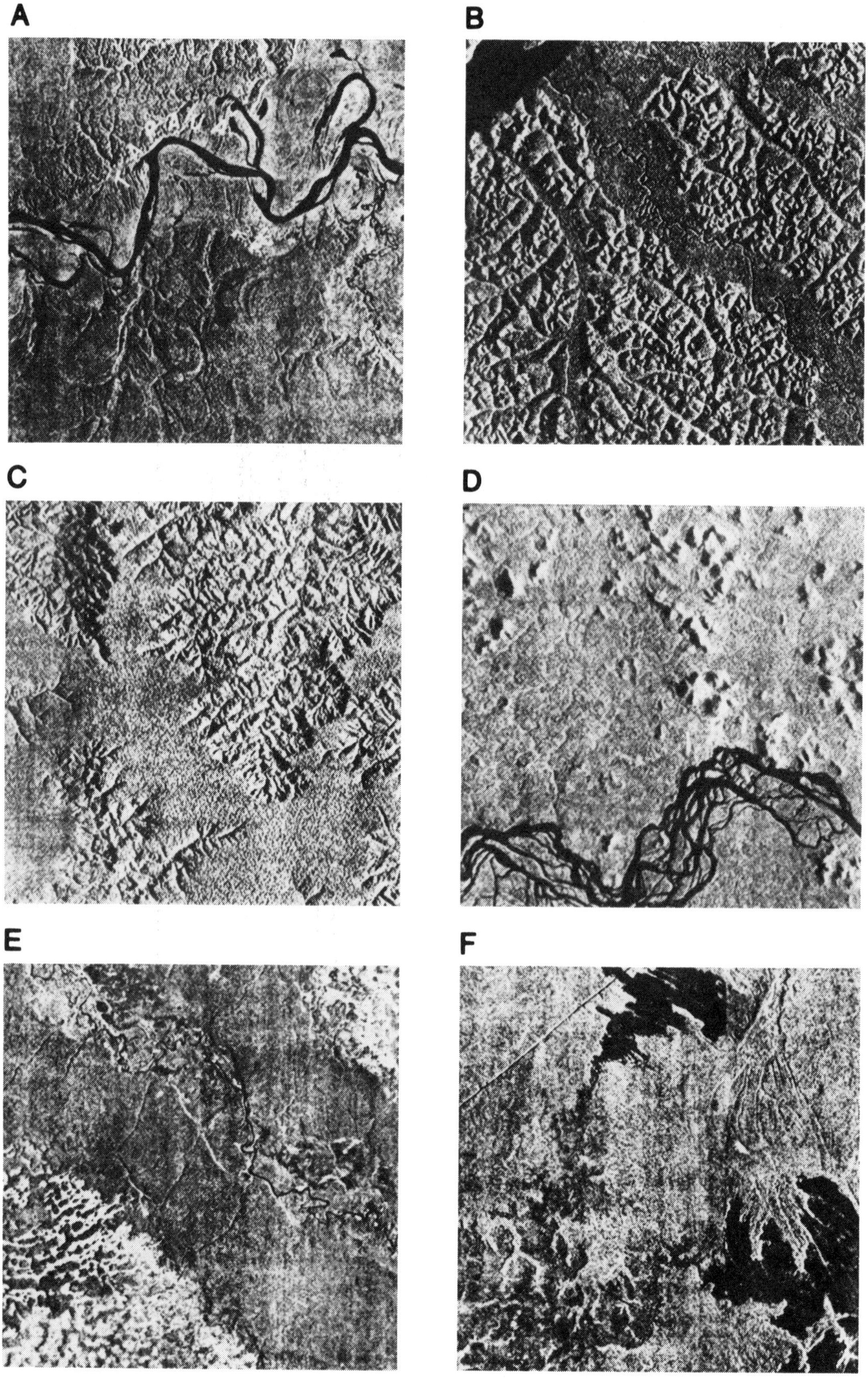
A
B
C
D
E
F

Clay particles are often cemented by iron and the iron oxides have an important positive effect on maintaining a good soil structure, built up by a lively soil fauna. The yellowish (xanthic) Ferralsols have less or less-well oxidized iron oxides compared to the red (orthic and rhodic) Ferralsols. Xanthic Ferralsols are thus more susceptible to degradation of soil structure when the forest cover is cleared and the soil fauna diminished by lack of fresh organic material. Moreover, the surface layer is subject to 'hard setting' which may lead to sheet and even gully erosion. Examples of such degradations are found in the Zanderij area of Suriname, around Belem in Brazil, and in the Congo basin.

Ferralsols are chemically very poor. Organic matter is of paramount importance, because the cation exchange capacity of kaolinitic clays is very low and thus available plant nutrients are in fact largely linked with the organic matter which is for a good part concentrated in the topsoil. The removal of the forest by felling and burning for peasant farming of the shifting cultivation type, may not have a serious detrimental effect on the recuperative capacity of the vegetation when fallow periods of 15-20 years are maintained. However, when fallow periods become too short a serious impoverishment and decline in soil structure may develop, resulting ultimately in anthropogenic shrub savanna.

A second group of major importance are the *Acrisols*. They cover half of Southeast Asia (mainly orthic Acrisols), but also occur in West Africa and on extensive areas in Amazonia. Their macrorelief ranges from nearly level to steeply dissected or mountainous. They are formed on a wide range of predominantly acid parent materials. The textural change in the soil profile is often quite definite as a result of clay accumulation in the subsoil (argillic B-horizon) with either low-activity (kaolinitic) or high-activity clays. The classification varies accordingly from ferric Acrisols to orthic Acrisols. In places the Acrisols are shallow on steeply dissected mountainous slopes (lithic phase). They are chemically poor, being acid, low in organic matter content and bases, and lacking natural fertility if weatherable minerals are exhausted. But the latter may vary considerably, due to the wide range of parent materials. Physically they are often fairly good, but compactness of the argillic B-horizon or a lithic phase limit root distribution and make them susceptible to erosion, especially on slopes.

On Ferralsols and Acrisols the rain forest developed in its most common appearance, due to stable and favourable environmental conditions. As to their (forest) land-use possibilities, Acrisols pose about the same problems as the Ferralsols, except that their natural fertility may be somewhat

Fig. 14 Examples of some important geomorphological characteristics in Amazonia, by radar mosaic images at 1 : 250,000.

A. Holocene flood-plain with point bars along meandering river in the lower Rio Purus area. South of flood-plain younger non-dissected terrace with old meanders (ox-bows). North of flood-plain older slightly dissected Pleistocene terrace.
B. Strongly dissected Early Pleistocene terrace, and narrow strips of swampland (igapó) along small tributaries of the Rio Tapajós.
C. Late Tertiary plateau land ('Belterra clay surface') and in Pleistocene periods strongly dissected and remodelled Tertiary/Cretaceous sediments; south of the Paragominas area.
D. Remnants (Inselbergs) of hilly crystalline basement, with shallow soils, in between Pleistocene terrace land with deep soils, crossed by a minor river; upper Xingú area.
E. Natural savanna vegetation (campina) on imperfectly drained water divide areas in the catchment area of the Rio Negro.
F. Old (dark grey) and new (black) burned-over areas on low forest/savanna vegetated Late Pleistocene terraces near major road (NW) in the Humaitá area.

Source: Projeto Radambrasil, 1972 – 1978.

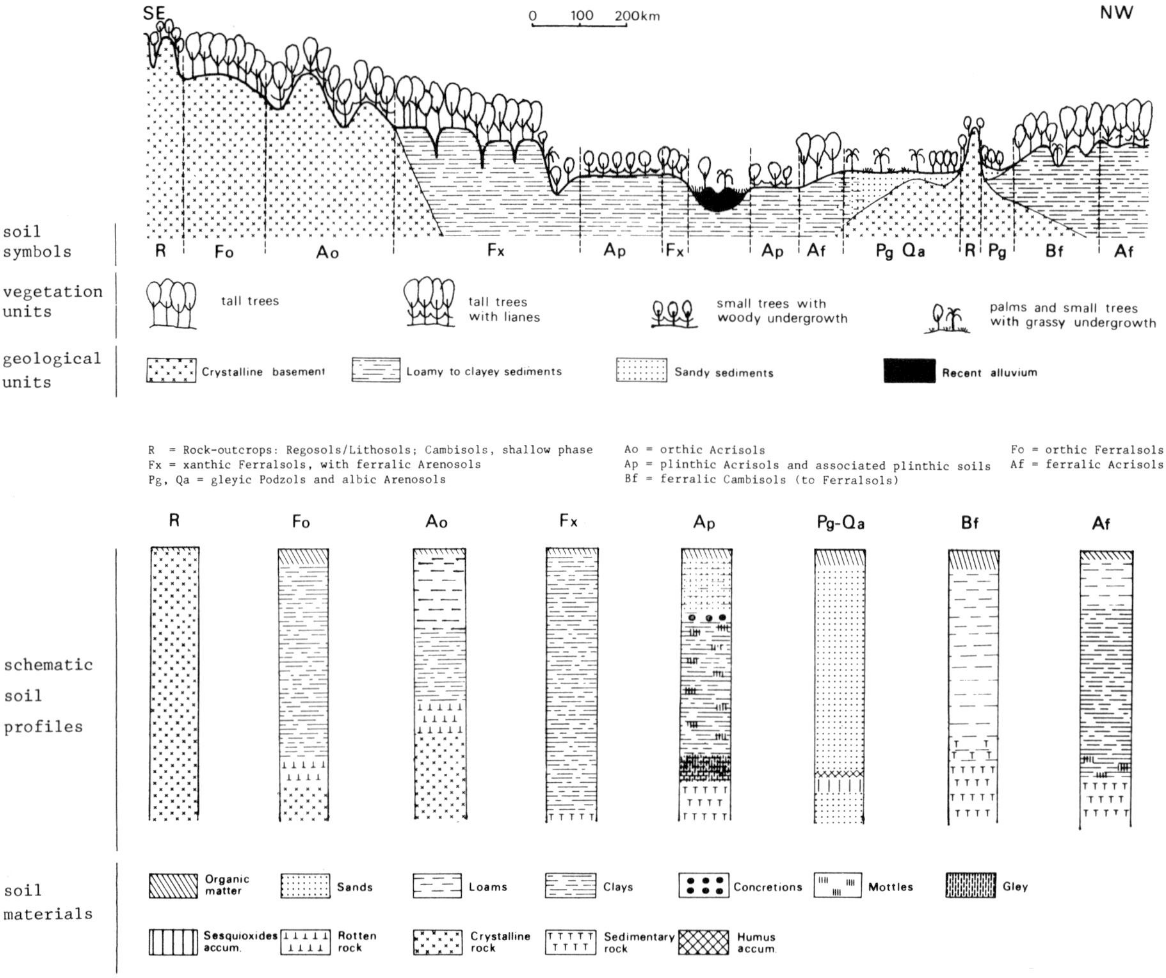


Fig. 15 Schematic cross-section of the Amazon region, showing the geology-land forms-soils relationship (adapted from Sombroek, 1984).

better, depending on the parent material, and that due attention should be paid to higher erosion hazards. Shifting cultivation has been practised over wide areas in Southeast Asia since ancient times, often leading to the development of a fire climax of anthropogenic savanna (dominated by *Imperata cylindrica* (alang alang)). However, extensive areas have been brought under permanent crops, of which rubber and oil palm are the most important.

To the west and southwest of the bottom of the Congo basin a major group of soils are the *ferralic Arenosols* on a substratum of Kalahari sands (of aeolic origin). They are poor soils; the clay content is usually below 10 per cent; the organic matter content is very small and the acid pH reveals the very low content of exchangeable bases. Due to the sandy character of these soils the water-holding capacity is low, leading to a more semi-deciduous type of rain forest, susceptible to degradation into a savanna type.

*Cambisols* constitute a collection of soil types intermediate between young soils and the very old deeply weathered ones. They are fine to medium textured. They may be in a recent phase of ferralitic weathering and occur on dissected sedimentary plains in Colombia, Ecuador, and on the colluvial soils of undulating regions in western equatorial

Africa, Sarawak and Kalimantan. These ferralic Cambisols maintain a degree of mineral reserve and their exchange capacity is higher than the capacity of the Ferralsols. Nevertheless they are chemically poor. A richer type (eutric Cambisols) occurs for example in limited areas of Java, Sumatra and Sulawesi, developed from basic to intermediate parent materials of volcanic origin and found on mid-slopes of volcanoes, but also in Acre State of Brazil. They offer fairly good land-use possibilities when protected against water erosion.

Among the best soils of the humid climates are the deep clayey, porous, purplish red or chocolate-coloured soils with a uniform profile, i.e. *Nitosols.* They are fine-textured and well-drained and are developed from rich, basic parent materials, often of volcanic origin. But they often occur on a rolling to steeply dissected macrorelief. Examples of occurence exist in the hills in the upper reaches of the Rio Huallaga (Peru) and the Rio Putamayo-Napo (Ecuador), in Central America, in southern Cameroon, and particularly in the Philippines and Indonesia.

Soils on recent volcanic ash materials, with a very dark to black colour and found on mountain slopes in volcanic regions, are called *Andosols.* The ash material is very light and possesses a high natural fertility. They occur, for example, within the circum-Sunda orogenic system, Ecuador, Costa Rica and Cameroon.

*Lithosols* are mineral soils less than 10 cm thick over hard rock. They occur everywhere, particularly on steep slopes. Sometimes they are the result of soil erosion after the removal of the original vegetation (forests). Lithosols are not suitable for agriculture and should be left under natural vegetation to serve other purposes such as the prevention of erosion.

Present or past hydrological conditions play or played an important role in soil formation and strongly determine natural vegetation cover and land-use possibilities. Acrisols with plinthite (*plinthic Acrisols*) develop as imperfectly drained and strongly weathered soils on more or less clayey parent material with a seasonally oscillating ground-water table. The profile consists of a relatively light textured topsoil over a relatively heavy textured subsoil with prominent coarse and abundant mottles of reddish colour in a white or light grey matrix. Upon exposure to open air the mottles become irreversibly hardened to slag-like material. Therefore artificial drainage measures are impractical. They have developed extensively on low-lying terraces along the lower Amazon, the Solimões, and the lower portions of their tributaries. They also occur in southern Sumatra and southern Irian Jaya and may be present in northwestern Zaire and Congo as well (not recorded on FAO/UNESCO map). The natural vegetation consists either of a poor and low type of forest, often with predominance of a palm species, or of a type of savanna. Low fertility, impeded drainage, and rooting limitations have taught local populations that arable farming is not feasible. When used as grazing lands erosion and irreversible hardening of the plinthite are likely to occur. These soils should not be confused with ferric Acrisols or xanthic Ferralsols containing some ironstone in between their friable earth, either from the surface downward or as distinct layers at varying depth (petroplinthic phases). They normally have a forest coverage and do not turn into massive rock upon its removal.

On more continuously imperfectly drained soils on sandy sediments podzolized soils develop. These profiles are characterized by a subsurface horizon of strongly variable thickness (from 20 cm to over 20 m), consisting of light grey to white sand or loamy sand. This is underlain by a dark brown or black subsoil with a firm consistence or even cementation - resulting in a low permeability and penetrability - and some accumulation of humic substances and of sesquioxides. Throughout the profile the base saturation is very low, and the aluminium saturation is high in the cemented subsoil. They are classified as (*gleyic*) *Podzols*, or, when the bleached sand layer is very thick, as *albic Arenosols.* They develop on low-lying terrains (e.g. flat to slightly concave interfluves or narrow, low river terraces and abandoned river-beds). They occur, for example, on Borneo and extensively in the upper Rio Negro area and the middle reaches of the Rio Branco drainage system in the Amazon region.

The natural vegetation type is either a savanna-forest type consisting of dense stands of thin and low trees with little differentiation (caatinga, kerangas), or a savanna (campina, campina-rana). Because of the very poor soil qualities the agricultural value of these terrains is nil. Regrowth after removal of the natural vegetation is very slow. Nutrients cannot be held by the mineral soil and are quickly washed down in the soil profile and drained off to the rivers. Such rivers (e.g. Rio Negro) carry often in fact 'black' water, because of the presence of humic acids originating from Podzol areas.

Poorly drained soils occur in extensive areas in the flood-plains along the main rivers and in the bottomlands within upland areas. Although the soils can be broadly grouped as 'Alluvial soils' and have in common little or no apparent profile development, they vary much in their internal drainage condition, their texture, organic matter content, acidity and clay mineralogy, depending on the local flooding conditions and the source of the sediments:

- relatively highly situated parts have soils with sedimentary stratification and free internal drainage (*Fluvisols*). Flooded only briefly or exceptionally, they make very good agricultural soils;
- the lower stretches have predominantly clayey soils with restricted internal drainage (*Gleysols*). They are seasonally waterlogged and inundated, but dry out to some depth during certain periods of the year;
- in the flood-plain of rivers that originate in mountainous areas and hence carry a considerable load of rich sediments, the Fluvisols and Gleysols are less acid to neutral with high-activity clays (eutric groups). On such soils a luxurious flood-plain forest prevails, or rich natural grassland when the hydrological regime impedes tree growth. It is also on these soils that the seasonal growing of dry-foot crops and of paddy rice as well as cattle grazing is very successful and in fact already extensively practised, especially in Indo-Malesia;
- the rivers that originate in crystalline shields or in the sedimentary basins themselves carry little or no sediments and may contain high percentages of humic acids as does the Rio Negro. The flood-plain soils in these areas are acid, have clay minerals of lower activity and are often also deeper and longer submerged (dystric groups). Hence a poorer flood-plain forest prevails and agricultural use is limited;
- in coastal areas the flood-plain soils are, or have been, subject to the influence of brackish or salt water (e.g. coastal swamps). They often contain detrimental percentages of salts, sodium, magnesium and/or sulphides. Their natural vegetation is often mangrove forest. Some of these soils may develop into acid sulphate soils upon drainage and aeration of originally waterlogged and reduced parent material. Their agricultural use is very restricted, both because of flooding conditions and of soil chemistry;
- in bottomlands and in older coastal swamps, where drainage is permanently poor, thick layers of acid peat (non-decomposed organic material) may have developed (*Histosols*). They occur, for example, on extensive low coastal areas of Sumatra, Borneo and Irian Jaya, but locally also in Amazonia, the Congo basin and near the coasts of Peninsular Malaysia, Thailand and Vietnam. Most remain under peat forest. Land use is mainly restricted to fish breeding and the gathering of useful natural products, which are plentiful in certain areas, especially Southeast Asia (nipa, sago, rattan, and raffia palms).

## 5. Survey and mapping

Survey and mapping of environmental conditions is an indispensable tool for land evaluation and land-use planning. Of the many ecosystem characteristics in tropical forest areas, the physical parameters, such as climate, topography, geology, hydrology and soils, are in fact much more stable with respect to human action than the biological parameters vegetation and fauna. This is why it is important, at land-use planning, to carry out a systematic physiographic soil survey - a survey method relating soils to the major land-form and the type of parent material. Thus Breimer et al. (1985) used a three-level hierarchical system of legend construction, with a land-form subdivision at the highest level, a geological subdivision at the

Table 6 Various types of soil surveys and related characteristics.

| Type of survey | Exploratory | Reconnaissance | Semi-detailed | Detailed | Intensive |
|---|---|---|---|---|---|
| scale range | 1 : 5,000,000 to 1 : 500,000 | 1 : 500,000 to 1 : 100,000 | 1 : 100,000 to 1 : 25,000 | 1 : 25,000 to 1 : 10,000 | 1 : 10,000 and larger |
| area represented by 1 $cm^2$ of map | 625 $km^2$ to 25 $km^2$ | 25 $km^2$ to 1 $km^2$ | 100 ha to 6.25 ha | 6.25 ha to 1 ha | 1 ha and less |
| approx. number of observations, 0.5 $cm^2$ of map* | 1/1,250 $km^2$ to 1/50 $km^2$ | 1/50 $km^2$ to 1/2 $km^2$ | 1/200 ha to 1/12.5 ha | 1/12.5 ha to 1/2 ha | 1/2 ha and less |
| accuracy of boundaries | all boundaries inferred | almost all boundaries inferred | some boundary checking - most inferred | position of almost all boundaries checked troughout length on the ground | position of all boundaries checked troughout length on the ground |

* Figures represent the density of all observations averaged over the entire area of the map (acceptable density usually ranges between 0.25 and 1.0 observations $cm^{-2}$ of map on this basis).

Source: derived from Breimer et al., 1985.

second level and soil mapping units (thus not necessarily identical to soil classification units) at the third level. Vink (1983) gives a short overview of various systems and methods used in landscape-ecological survey and mapping.

Soil survey can be done at very different scales, covering very different extents of land and needing various intensities of observations. A strict relationship exists between the accuracy, scale and purpose of soil maps. In general it may be stated that the purpose of a survey determines the accuracy required from the map; the accuracy determines the mapping scale, which in turn sets the limitations to the possible uses of the soil map. Some characteristics in relation to the type of survey are given in Tables 6 and 7.

The execution of a complete soil survey includes office activities, field work and laboratory analysis. Office activities include the collection and interpretation of basic information on environmental conditions, scrutiny of any previous studies in the area, acquisition and study of remote-sensing imagery, and at a later stage, map compilation and survey report writing. Remote-sensing techniques vary according to the extent of the survey from satellite images (Landsat; exploratory and reconnaissance surveys), via radar images (SLAR; reconnaissance surveys), to aerial photography (larger scales). With respect to the often very cloudy tropical rain forest areas, special attention must be drawn to radar images, normally produced on a scale of 1 : 250,000. The great advantage of this type of imagery is the all-weather ability (clouds do not reflect radar waves). They give an excellent view of geomorphological-hydrological conditions (Table 7). Field work consists of measuring soil properties at many sites in the landscape through soil augering and profile description, and sampling

Table 7 Some possible interpretation potentials and uses of different soil survey types.

| | Exploratory | Reconnaissance | Semi-detailed | | Detailed | Intensive |
|---|---|---|---|---|---|---|
| Map interpretation potential | 5,000,000 to 500,000 | 1 : 500,000 to 1 : 100,000 | 1 : 100,000 to 1 : 50,000 | 1 : 50,000 to 1 : 25,000 | 1 : 25,000 to 1 : 10,000 | 1 : 10,000 and larger |
| *Indications* | | | | | | |
| a. indicates susceptibility of soils to deterioration | | * | ** | *** | *** | *** |
| b. indicates suitability of soils for management and land preparation | | * | * | ** | *** | *** |
| c. indicates constraints to land use | | * | * | ** | *** | *** |
| *Uses of soil map* | | | | | | |
| a. Master planning | | | | | | |
| 1. national planning | *** | ** | * | | | |
| 2. regional planning | *** | *** | ** | * | | |
| b. Project planning | | | | | | |
| 1. pilot projects for agricult. development | | | * | ** | *** | *** |
| 2. planning of large-scale farm units | | | * | ** | *** | *** |
| 3. land settlement scheme | * | ** | *** | ** | ** | * |
| c. Operational planning | | | | | | |
| 1. siting of experimental plots | | | | * | ** | *** |
| 2. siting of drainage and irrigation schemes | | | * | ** | *** | *** |
| 3. siting of buildings | | | * | ** | *** | *** |

* minimum ** moderate *** maximum

Source: Breimer et al., 1985.

in representative soil pits. Delineation of mapping units is done in the field, normally using preliminary delineations made after interpretations of aerial photographs or other remote-sensing imagery. Laboratory analysis of soil samples is an indispensable part of a soil survey as it provides the basic data for the characterization of the soils in the field (Breimer et al., 1985).

The soil map resulting from a physiographic survey will be directly comparable with vegetation data plotted on the same physiographic base, to produce a fairly comprehensive picture of the biotic and abiotic features of a given area (Breimer et al., 1985). In contrast to common procedures in agricultural lands, soil studies in areas with original or modified tropical forest vegetation should give prominent attention to the properties of the vegetation-soil interface, i.e. the litter layer and the soil surface layer. On the other hand numerous methods and classifications exist with respect to vegetation survey and mapping. Most often, legend construction is on the basis of physiognomy and structure combined with abiotic environmental factors (e.g. geomorphology, topography, hydrology). These classifications then are formulated for a specific project and their use is limited to a specific region or country (e.g. Projeto Radambrasil, 1972 – 1978; Proradam, 1979; Blasco et al., 1983).

Concerning more general systems of classifying tropical forest types two approaches to classification should be mentioned:

- in 1972 UNESCO proposed an 'International Classification and Mapping of Vegetation' (UNESCO, 1973), which is theoretically universal. It can be described as being basically physiognomic-structural in character, with some supplementary ecological information integrated into its various categories and applicable to natural and semi-natural vegetation;
- a second approach is a classification on floristic characteristics (sociological plant communities). Such a system can be applied on a large scale, but also on a small scale with legend units of more complex character (Zonneveld, 1979).

Both systems have the important advantage (besides general applicability) of permitting the addition of further categories and subdivision whenever desirable. Moreover, structural and floristic systems can be combined, which often will be recommendable. Survey methods are again largely based on interpretation of remote-sensing imagery and field surveys. Unfortunately a standardized approach to vegetation classification has so far not yet been generally adopted.

A map indicating the distributional pattern of the various vegetation types or plant communities is not the ultimate aim, however, but meant to serve as a basis for resource inventory (Verstappen, 1983). Such a resource inventory has, for example, been carried out by the impressive FAO/UNEP 'Tropical Forest Resources Assessment Project' (FAO, 1981), but it mainly focused upon wood production potentials and factors directly influencing these potentials. The resource inventory should have its roots in the land-use objectives and, as far as possible, in specific relevant and sustainable land-use alternatives. This way the inventory will bear a more pragmatic character. The vegetation, for example, may have qualities indicating certain land-use potentials, or qualities valuable to and to be incorporated in certain land-use types (see Boerboom and Jonkers, this volume).

The conservation of production potentials and the values of the primeval forest vegetation will always be aspects to be duly reckoned with. This is because conservation or restoration of the original ecosystem will be always one of the land-use alternatives to be considered. The loss of qualities that are inherent to the primeval forest vegetation should be accounted for, whenever arriving at a recommended non-forest land use.

Authors' address: W.J. van IJssel and Dr. W.G. Sombroek, International Soil Reference and Information Centre, P.O. Box 353, 6700 AJ Wageningen, The Netherlands.

## REFERENCES


Aubert, G. et al. (1967). *Classification des sols.* Grignon: Laboratoire de Géologie-Pedologie de l'ENSA.

Blasco, F., Laumonier, Y. and Purnajaya (1983). Tropical vegetation mapping: Sumatera. Biotrop. *Bulletin in Tropical Biology* 22.

Breimer, R.F., Kekem, A.J. van and Reuler, H. van (1985). Guidelines for soil survey and land evaluation in ecological research. *MAB Technical Note* 16.

Buringh, P. (1979). *Introduction to the study of soils in tropical and subtropical regions.* Wageningen: PUDOC.

D'Hoore, J.L. (1964). La carte des sols d'Afrique au 1:5,000,000. Lagos: CCTA.

FAO (1978). Report on the agro-ecological zones project. I. Methodology and results for Africa. *World Soil Resources* 48. Rome.

FAO (1981a). Tropical forest resources assessment project: Tropical Asia. Rome.

FAO (1981b). Tropical forest resources assessment project: America Tropicale. Rome.

FAO (1981c). Tropical forest resources assessment project: Afrique Tropicale. Rome.

FAO/UNESCO (1971). Soil map of the world at 1:5,000,000. 4: *South America.* Paris: UNESCO.

FAO/UNESCO (1977). Soil map of the world at 1:5,000,000. 6: *Africa.* Paris: UNESCO.

FAO/UNESCO (1979). Soil map of the world at 1:5,000,000. 9: *Southeast Asia.* Paris: UNESCO.

Jacobs, M. (1981). *Het tropisch regenwoud: een eerste kennismaking.* Muiderberg: Coutinho.

Kira, T. (1978). Community architecture and organic matter dynamics in tropical lowland rain forests of Southeast Asia with special reference to Pasoh Forest, West Malaysia. In *Tropical trees as living systems,* ed. P.B. Tomlinson and M.H. Zimmerman. New York: Cambridge University Press. Pp. 561-590.

Papadakis, J. (1966). *Climates of the world and their agricultural potentialities.* Buenos Aires: Papadakis.

Projeto Radambrasil (1972-1978). *Levantamentos de recursos naturais* 1-15. Rio de Janeiro: Ministério das Minas e Energia, Departamento Nacional da Produção Mineral.

Proradam (1979). *La Amazonia Colombiana y sus recursos* 1 (report), 2-5 (maps). Bogotá: IGAC-CIAF.

Richards, P.W. (1964). *The tropical rain forest.* Cambridge: Cambridge University Press.

Sombroek, W.G. (1966). Amazon soils. *Agricultural Research Reports* 672.

Sombroek, W.G. (1984). Soils of the Amazon region. In *The Amazon,* ed. H. Sioli. Dordrecht: Junk Publishers. Pp. 521-535.

UNESCO (1973). International classification and mapping of vegetation. Paris.

United States Soil Survey Staff (1975). Soil taxonomy: a basic system of soil classification for making and interpreting soil surveys. *Agricultural Handbook* 436. Washington D.C.: Soil Conservation Service, US Dept. of Agriculture.

Vanzolini, P.E. (1973). Paleoclimates, relief and species multiplication in equatorial forests. In *Tropical forest ecosystems in Africa and South America: a comparative review,* ed. B.J. Meggers, et al. Washington D.C.: Smithsonian Institution. Pp. 255-258.

Verstappen, H. Th. (1983). *Applied geomorphology.* Amsterdam: Elsevier.

Vink, A.P.A. (1983). *Landscape ecology and land use.* New York: Longman.

Walter, H. (1979). *Vegetation of the earth.* New York: Springer Verlag.

Walter, H. and Lieth, H. (1967). *Klimadiagramm Weltatlas.* Jena: V.E.B. Gustav Fischer Verlag.

Whitmore, T.C. (1974). Change with time and the role of cyclones in tropical rain forest on Kolombangara, Solomon Islands. *Commonwealth Forestry Paper* 46.

Whitmore, T.C. (1975). *Tropical rain forests of the Far East.* Oxford: Clarendon Press.

Zonneveld, I.S. (1979). Aspects of the ITC approach to vegetation survey. *Documents Phytosociologiques, Nouvelle Serie* 4, 1029-1063.

# Suitability of tropical forests for relevant use

by C.P. van Goor*

## 1. Introduction

Each year millions of hectares of tropical rain forest give way to the pressure of the ever increasing population in tropical countries. Since much of these forests are of vital importance for the quality of the environment, it is urgent that this destruction is halted and a land-use policy developed, by which forests can be maintained or at least utilized in an ecologically sound way (Wiersum, 1984). In most tropical countries, society needs forests as a reserve of land to be used for food and fuelwood production. When forest is converted to land that can support sustainable agriculture, this conversion might be beneficial. But this mostly is not the case, particularly because large areas of forest land are situated on poorer soils. So the land will be abandoned after some years of agricultural use and becomes covered by grass, shrubs or secondary forest of low quality.

Decisions about land use will be mostly related to the question of whether or not forest is to be converted to agricultural land. However, using forest land for forestry always implies opening up the forest by a network of roads, which mostly results in encroachment by local people applying shifting cultivation or grazing. On poor soils this will be the lethal blow for forests and soils. In tropical areas forest land in general might be classified as undisturbed forest, secondary forest, man-made forest, agricultural/grazing land and unproductive land. For a great number of reasons, in particular the still incomplete knowledge of natural forest ecosystems in the moist tropics and their significance for mankind in general, undisturbed forests are of paramount importance for nature conservation. Although some technology is already developed for protecting stretches of undisturbed natural forests, these do not give sufficient certainty for consistent achievement or realization. The actual situation is not encouraging. Maintenance and ecologically sound utilization of tropical forests, however, is essential for the survival of people living in forest areas.

This contribution deals with an approach for planning sound utilization of tropical forests and tropical forest land. This approach is elaborated on the basis of suitability classification of tropical forest land for relevant use, relating to the framework for land evaluation developed by FAO in 1976. The applicability of this framework for forestry purposes has been studied by a workshop of IUFRO and ISSS (Laban, 1981). Recently FAO issued guide-lines for land evaluation for forestry, which are based on the studies of the IUFRO/ISSS workshop (FAO, 1984).

In this paper the following steps of the system of land-use planning by land evaluation are dealt with:

- procedure;
- initial consultations;
- land mapping units (LMU);
- land utilization types (LUT);
- matching LMU and LUT;
- suitability classification;
- presentation of the results.

## 2. The procedure

Characteristic for the procedure is the two track system (Beek, 1978 and Fig. 16). One track is dealing with the socio-economic, cultural and political setting of the land evaluation. From this setting an analysis is carried out, identifying the needs of society for forests and forest produce. The second track deals with the general physical conditions, in particular the land. Land in terms of land evaluation is an integrated system, comprising not only the soil, but climate, vegetation, relief, fauna and man as well. The definition of land given in the

* Constructive criticism and valuable suggestions were gratefully received from K.J. Beek, R.L. Busink, C.F. van Beusekom, H.J. Gelens, W.B.J. Jonkers, C.F.W.M. von Meijenfeldt and D.C.P. Thalen.

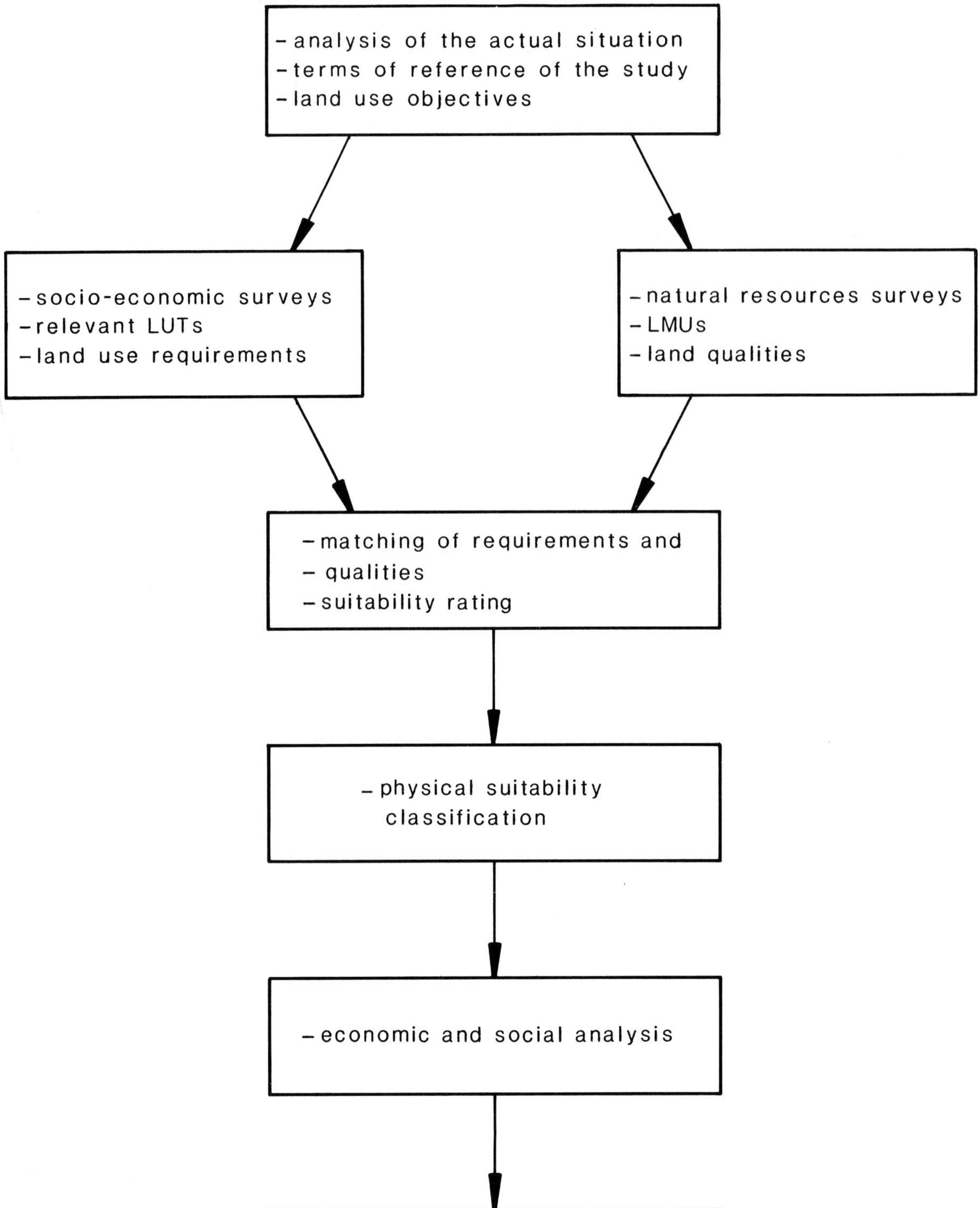


Fig. 16 Procedure of land evaluation (source: Gelens, 1984).

FAO framework is complete and reads: 'An area of the earth's surface, the characteristics of which embrace all reasonably stable or predictably cyclic attributes of the biosphere vertically above and below this area, including those of the atmosphere, the soil and the underlying geography, the hydrology, the plant and animal population and the results of past and present human activity to the extent that these attributes exert a significant influence on present and future uses of the land by man.'

The land is classified on the basis of these properties in LMUs (land mapping units) in such a way, that these properties can be related to the requirements of the types of land use. These types of land use are described as LUTs (land utilization types), a specific way of using the land relevant for the land evaluation region or country, in terms of key attributes, reflecting the physical, economic and social setting. The requirements of the LUTs are expressed in terms of soil, management and conservation.

The next step in the procedure comprises the confrontation of the requirements of the LUTs and the properties of the land, or, in other words, the mating of LUTs with the LMUs. By this action the suitability of the LMUs for the relevant LUTs can be determined. In general two kinds of suitability classifications are carried out: a suitability classification based on performance in physical terms and an integrated suitability classification. The latter is the physical classification completed by economic and social analyses and expressed in physical and socio-economic terms.

Mostly the LMUs will be suitable for more than one LUT. Therefore it is recommendable to present the results of the land evaluation in combination with a number of tropical land-use policy options to facilitate the process of decision making. One of the case studies (Thalen, this volume and Appendix 3) has adopted this procedure of land evaluation as the basis for land-use planning.

## 3. Initial consultations

Before defining and describing the land utilization types, initial consultations are executed, comprising an inventory and analysis of so-called fundamental references related to the socio-economic and physical situation of the land evaluation area. This is a time-consuming activity, which should be initiated in the very early stage of the land evaluation. The data collection and analysis of fundamental references is aiming at the selection of relevant land utilization types. The most important items of these fundamental references are:

- the terms of reference of the land evaluation. In some cases preliminary land utilization types - relevant for the study area - are given in a global description;
- the actual development situation of the region or the country, in particular regarding the actual land use, employment, population, infrastructure, income, technology, etc.;
- the formal development objectives regarding ecology, economy, employment, training and education, research, etc.;
- the time period for which the results of the land evaluation study are expected to remain valid. Land use will change during time so adaptation is essential;
- the socio-economic conditions of the land, regarding, for instance, ownership, location, size, etc.;
- the general physical conditions of the land, in particular climate, soil, hydrology, topography, vegetation, etc.

A great help for the compilation of the gathered information is a so-called structured list of major and minor determinants. These are the background for the land evaluation study and can be listed in nine major determinants:

- government;
- location;
- technology;
- produce;
- labour;
- capital;
- management;
- land: socio-economic aspects;
- land: physical aspects.

The checklist of these determinants is to be elaborated in more detail as is demonstrated in Appendix 1. The land utizilation types are developed on the basis of this checklist.

## 4. Land mapping units (LMUs)

The LMU is a mapped area of land with specified characteristics, homogeneous with a limited internal variation. They are delineated after surveys of natural resources such as soils, forests, geography or others. The LMUs have specific properties, which can be measured and which are called 'land characteristics'. For the process of land evaluation the land characteristics cannot be used directly, because of interactions. Therefore 'land quality' is introduced as a complex attribute of land, which acts in a distinct manner in its influence on the suitability for a specific use. In general land qualities are divided in four categories which are directly related to the use of the land:

- qualities related to growth, yield, such as availability of water, nutrients, and energy;
- qualities related to management, such as accessibility, location, trafficability, stoniness;
- qualities related to the sustained maintenance of the natural resources;
- qualities related to natural values and recreation.

In Appendix 2 a number of land qualities which are relevant for forestry are summed up. This list might not be complete, in particular in relation to nature conservation aspects. It should be worthwhile if nature conservation organizations initiated a study on land qualities essential for land evaluation for this particular field. In that case, an integration of land evaluation for agriculture, forestry and nature conservation, which is so badly needed in countries with tropical forests, is achievable.

The scale of land evaluation influences the aggregation level of the land units and the land-use units. Generally land-use planning starts with a broad concept for large areas after which, depending on the aim of the study and the presence of facilities and data, more detailed studies follow. Land evaluation mostly begins on a reconnaissance level on scales as 1 : 1,000,000 or even smaller, followed by a semi-detailed level to end with a detailed level on a local scale of 1 : 10,000. The case studies demonstrate the way various situations dictate the scale and level of aggregation.

## 5. Land utilization types (LUTs)

The land utilization types (LUTs) are formulated with the help of the results of the initial consultations and described with the key attributes - related to the major determinants of Appendix 1 - produce, labour, capital, management, technology, and scale of operations. Only then will the LUTs fit into the socio-economic and political context of the land evaluation area. Moreover, such description makes it possible to determine the specific requirements of the LUTs to the land. These requirements are directed to the following groups:

- requirements for organic production and yield;
- requirements regarding management;
- requirements related to the maintenance of the resources;
- requirements regarding nature conservation and recreation.

For forestry the key attributes are quite specific. Produce for instance has two main forms. The material produce, such as wood, resin, fruits, rattan and other minor products on one hand, and the immaterial produce, such as nature, protection of land and water, recreation, religion, etc. on the other hand. The latter is mostly indicated as function and not as produce. The multiple-use principle involves a combination of produce and functions on the same kind of land. Nevertheless it is possible to group the LUTs for forestry in some broad combinations:

- protection of forest, vegetation and fauna;
- protection of soil, water and microclimate;
- commercial production of wood and minor products;
- collecting minor products of the forests;
- production of wood, minor products and food crops;
- recreation, tourism and other social benefits.

In the paper by Boerboom and Jonkers (this volume) a number of land utilization types are given. These are derived from the actual types of utilization of forests in the tropics, but not formulated for the purpose of land evaluation. In the case study of

Kali Konto (Thalen, this volume) land utilization types are described for land-use planning (see Appendix 3). However, also in these examples the aggregation level is still so high, that requirements for the land are not elaborated in detail.

## 6. Matching LMU and LUT

An important step in the process of the land evaluation is the matching. All relevant LUTs with their requirements are combined with all LMUs. Each combination of a LUT with a LMU is analysed. This analysis contains the following items:

- the rate in which a certain LMU is suitable for a certain LUT;
- a study how the suitability of a LMU for a specific LUT can be improved, e.g. by the improvement of certain land qualities with a certain input and/or adaptation of the LUT and consequently changing the land requirements. For forestry, this is important regarding road building and opening up;
- a forecast of the effects of the improvement of land qualities;
- a study of the input/output relation regarding the LUT/LMU combinations or land-use systems.

For forestry, it is necessary to include also the effects and influences on both the surrounding and more distant land, which belongs to the land evaluation region. This is particularly valid in catchment areas of river systems where land use upstream effects land use downstream. But also in those cases where storage lakes are built, silt deposits are effected by land use upstream. From the analysis of the matching process the most optimal combinations of LUTs and LMUs are chosen. This is a kind of iterative process, which, with the progress of the inventories, studies and information, makes continuous adaptation possible.

In the process of matching, three steps can be distinguished: setting of factor ratings for each land-use requirement, comparison of these ratings with the land units, and subsequent determination of land suitability ratings.

Moisture availability as a land-use requirement can be rated, for instance, in mm available water in the soil as more than 120 mm; 80 – 120 mm; 40 – 80 mm and less than 40 mm, being, for instance, respectively very suitable, suitable, moderately suitable and not suitable. For estimates of produce as diagnostic factor for land suitability, site classes can be rated. Site class I means very suitable, site class II suitable, site class III moderately suitable, and site class IV and V not suitable. An example is given in the case study of Kali Konto (see Appendix 3).

As far as is known, factor rating related to the immaterial produce of forests is still in a process of development and needs more studies.

## 7. Suitability classification

From the foregoing it is clear, that after the factor ratings setting, each land utilization type can be compared with each land unit by means of these ratings. This will lead to land suitability ratings. These suitability ratings are referring to one land-use requirement alone, but the complete set of land suitability ratings of one LUT and one LMU will give the suitability rating for that specific land use. This will generally include the conditions for growth and yield, for management and for sustained maintenance and conservation.

Suitability classification can be carried out on the base of the existing situation, but also by taking into consideration minor and major improvements. In forestry, this is important regarding infrastructure, determining the current and potential suitability.

Besides, internal and overall land suitability classification can be distinguished. The internal suitability classification is restricted to the land evaluation area, whereas the overall classification also considers the effects land use may have on a wider environment.

The heart of the matter of the land suitability classification is the way in which, and the extent to which, the land-use objectives are met by this classification, and how this is applied in the land-use planning.

## 8. Presentation of results

Land evaluation for forestry and suitability classification of forests for relevant use are not independent goals, but the basis for planning forest use. To promote the application of the results of the land evaluation by planners it is recommendable to translate these results into a number of proposals for land-use planning, related to the socio-economic situation and political options. The relevant LUTs are brought together in management models, which are elaborated in detail regarding produce, labour and input/output ratios to be expected now and in the future.

With the help of such socio-economic and political analysis the management models will be realistic. From these models the consequences of decisions are made clear. Even the consequences of the execution of minor and major improvements become evident. The effect of current policy may be introduced, for instance, when nature conservancy is primary objective, or highest profit per unit of area or employment rate. Such an approach, in which the results of land evaluation are explained from various options, will facilitate the decision making of the land-use planners (see again Thalen, this volume).

## 9. Final remarks

The development of a plan for land use with the help of land evaluation is not a simple matter. Not only is a great number of data, to be collected by inventories and studies, needed, but a good team of experts in various disciplines working in a strongly integrated programme is essential. This integration and team-work appears always to be an obstacle or at least a serious handicap. The different kinds of land use - agriculture, forestry, nature conservation - always tend to plan from their own narrow standpoint and interest. In situations where the pressure on the land and the natural resources has reached the point at which the natural resources are endangered - already the situation in many places in the world - only an integrated approach for land-use planning offers relief. As elaborated before, such an approach must start from the socio-economic and political situation of the country, region or area (see again Thalen, this volume, but also a similar land-use planning exercise for forestry in Burkina Faso in Wiersum, 1984).

However, when such an integrated plan is developed, adopted and implemented, it is of paramount importance to maintain the plan. Plan maintenance is possible by the systematic feed back of data and results. Plan maintaining comprises monitoring after the implementation and evaluation of the collected information. This being the case, measures for improvement or adaptation are developed and the land-use plan is updated. In particular in forestry with its long production periods, continuity is essential, which means that plan maintenance should be given serious attention.

# GLOSSARY

*Land*
An area of the earth's surface, the characteristics of which embrace all reasonably stable or predictably cyclic attributes of the biosphere vertically above and below this area, including those of the atmosphere, the soil and underlying geography, the hydrology, the plant and animal populations and the results of past and present human activity to the extent that these attributes exert a significant influence on present and future uses of the land by man.

*Land mapping unit*
An area of land demarcated on a map and described in terms of land properties and/or qualities.

*Land quality*
An attribute of the land which acts largely as a specific factor on the performance of a certain use, e.g. available water, available nutrients, resistance to erosion. The expression of each land quality is determined by a set of interacting single or compound land characteristics with different weights in different environments depending on the values of all the characteristics in the set.

*Land requirements*
The specific land conditions required for the proper functioning of a certain crop or agricultural implement, e.g. water requirements, workability requirements.

*Land suitability*
The fitness of a given type of land for combination with a specified type of land utilization.

*Land utilization types*
A specific way of using land, actual or alternative, described for the purpose of land evaluation in the following key attributes: a. produce, b. labour, c. capital, d. management, e. technology, f. scale of operations. It is a technical organizational unit in a specific socio-economic and institutional setting.

*Land evaluation*
The process of assessment of land-use performance, involving the execution and interpretation of surveys and studies of land forms, soils, vegetation, climate and other aspects of land in order to identify and make a comparison of promising land uses in connection with specific land units in terms applicable to the objectives of the land evaluation.

## REFERENCES


Beek, K.J. (1978). Land evaluation for agricultural development. *ILRI Publication* 23. Wageningen.

FAO (1976). A framework for land evaluation. *Soils Bulletin* 32. Wageningen.

FAO (1984). Land evaluation for forestry. *Forestry Paper* 48. Rome.

Gelens, H.F. (1984). Land evaluation for forestation. In *Strategies and design for afforestation, reforestation and tree planting,* ed. K.F. Wiersum. Wageningen: PUDOC. Pp. 219-230.

Laban, P., ed. (1981). Proceedings of the Workshop Land Evaluation for Forestry. *ILRI Publication* 28.

Wiersum, K.F., ed. (1984). *Strategies and designs for afforestation, reforestation and tree planting.* Wageningen: PUDOC.



Author's address: C.P. van Goor, State Forest Service, P.O. Box 20020, 3502 LA Utrecht, The Netherlands.

# Appendix 1. Checklist of major and minor determinants of land utilization types (an example oriented to forestry, see Laban, 1981)*

*Government*

Existing development situation:
gross national product, income/head for different groups of society; general level of education, health, housing, etc.; political system, structure, power relations; present land use.

Existing development prospects:
plans and targets, such as projections for scales of operation, land reclamation, reforestation and consolidation, forest inventories and classification (nature reserve, protection forest, other).

Labour:
absorption and labour income targets.

Production:
targets in relation to export, consumption and import substitution of specific produce such as wood, energy, water-supply, outdoor recreation and tourism, nature conservation, food and fodder crops.

Policies:
as regards energy, environmental control (e.g. soil conservation, flood control, water and air qualities, buffer zones) and legislation (e.g. felling prohibitions, use of state-owned lands, reforestation requirements of exploitation concessions, sustained yield); financial policies as regards subsidies, taxation, foreign exchange.

Status of government services:
research, education, extension, management, credit, supply of inputs, output processing, transport, storage, marketing.

Status of government organization:
structure, hierarchy and relationship between ministries, departments, executive bodies, planning commissions.

*Location*

Critical distances:
residence to campsite, campsite to food-market/health service, campsite to working place in the forest, campsite to wood-market/processing point and mill to sales/export point, servicing/repair centre to forest.

Urban influence:
availability of labour, turnover of personnel to urban workshops, distances.

Status of infrastructure:
types of roads, road density, surfacing, maintenance; hazards such as susceptibility to obstructions, e.g. snow, flooding and landslides; raftability of rivers in different seasons; number of ferry-crossings; regulations regarding weight of vehicles, speed limits, tolls; capacity of harbours and airports.

Means and cost of transportation:
external (road, rail, river or combinations), internal (drag roads, railways, skidding, cable-yarding); by own, hired or contracted equipment; transport losses due to decay, long transporting time, poaching; cost of transportation (external and internal); cost of intermediate handling, storage.

Availability and local prices of inputs:
cost of new and second-hand equipment; distance to second-hand markets, to fuel depots; available water-supply (paper); variations in prices compared with other areas.

Other local costs:
land premiums, land taxes, boundary maintenance.

Environmental factors:
topographical features (steepness and irregularity of relief, roughness of terrain); ad-

* Note: When reporting on major and minor determinants, a sharp distinction should be made between the present situation and the options for development. Determinants should be assessed as quantitatively as possible and be reasonable, given the scale and terms of reference of the project.

vantages compared to other areas (healthy mountain areas versus hot tropical coastal swamps).

Natural interdependencies with other areas:
(subsurface) water storage, water-supply, drainage, erosion and flooding impact on downstream areas; effect of deforestation upstream.

*Forest produce*

Removable produce:
timber, industrial wood, firewood, charcoal, leaves and branches, bark, fruits, resin, game, fish, honey, rattan, bamboo, medicinal plants, woodcarving products.

Non-removable produce:
healthy environment, soil protection, space for recreation, knowledge about natural ecosystems, gene pool conservation, grazing possibilities, land for shifting cultivation, water-supply, scenery.

Observed and potential yields:
from mixed or pure forest, from hardwoods or conifers; potential yield increases, trends.

Age and overall condition of forest in relation to specific produce:
defects; possibility for natural or artificial regeneration or coppicing; phytosanitary conditions (required treatment for improvement); environmental conditions (degree of forest degradation); degree of tree stocking; quality of specific produce.

Scale of operations required in relation to specific produce:
felling systems, quality of produce, exploitation intensity.

Availability of seeds and plants:
quality and source of seeds; commercial, certified or selected seeds, existence and quality of commercial, government or other tree nurseries.

Destination of produce:
own saw-mill, local or national market, export; raw, semi-final or final product.

Marginal distances of specific produce to input and output market:
dependent on form, size, quality and on prices of semi-final and final products.

Demand for specific produce:
on local or national market; quality and quantity required; export prospects; shipping, government export regulations, competition with other countries; income and price elasticities; price and price structure of outputs, trends.

*Labour*

Total availability:
labour density: man/land and man/capital ratios per operational unit, e.g. family, farm, co-operative forest enterprise, communal forest land; differences per region; competition with other sectors; seasonal distribution; mobility of labour.

Kind:
male, female, child, cultural and social restrictions; full-time or part-time; local or migrant; on/off-farm.

Education and specialization:
skills, available and required levels; existence of various levels of education facilities, motivation and work attitudes in government and other institutions.

Limits to scale of operation:
due to labour availability and distribution in relation to various forestry activities such as afforestation, road maintenance, harvest and other operations.

Labour income:
in forestry but also in other sectors; per unit of land, time or capital; labour income from forestry activities as a percentage of income derived from other activities.

Labour conditions:
existence of government or other cultural regulations; strength and behaviour of labour organizations; preference of labour for specific kinds of work; status of labour in forestry activities; value of leisure as compared to labour.

Labour productivity:
per time unit, per unit of land, per unit of invested capital.

Relationships with other production factors:
capital invested per labour unit; available and occupied land per labour unit; effective animal and/or mechanical labour inputs.

Trends and prospects:
relating to above-mentioned aspects.

*Capital*

Available and invested capital:
per operational unit and per ha.

Present capital investments:
in roads, bridges, buildings, in plant and equipment, and in drainage/water-regulation; value of these investments.

Price of capital for investment and financing:
interest rates, inflation, alternative investment opportunities; amortization, annuities, taxes; in forest operations, in forest protection, in processing; trends.

Price structure and policy:
free or state-controlled market, control of maximum prices, quota control, import and export regulations; difference between nominal and real exchange rates of foreign currency; shadow prices; price ratios of inputs and outputs; observed trends.

Availability of capital inputs:
non-recurrent and recurrent input; availability for maintenance and repair of machinery and equipment; quality; scarcity; prices, kind of availability (own, hired, contracted, purchased); locally available or to be imported.

Investment financing:
existence and willingness of development banks to invest; existence and status of credit institutions; credit regulations and conditions; alternative investment opportunities.

Investment incentives:
government subsidies, temporary tax exemptions, tax rebates for re-development (planting); soft loans; investment conditions.

*Technology*

Kind of techniques applied:
use of fertilizer, insecticides, herbicides; shortwood, tree length, full and total tree harvesting concepts, at different levels of mechanization; intensity of labour used in forest operations.

Specification of available traction and implements:
manual and animal power (hand tools, horses, oxen); manually operated machinery (brushcutters, power saws, insecticide sprays); tractor-operated mobile and semi-mobile machinery; stationary machinery.

Supply of readily available and applicable techniques:
choice of systems and mechanizational level; availability of implements, machinery and spare parts; availability of educational facilities for forest workers and machine operators; physical properties of land; capital/labour situations; status and orientations of research and educational facilities.

Scale of operations required for the application of specific techniques:
technical components: machine manoeuvrability, character of operations (selective *vs* clearcutting); economical component: machine utilization costs.

Predictive capacity of climate and other environmental hazards:
presence and sophistication of research and 'routine' institutions; quality and density of network for recording data on climate, soils, vegetation, hydrology, erosion, fire, etc.

Predictive capacity of market fluctuations and price relationships:
access to international and national information sources; sophistication of data handling; flexibility to adapt to changing situations.

*Management*

Surveying and inventory:
experience with survey-flying, aerial photograph interpretation, air-calls, groundcalls, sampling and mapping.

Planning:
necessary know-how and experience at different levels in relation to:

- formulating goals, ways, time limits as regards: orientation of specific produce components and overall production; harvesting and regeneration methods; tracing and constructing roads; recreation facilities;
- determining requirements of: men, machines, buildings, logistics, short-term and long-term credit in relation to time limits and seasonal availability;
- degree of centralization of management decisions: communicating systems; freedom of timing of operations.

Operational experience:

- capacity utilization of men and machines: efficiency in use of specific inputs; feeling for the use of equipment; degree of specialization; technical experience; feeling for social contacts and stimulating people; care of personnel; bearing isolated living conditions;
- processes and network planning: level and organization of product processing; feeling for timing of operations related to climatic variation; feeling for the tolerance for specific operation of trees and forests; feasibility and adoption rate of new techniques; ability to absorb inefficiency;
- efficiencies in specific operations such as access and transport system, forest protection against insects, diseases and fire, site improvement (fertilizer use, irrigation/drainage, tree species composition).

Commercial experience:
in marketing and storage; capacity utilization of capital and money affairs.

Specific social, cultural and religious values:
individual attitudes and outlook; solidarity and other group attitudes, public relations (information and interpretation).

*Land (socio-economic aspects)*

Available land per inhabitant:
man/land ratio.

Land/ownership and land tenure:
transferability of land titles, security of land titles; land prices and trends; extent and use of community lands, extent of government land and national parks, reserves; ethnic claims on land; land tenure systems, status of unused land and amounts available.

Land use:
patterns, rotational cycles, shifting cultivation; existence of extensive grazing in forest areas; legislation and rights of local population as regards use of government-owned (forest) land; traditional division of tasks between men and women; need for subsistence food crops.

Status of physical infrastructure:
form and size of land parcels, farm sizes, size of operational units; percentage share of different farm size groups.

Status of institutions and legislations:
cadastral and extension services, water board, irrigation authority; soil conservation law and services, forestry laws, regulations on grazing; government strength in implementation and execution of laws; credit facilities.

Trends:

- in land prices, farm size, land occupation, land productivity, changes in land use, scale of operations and land-use intensity;
- in physical aspects: topography, accessibility, interdependency; biophysical conditions.

# Appendix 2. Land qualities for forestry

| Land quality | Land characteristics |
|---|---|
| *Qualities related to growth and yield* | |
| Radiation regime | Total radiation, sunshine hours, aspect; day length: latitude, climatic type. |
| Temperature regime | Temperature - mean annual, mean for growing season, hottest, coldest months: altitude, aspects, climatic type, major climatic region. |
| Moisture availability | Relative evapotranspiration deficit, rainfall/evaporation ratio, depth to groundwater, rain aspect, vegetation indicators, soil moisture storage capacity. |
| Soil drainage | Soil drainage class, depth to mottling: vegetation indicators (communities or species). |
| Nutrient availability | Mean levels of N, P, K, etc., soil pH: topsoil thickness, soil type. |
| Rooting conditions | Effective soil depth, stones and gravel, rock outcrops and boulders, soil structure: soil type. |
| Conditions affecting germination and establishment | Soil texture, stones and gravel, surface sealing or capping. |
| Salinity/sodicity | Electrical conductivity of saturation extract, exchangeable sodium percentage: soil type, vegetation indicators. |
| Other toxicities | Observed toxicities, soil pH: soil type. |
| Climatic hazards | |
| ■ fire | Observed frequency; length of dry season, rainfall/evaporation ratio, combustibility of ground vegetation. |
| ■ frost | Mean frost days: altitude. |
| ■ wind | Frequency/severity of high winds, typhoons; exposure index, aspect. |
| Physiographic hazards | |
| ■ flood | Observed frequency/severity: topographic site. |
| ■ landslide | Observed frequency/severity: slope angle, rainfall intensity, soil depth. |
| Incidence of pests and diseases | Observed incidence; relative humidity; temperature, soil factors of known influence. |
| Present timber volume | By species, from forest inventory. |
| Predicted timber yield | By species, from forest yield prediction or growth-site correlation: site index. |
| Seedling survival rates | Recorded averages for site types or area as a whole, by species. |
| Predicted yield of non-timber products | From forest inventory or prediction. |
| *Qualities related to management* | |
| Terrain factors affecting mechanized operations and internal access | Terrain class; slope angle, relative relief, stream frequency, microrelief, soil bearing capacity, presence of swamps, cracking clays. |

| | |
|---|---|
| Conditions effecting nursery sites | Available water-supply (surface or ground water), soil texture. |
| Present vegetation cover | Ease of clearance. |
| Size of potential management | Size of blocks of suitable land. |
| Location | Distances from earth road, tar road, rail, river; and from saw-mills or other markets. |
| *Qualities related to maintenance of resources* | |
| Erosion hazard | Estimated soil loss, t $ha^{-1}$ $y^{-1}$; slope angle, rainfall erosivity, soil erodibility, rainfall. |
| Water yield | Recorded or estimated. |
| Predicted response of streamflow | Hydrological modelling. |
| Tolerance to vegetation degradation | Observed or estimated; present condition of vegetation, vegetation type. |
| Presence of valuable rare/endangered plant and animal species | Presence, rarity; minimal areas; presence of refugia. |
| *Qualities related to natural values and recreation* | |
| Scenery | Esthetic or scientific value, and variety, of lands and vegetation. |
| Resources for recreational and tourist activities | E.g. rock climbs, fishing resources, wildlife, wilderness traveling. |

Source: derived from FAO, 1984.

# Forestry and agriculture: an alliance for survival

## Some observations on tropical forest policies

by W.M. Otto*

### 1. At last the world discovers its forests

The process of deforestation in the tropics is not a recent phenomenon. Especially in the last century, colonial powers promoted export-oriented agriculture to meet the demands of a growing world market. As a result, large tropical forest areas, usually the most fertile on flat lands and gentle slopes, were cleared and reclaimed into plantations for cash crops like sugar cane, tobacco, coffee, rubber, etc.

In the 20th century, however, the deforestation began to get into an ever greater acceleration, showing alarming dimensions in the last decades. Many foresters, ecologists, conservationists, biologists, soil scientists and other experts have been warning time after time of the fatal consequences of deforestation, but until recently, their warnings have fallen on deaf ears. The indifference in public opinion began to change slightly only after some widely publicized studies. One of these certainly is The Global 2000 report to the President (1980), because it described the vital importance of the tropical forests for the life support system of our earth.

Another important signal to public opinion was the publication in 1982 of the first results of the FAO/UNEP *Tropical Forest Resources Assessment* project. For the first time in history a systematic and continuous monitoring of the extent, condition and deterioration of tropical ecosystems, including tropical forests, was made possible and practical.

The first results were very revealing if not alarming. So in the eighties in national and international political and administrative circuits, gradually it became common knowledge that nowadays every year more than 10 million ha of tropical forest area is falling victim to other use and abuse, and also that the consequences could be very serious in economic and ecological terms, both nationally and globally. Apparently something had to be done.

It seems that 1985, the International Year of the Forest, shows the beginning of a break-through in the consciousness of the international community about the importance of tropical forests. The Ninth World Forestry Congress, held that year in Mexico, concentrated on 'Forest Resources in the Integral Development of Society' as the central theme and special attention was given to tropical forests.

FAO and World Bank, together with UNEP and a group of donor countries, established the *Tropical Forestry Action Plan.* In November 1985 in the Hague, The Netherlands, a meeting was held on 'Harmonizing International Forestry Development Co-operation in support of the Tropical Forestry Action Programme'. For the first time in history the political leaders of Europe and Africa in February 1986 convened in Paris for a summit meeting, the 'Silva Conference', to consider long-term forest policies to rescue the world's forests. So, at last the international community is beginning to understand what is going on with tropical forests and what is at stake.
Consequently tropical forest policy more than ever will be an issue of national and international debate, if only to direct increased efforts and financial means to the right objectives. In the following observations forest policy is placed in a wider framework of the development of rural areas and the management of natural resources.

### 2. Driving forces behind deforestation

Discussions about rate of and reason for deforesta-

* The author expresses his thanks to R. L. Busink for his valuable assistance in the literature research for this article.

tion have often been dominated by wild accusations, persistent misunderstandings and gross simplifications. It might have been very easy if we could simply put the blame for deforestation on multinationals, corrupt regimes, over-population or demand for tropical timber in industrial countries. However, things are a little bit more complicated.

Regarding the rate of deforestation, important factual information is provided by the first results of the UNEP/FAO *Tropical Forest Resources Assessment* projcct. Although still subjcct to unccrtainties due to different definitions and poor national statistics, the rate of deforestation is now considered to be 11.3 million ha of tropical forests annually being converted to cropland and an additional 4.4 million ha seriously affected by timber logging operations. Along the new logging roads afterwards in many cases the remaining forests are cleared for subsistence farming.

However, what has been registered here does not present the causes but only the visible symptoms of deforestation. The pressure upon the forests is exerted by a great number of different driving forces, which arise from economic and social conditions, such as:

- poverty;
- population growth;
- landlessness;
- unemployment;
- iniquitous land tenure systems;
- shortage of food;
- shortage of fuelwood;
- agricultural practices like shifting cultivation;
- erosion or desertification;
- national or international demand for timber;
- national or international demand for food;
- and last but not least, the omnipresent need, both public and private, for short-term benefits, no matter the long-term consequences.

These driving forces, although manifesting themselves in rural areas, in their turn are the outcome of underlying structural conditions in the countries involved, such as:

- a weak financial and economic position;
- a weak management of the national economy;
- a weak structure of public sector institutions;
- subordination of the interest of rural areas to those of the cities;
- subordination of long-term interests to short-term policy;
- political and military instability.

All these driving forces and underlying conditions - also influencing each other - manifest themselves in a certain 'mix' which varies between countries and regions within countries. The composition of this 'mix' can also change as time passes. For instance, in a number of countries rising populations and incomes probably will increase domestic demand for timber and fuelwood, resulting in increasing pressure on the forests.

So deforestation is a complicated and changing process varying from country to country and from region to region. It is the result of economic and social forces, manifesting themselves in rural areas but in their turn determined by the balance of economic, political and administrative powers within the countries involved and sometimes also by international economic and political powers. Therefore, at short notice there are no feasible means to get control over the deforestation process, let alone to stop it. The deforestation process no doubt will go on for some time to come. So the question is not whether deforestation can be stopped, but how to get control over this process in the coming decades in such a way that it proceeds in a less chaotic and, if possible, more planned manner. Only then it could be canalized, slowed down and eventually reversed. But certainly this will be a race against time.

Although this prospect is gloomy, especially European observers might well remember their own forest history. The cold facts are that the European forests have been cut almost to the last tree and reforestation started only when shortage of fuelwood and timber made it an economic necessity. Moreover, this history might repeat itself in another way. The European forests again are in great danger, now because of the threat of acid rain and other pollutants, the by-products of an industrial civilization almost completely relying on fossil fuel combustion. Although the facts are well-documented and widely known, the industrial countries of Europe still have a long way to go before their industrial civilization has been made compatible with the preservation of their forests and other natural values. At stake are great economic, financial and political interests both public and private. But if another catastrophy for the European forests is to be prevented, it is clear that also here time is running out.

So, when the problem of tropical deforestation is discussed in the western industrialized world, some modesty and understanding are appropriate. Both because of our failure in the past to protect our own forests and because of our share in the responsibility for tropical deforestation during the colonial period.

## 3. Many proposals to rescue the tropical forests

Many institutes and experts have been advocating for years policies, ways and means to halt the process of deforestation and to manage the forestry resources.

To mention very briefly some recent views, Rubinoff (1983) for instance proposed a plan to preserve a sample of the world's remaining moist tropical forests through the establishment of an internationally financed system of 'Tropical Moist Forest Reserves'. The plan provides for 1,000 forest reserves covering in total about 100 million ha. The costs, estimated at US $ 3 billion annually, should be financed by all the developed temperate zone nations.

Guppy (1984) tackled the problem from another side and stressed the necessity to stimulate change in social and economic conditions in general in the countries with tropical forests. More specifically he advocated to establish, analogous to the OPEC, an Organization of Timber Exporting Countries (OTEC). These countries could by co-operation increase the price of tropical timber. The tropical forest would then become a greater economic value, which in turn is a prerequisite for a better management of these forests. And OTEC also could provide the necessary financial support.

A broader approach, endorsed by a group of prominent scientists and conservationists, was outlined in the *World Ecological Areas Programme* (WEAP) of 1980. According to this programme the fatal trend in deforestation should be reversed along different lines such as:

- an increase in the rate and scale of commercial afforestation in tropical areas;
- the setting up of local wood-processing enterprises;
- an increase in the rate and scale of commercial afforestation in the temperate industrial countries;
- a shift from destructive to sustainable agricultural systems.

WEAP (1980) offers an additional option, that is the possibility to promote rural employment, food self-sufficiency and a sound secondary industrial sector, both to relieve the pressure on the forests and to contribute to the solution of other existing major problems in the countries involved.

On the basis of the experience of many World Bank projects, Spears (1979, 1983) advocates more control over deforestation by better planning and more cohesion between the different parts of rural development. He also warns of the tension between the lower and higher parts of river basins which make increased development of agriculture, especially in the lower areas, a necessity.

The FAO and World Bank together with UNEP and some donor countries drafted a *Tropical Forestry Action Plan* (TFAP), supported by the World Forestry Congress in Mexico 1985. This TFAP concentrates on five priority areas for action:

- fuelwood;
- forestry's role in land-use planning;
- forest industrial development;
- conservation of tropical forest ecosystems;
- institution strengthening in research, training and extension.

This review of proposals, however brief and incomplete, shows clearly the wide diversity of the different approaches. Certainly these proposals contain many of the necessary elements of any forest policy. But in most of these views and proposals one major aspect receives too little attention, if not ignored altogether, namely that almost all the forces behind deforestation are acting outside the forests. If these forces are not contained, in most cases forest policies will be of little use and probably will be swept away together with the forests they intend to manage. So forest policy has to be much more than policy for forests.

## 4. Deforestation closely connected with hunger and poverty

A lively picture of the complex nature of the deforestation process has been given by Guppy (1984). He compared deforestation with a cake of which the top layer is formed by population growth and land hunger. The second layer consists of social conditions, covering a third layer where local political motivation is mixed with unwillingness to face realities. The fourth layer contains all imaginable financial problems. Unfortunately, as described before, the reality is even more complex and cutting a slice of the deforestation cake will disclose many other layers, colours and tastes.

It is obvious that for complex problems there are no easy solutions. The traditional forest policies usually are directed at the protection, conservation and management of existing forest areas. If the mere survival of the forests is at stake, then the first priority in forest policy should be to make a connection with policies which can relieve the pressure. Forestry therefore should be deeply concerned about the conditions outside the forests from which the driving forces leading to deforestation arise. The most dangerous condition in many cases is the neglect of rural areas and the people living there. The answer for this situation is well-known. There has to be a shift in policies and priorities from the cities to the rural areas.

There are two important reasons for the urgent priority of rural development. The social reason is that in Africa, Asia and Latin America hunger and poverty are mainly prevailing in the rural areas. The economic reason is that weak economies in these countries can only be improved by economic growth preceded by or simultaneously with agricultural development.

The race between growing populations and the increase of agricultural production to provide the necessary food (and fuel) will be decided in the rural areas. But also the fate of the forests and other natural resources to a large extent will depend on the success or failure of rural development policies. So forestry has a big stake in the development of rural areas. Fortunately there is a broad international consensus on the necessity and urgency of rural development as one of the most important tools to combat hunger and poverty in the developing countries. This consensus has been confirmed formally and unanimously at the UN World Conference on Agrarian Reform and Rural Development held in Rome in 1979. But from acceptance of principles to their realization there is still a long way to go. Moreover, rural development is not a simple remedy to all kinds of economic and social diseases.

In the first place, it covers a broad range of technical, economic, social, legal and administrative activities, varying widely and dependent on conditions and circumstances. Even more tricky are the differences in fundamental approach to rural development from economic, social and political points of view. Rural development therefore is not one single prescription but can have varying approaches and forms. So the inevitable connection between forestry and rural development is not making things easier. But as already mentioned, there are no easy solutions for complex problems.

## 5. The interdependence between forestry and agriculture

Traditionally forests have been a reservoir to meet the agricultural expansion demanded by economic development and population growth. Since in many places the process has gone too far and the equilibrium between agricultural land and necessary forests has been disturbed, a new task lies ahead. The real issue for the coming decades therefore is how to combine agriculture and forestry to raise the production of food, fuel and timber and, above all, how to raise incomes and living standards for the rural population. This issue is especially complicated, because the forests also have to maintain the environmental stability on which continued agricultural production depends.

If forestry and agriculture should forget their traditional rivalry and together participate in rural development, where do they meet, support and complement each other? From the forestry point of view it is important that each hectare of agricultural land can produce more products on a permanent base. Only then can the need to convert more forests into agricultural land be reduced. From the agricultural point of view it is important that sufficient forests are available near the villages and settlements to meet the need for fuelwood, timber and other non-wood products. Also it is important that the productivity of agricultural land is protected by forests against erosion, floods, droughts and silting up of irrigation systems.

Both agriculture and forestry also have an interest in planting new forests near the villages for fuelwood and timber and in the reforestation of eroded land not suitable for permanent agricultural use. For agriculture, the future supply of fuel and timber can be secured and the productivity of agricultural land better protected. For forestry, the planting of forests near the villages can compensate for earlier losses and reduce the pressure on existing natural forests. Moreover, the reforestation of eroded areas can restore the ecological balance. Tree planting and reforestation can also provide an important contribution to the increase in and diversification of products, employment and incomes in rural areas. So to relieve the pressure on the remaining forests rural development should contain two major elements:

- the increase and diversification of agricultural production on existing cropland and pastures;
- the planting of new trees and forests near villages and the reforestation of eroded lands unsuited for agricultural use.

Both elements should fit into a development of rural areas not only leading to an increase in food production, employment and incomes, but simultaneously leading to the conservation and rehabilitation of natural resources of which the forests are essential to protect sustained agriculture. So agriculture cannot have a sustained production without forests to protect its soil and waters and to meet the demand for fuel and timber. Also, the converse is true, that is, forestry cannot hope to protect its forests without an improvement in the living conditions of the rural population.

## 6. Reforestation: a major challenge for forestry

Reforestation, which in the tropics is only in its initial stage, needs special attention in the coming decades, because reforestation will become an important element of rural development. According to the FAO assessment of Tropical Forest Resources of a total area of tropical forests of 1.8 billion hectares, by 1985 planted forests are expected to cover 17 million hectares, that is only 1 per cent. Estimates of existing plantations and current planting programmes indicate that about 60 per cent of the plantations consist of trees for industrial timber while the remaining part will provide fuelwood and non-wood products or focus on stabilizing soils and water supply.

The present annual rate of planting is 1.1 million hectares, so for every ten hectares of tropical forests cleared, only one hectare is replanted. In the tropics the plantations together with natural regrowth are therefore far from compensating the conversion of forest into agricultural land. To meet the projected demands for domestic fuelwood and industrial timber a dramatic increase of the current rate of planting will be necessary. FAO estimates that to meet the demands of the developing world only for fuel wood in the year 2000, an increase of 18 times the current annual rate of planting is required. Meanwhile experience shows clearly that unmet demands for fuelwood immediately are converted into destructive pressure on the forests.

So it is obvious that the present annual rate of planting of 1.1 million hectares will have to be increased to somewhere between 10 and 20 million hectares yearly. This is in itself a gigantic task technically, organizationally, financially and politically. If one is aware, moreover, that in one way or another most reforestation has to fit into the development of the adjacent rural areas, then it becomes clear that for the coming decades reforestation will be the major challenge for forestry.

Of course this does not mean that the concern for protection of the existing natural forests is less urgent or could be neglected. The tropical forests of the future certainly should contain sufficient well-protected undisturbed virgin stands if only to safeguard genetic plant resources, wildlife and other irreplaceable values. To attain this end, inevitably also other natural forests will have to be managed. Not only to put the exploitation of timber on a sustained-yield base but also to sustain the availability of a variety of other products like resins, tannins, gums, camphor, etc.

Apart from the many technical aspects of reforestation, such as the difficult choices of tree species and silviculture, there are some fields where special attention is needed such as:

- the legal status of the trees and the land on which they are planted, the responsibility for the maintenance of the stands, the right to future benefits, and in general the participation of the local communities in the reforestation activities;
- the organization of reforestation activities as 'rural public works' providing employment in rural areas with much unemployment and landless labour;
- the possibilities to combine reforestation - at least temporarily - with agriculture in an agro-forestry system, providing land to agriculture and maintenance to the forest. For instance the successful 'tumpang sari' system on Java in Indonesia.

## 7. Difficult steps from principles to practices

The difficulties from the forestry point of view concentrate mainly on three fields:

- the conversion of existing natural forests into managed forests, producing timber and non-wood products on a sustained-yield basis;
- the creation of new forests by reforestation of eroded areas;
- the integration of forestry into rural development.

For forestry especially this integration creates new problems, for the role of forestry in rural areas of course has to be translated into feasible policies, programmes, projects and guidelines. The difficulties will be tremendous. One basic problem, for instance, is the inevitable land-use planning, technically complicated and politically very sensitive. On the basis of surveys and inventories every rural region or river basin needs defining which areas are suitable for permanent agriculture and which areas need to remain under or to be planted with forest in order that present and future demands for fuel and timber can be met without depleting the forest resource and without destroying the forest ecosystem protecting the agricultural lands. An additional complication is the possible gradual shift in the composition of forests from natural forests towards higher yielding plantation forests.

Countless other social, economic and legal problems will arise from changes in land use related to new agricultural methods and systems and reforestation. Step by step solutions have to be found, tailored to specific situations. In this respect World Bank and FAO have been doing important pioneering on the integration of forestry into rural development.

The World Bank and other UN agencies in recent years have been giving increasing priority to community forestry, watershed protection and forestry's integral role in rural development. From various projects distributed all over the world FAO has assembled and analysed documentation on the role of forestry at the local rural level, the problems encountered and the possible solutions.

It is becoming clear that the nature of the problems is so many-sided that a comprehensive approach is needed by forestry experts joining efforts with colleagues of other disciplines such as agronomy, soil science, ecology, economy, anthropology, law and public administration. For real progress in this field new research efforts are needed, focussed on the coherence and interdependence of agriculture and forestry. In addition careful documentation and analysis of past and ongoing projects could improve the set up of new projects in the field. But even if forestry succeeds in mastering the technical difficulties associated with reforestation and with the integration of forestry into rural development, other political and institutional bottle-necks are lying ahead.

## 8. A first prerequisite: priority in the national long-term development plans

Widespread hunger, poverty and unemployment in developing countries have brought most of their governments into an activist role in development. In those countries multi-year development plans and special ministries or planning agencies for medium- and long-term planning are common practice. Although development plans in many cases show poor records and do not always play a major role, the World Bank stresses that the process of planning is useful because it brings together different government agencies and sections of society to think about national development. It also can provide the political argumentation needed to mobilize public support for development plans.

Now rural development and management of resources inclusive forests are typical elements of long-term policies. So if countries do have medium- or long-term development plans - even if they might not be very effective - a first prerequisite to manage the deforestation process is for forestry together with rural development to have clearly their share and priorities in these plans. The same holds for their position in the connected multi-year public investment programmes. Only in this way the conservation of forests as part of a development policy for the rural areas can become a vital part of government policy. To this end the interests of rural development and forestry should be promoted on the highest political levels within the government by strong ministers and politicians as well as by the relevant ministries.

Right here, however, two big political obstacles are looming up:

- the prevailing neglect and subordination of the rural areas and its population to the cities;
- the usual neglect and subordination of long-term interests to short-term policies.

Although most developing countries have accepted the necessity for rural development to combat poverty and hunger and have accepted the necessity for management of resources on a sustained basis, there is still a wide gap between theory and practice. In most countries only 10 to 20 per cent of the government budgets are spent for rural development. And indeed an increase of this share would inevitably affect the vested commercial, industrial and political interests concentrated in the cities. So, overcoming the 'urban bias' will be a big political problem in many countries.

The same holds for the establishment of long-term policies. Sometimes only greed prevents a government from enforcing cutting regulations in its forests, and stimulating reforestation and local processing of timber instead of exporting logs. In this case the 'goose with the golden eggs' is simply killed. However, in many countries the urgent problems of today indeed do require major efforts of the governments. Therefore politically and financially there is often only a narrow margin for tackling the problems of tomorrow. In other words, the problems of the present generation are so acute that apparently it is impossible to solve simultaneously the problems of the next generation. The tragedy, however, is that the next generation is already with us. Almost half of the population of the developing countries is younger than 16 years and will have to start to make a living in the coming decade.

The fate of the tropical forests is closely connected to the success or failure in obtaining sufficient political and financial priority for development of rural areas and the responsible management of natural resources. In this sense one can agree with Westoby (1985) that deforestation is primarily a political problem.

Although at present forestry sees agriculture as a competitor in land use and a threat to its forests, their long-term interests in the rural areas run parallel. So politically and psychologically forestry and agriculture should build an alliance for their joint survival.

## 9. Management of policies, programmes and projects by public institutions

There are of course also many other important policies to be decided upon, which are vital for rural development and resources management, for instance:

- legislation regarding land rights, land use and land-tenure systems;
- legislation regarding the protection and exploitation of forests;
- fiscal policies for the forestry sector;
- pricing policies for food and agricultural products;
- agricultural credit policies;
- the distribution of power between different ministries, and the level on which agriculture, forestry, environment and natural resources are fitted into governmental organization.

But any policy, whatever its nature, has to be designed and translated into programmes, projects and budgets. Also, these policies have to be implemented, operated, evaluated and, if necessary, adjusted.

In the case of rural development and forestry there is also a strong need for sectoral co-ordination on different levels between the ministries, agencies and institutions involved, and, last but not least, during the whole process the people and interest groups involved have to be consulted, their co-operation secured and their participation mobilized.

Since in many developing countries the public institutions not always have the disposal of sufficient man-power, skills and motivation to carry the managerial burden of accelerated development, special attention should be given to the balance between policies and the possibilities to implement them. In the meantime reinforcement and improvement of the public institutions is as important and urgent as the promotion of the right policies, legislation and planning.

Many suggestions for the reinforcement of the public institutional infrastructure have been given by the World Bank. Some should be mentioned especially in relation to deforestation and rural development. The World Bank stresses the need for good information systems and reliable monitoring of current developments. The problems of planning without facts and the lacking of reliable statistics have proved to be very damaging for any development. In the case of deforestation and the resulting deterioration of rural areas by erosion, floods, silting up of irrigation systems, etc., the monitoring of current developments has not only a factual significance for designing development plans, but also a political meaning.

Although in public administration - also in the developed world - usually the long-term interests are neglected, there is one exception to this rule, namely in case of calamities. Only when the results of neglect of long-term problems become visible and tangible as disasters with many victims, great losses and economic impacts, only then are governments inclined to act and allocate means for long-term policies. There are many examples of this phenomenon. Now good monitoring of current developments can explain and even predict and announce disasters and thus influence public opinion, politicians and governments to pay more attention to long-term problems such as deforestation.

Another institutional constraint arises from the fact that rural development is a so-called 'people-centered' development. Typical problems are for instance:

- the uncertainty whether local people really want the improvements offered by the project;
- the necessity to mobilize the local people and to make use of their skills and experience;
- the prevailing tensions between different local interest groups and different localities;
- the varying patterns of human behaviour among cultures and localities.

So great attention is needed for the indispensable link between the government and the local people involved in the projects. This link has to be established on the spot and not from behind the desks in the ministries.

By education and tradition in forestry, interest is concentrated on the forest rather than on the people in and around the forest. However, as explained earlier, forestry has to co-operate with the people outside the forest, if only for its own survival. So there is a clear necessity to change its introvert character. The core of this problem once was summarized with crystal clarity by Soekiman Atmosoedaryo (1978) stating 'If you want people to love the forest, first love the people'. Forestry education should play an important role in this necessary change of orientation.

More in general the institutional constraints in the forestry sector constitute major obstacles to effective development. One aspect of strengthening forest administration is to ensure within the forestry sector more skill and understanding of agricultural and socio-economic problems in rural areas. Conversely too, however, in agricultural research, education and extension the vital role of forests in rural areas should also be better understood.

## REFERENCES


Brown, L.R. et al. (1984). *State of the world.* New York: Norton & Co.

Brown, L.R. et al. (1985). *State of the world.* New York: Norton & Co.

Committee on Forest Development in the Tropics (1985). *Tropical Forestry Action Plan.* Rome: FAO.

FAO (1978). *Forestry for rural communities.* Rome.

FAO (1983). Forest administration for development. *Unasylva* 35(142). Rome.

FAO (1985). Forests, trees and people. *Forestry Topics Report* 2.

Guppy, N. (1984). Tropical deforestation: a global review. *Foreign Affairs* 62, 928-965.

Lanly, J.P. (1982). Tropical forest resources. *Forestry Paper* 30. Rome: FAO.

Mergen, F., ed. (1981). Tropical forests: utilization and conservation. *Proceedings of an International Symposium held at Yale University.* New Haven: School for Forestry and Environmental Studies.

Myers, N. (1980). *Conversion of tropical moist forests.* Washington D.C.: National Academy of Sciences.

Palin, D. (1980). *Management of development forestry: a comparative study of public forestry administrations in the Asia-Pacific region.* Rome: FAO.

Rubinoff, I. (1983). A strategy for preserving tropical rain forests. *Ambio* 12, 255-258.

Soekiman Atmosoedaryo (1978). The role of forestry in local community development. Guest speaker's address, *Eighth World Forestry Congress.* Jakarta.

Spears, J.S. (1979). Can the wet tropical forest survive? *Commonwealth Forestry Review* 58, 165-180.

Spears, J.S. (1983). Tropical reforestation: an achievable goal. *Commonwealth Forestry Review* 62, 201-217.

The Council on Environmental Quality and the Department of State (1980). *The Global 2000.* Report to the President. Washington D.C.: U.S. Government Printing Office.

U.S. Interagency Task Force on Tropical Forests (1980). *The world's tropical forests: a policy, strategy and program for the United States.* Report to the President. Washington D.C.: U.S. Government Printing Office.

Westoby, J. (1985). Forest policy: one step forward. *Unasylva* 37(148), 55-57.

World Bank (1978). *Forestry sector policy paper.* Washington D.C.

World Bank (1982). *World development report.* Oxford: Oxford University Press.

World Bank (1983). *World development report.* Oxford: Oxford University Press.

World Ecological Areas Programme (1980). A plan to save the tropical forests. *The Ecologist* 10, 1-5.



Author's address: Dr. W.M. Otto, Jagersveld 2, 8222 AB Lelystad, The Netherlands.

# Epilogue

by C.F. van Beusekom

In this summary the general outline of the seminar as pointed out in the introduction is followed. From the contributions on the *demand* aspects (Luning, Boerboom and Jonkers) and on the *supply* aspects (Oldeman, Van IJssel and Sombroek) main points are selected and important statements are stressed. Next, essentials of land-use planning as described by Van Goor are shortly summarized, with special attention to particular difficulties which must be taken into account when applying this planning system to tropical rain forest lands. Finally, a survey is given of the main issues in the paper by Otto, which deals with the manifold underlying structural factors, factors which too often frustrate any promising attempt to better forest management. The priorities he gives for a strategy to relieve the pressure on the forest are stressed in particular.

## 1. Demands

In Luning's contribution the complexity of socio-economic needs and conditions affecting tropical rain forest is the central theme, as well as how to deal with this complexity in planning practice. Some needs are linked to the ecosystem and cannot, or at least much less effectively and probably only partly, be fulfilled otherwise. Other needs are not linked to rain forest in particular; such needs could - and generally should - be satisfied by shifting activities to other parts of the country or by finding alternative solutions.

Another way to look at needs is to take two complementary view-points: the angle of public interest and the angle of private interest. Both are manifold and often contrary. In both interest groups often short-term needs and long-term needs are conflicting. Here the difficulty arises that conventional economic analysis usually does not give sufficient weight to future scarcities and it is suggested by Luning that this analysis should be adapted accordingly.

The analysis of socio-economic conditions and requirements in land-use planning for tropical forest land should take into account the different aspects mentioned above. Neglect of this complexity of needs usually brings about a total failure of forest management and rural development projects.

All needs for tropical rain forest from whatever angle or interest group they may originate, cause pressure on this forest. Looking at this pressure on a world-wide scale, three major factors contributing to forest destruction can be singled out:

- the need for farming/livestock raising;
- the need for fuelwood;
- the consequences of the need for timber, meeting consumers' demand at the national and international level.

Especially the need for farm land, mostly linked to excessive population growth, is a predominant pressure factor in most tropical rain forest countries. Luning emphasizes that agricultural development by more intensive use of existing farm land should be highly preferred to 'development' through extension of farm-land area at the cost of tropical rain forest, at least in a number of countries with high population densities.
Depending on overall socio-economic conditions, as well as on rain forest area per head of population, a general typology of tropical rain forest countries has been made. Luning points out, however, that this classification must be refined to make it relevant for planning and policy making. It might be assumed that for those countries or regions in which similar overall socio-economic and forest conditions occur, likewise similar forest policy might be required. To this purpose general strategic development models could be developed. Of course every country has its own and specific problems, according to which such development models should be adapted into a master plan which meets the more specific circumstances of each country in particular. Such master planning should follow the principles of land evaluation as elaborated by Van Goor.

## 2. Land-use types

The various needs as analysed by Luning find expression in a multitude of types of forest land use. Many current use types are in fact to be considered forms of abuse. Other forest-use types are sustainable, but in this group several are neglected or still insufficiently recognized. The contribution by Boerboom and Jonkers describes and characterizes these various forest-use types as to their economic benefits on the one hand, and as to their impact on the forest ecosystem and their long-term prospects on the other hand. Sixteen land-use types are reviewed along that line and summarized in a table.

Boerboom and Jonkers point to the important fact that each form of forest use affects possibilities for other uses; many types are incompatible or may limit future use. Three types of interaction occur:

- harvesting one forest component affects development and viability of other components;
- eliminating or damaging forest cover affects land use elsewhere (externalities);
- groups of users can be incompatible, either in social or in economic respects.

Hence, choices have to be made and limitations accepted. When considering alternatives of forest land use, a primary criterion should be their impact on the ecosystem, since wise use of tropical rain forest as a natural resource can only be a reality if one knows whether, and to what degree, such forest systems can be modified. Unfortunately, there is much more experience in techniques and forms of use leading to ecosystem destruction than leading to balanced ecosystem management. Although our knowledge of tropical ecosystem management is lagging behind the vast destructive capacity of our technology, there is no time to fill this gap, since man has entered the tropical forest ecosystem and will continue to do so. Hence, there is no other way than to make use of the knowledge that is available now, and to absorb and use any knowledge that may come to us in the future. At any rate, it would be a vast gain if the limited ecosystem knowledge already at our disposal, would be applied consistently in current use of the tropical rain forest 'supply'.

## 3. Biotic properties

Oldeman's paper describes our knowledge about the dynamics of tropical rain forest ecosystems: what is their structure, how is this structure working, how does it react upon modification by man, and what rules should be observed. Oldeman's approach to the tropical rain forest ecosystem emphatically includes the human component. This component is not only a reality, but also most human activities have some natural equivalent in forest dynamics.

When dealing with the tropical rain forest ecosystems, for whatever purpose, one must have some basic knowledge about these systems:

- their composition (species and populations);
- their structure and architecture;
- their species relations, flows, reservoirs and feed-back loops of matter and energy.

Moreover, it is important to know that this ecosystem is composed of subsystems in different scales. For rain forest management two levels are essential and of practical significance, the eco-unit level and the forest-mosaic level (see Oldeman). The forest mosaic is the ecological equivalent of the land mapping unit (LMU) in land-use planning (see Van Goor). Forest utilization for whatever purpose can generally be expressed in terms of modification of the system on the forest-mosaic level and on the eco-unit level.

Species richness of tropical rain forest is especially linked with eco-unit architecture; in 'climax' eco-units there is an enormous variety in architecture, which leads to an immense diversity in species. Most rain forest utilization types (Boerboom and Jonkers) result in modification, mostly simplification, of eco-unit architecture. The more simplification of eco-unit architecture, the more impoverishment of forest flora and fauna. For instance, when forest utilization for gene pool purposes is planned, eco-unit architecture must not be changed.

Diversity of species of flora and fauna not only depends on eco-unit architecture. Many species need different eco-units for their survival as well as so-called minimal areas. Therefore, in the planning of undisturbed forest reserves minimal areas of species should be taken into account. Moreover, many tropical rain forest species only occur within limited geographical areas. Particular parts of the tropical rain forest belt are especially rich in species, which often occur nowhere else. These relic areas or refugia (see van IJssel and Sombroek) are usually known by zoologists and botanists. Forest land mapping and forest-use planning should take such refugia into account, as well as the evidence about minimal areas of occurring species.

Utilization of tropical rain forest not only means modification of its architecture, it also means modification of its balance of matter and energy. For instance, harvesting trees is removing stored energy and nutrients from the system. The balance of gains and losses of matter and energy is mostly expressed on the forest-mosaic level. In sound utilization of tropical rain forest this balance should not be disturbed too much; especially nutrients should be kept in the system in order to maintain its productivity. Since most soils of the tropical rain forests are poor and extremely vulnerable (van IJssel and Sombroek), and since the major part of minerals and energy is locked away in forest biomass, forest damage and deforestation can easily lead to rapid leaching, heavy erosion, freshets or mud streams.

From the foregoing evidence it becomes clear that everything depends on the degree in which modification of tropical rain forest ecosystems is effectuated. Depending on this dosage of influence some utilization types have only a slight impact on the system, other types may lead to a certain degree of impoverishment, and still others virtually cause its often irreversible destruction (Boerboom and Jonkers).

To prevent ultimate loss of the forest, some ecological rules must be applied in planning and management:

*The rule of functional shifting*:

a certain shift in species composition for commercial reasons may go along with natural forest dynamics, at least to some extent.

*The rule of reversibility*:

functional shifting should not cause the extraction of species and, still more important, it should not trigger self-reinforcing degradation cycles (leaching, erosion, impoverishment, diseases, pests and others).

*The rule of scale*:

scale of human interventions should be proportionate to the scale of natural forest dynamics.

Finally, it cannot be said too often, that good management of existing forests is economically much more interesting than first destroying them and afterwards restoring the degraded land by means of afforestation. Reafforestation is rebuilding a destroyed forest ecosystem. Rebuilding a stable system is a long-lasting effort, which has to obey the same rules as are mentioned above for management of existing forest. Under proper management the direct yield or supply of tropical rain forest ecosystems is usually modest, but may be of long duration, provided human requirements will respect the limits of these systems. Exceeding these limits in the long run never pays.

## 4. Abiotic land properties

In Oldeman's paper only the biotic part (vegetation, fauna) of the ecosystems has been elaborated. No less important, however, are the abiotic environmental factors, which are discussed by van IJssel and Sombroek. In tropical rain forest environmental factors such as climate, geomorphology, topography, soils and hydrology, may vary within a wide range. These variations affect, together with the natural vegetation, to a great extent the forest land-use possibilities. Hence, whenever land-use planning is concerned, these environmental factors should be thoroughly investigated.

The climate in tropical rain forest areas (rainfall and temperature) is in general no limiting factor to growth. An important feature is that these macroclimatic factors and the vegetative cover together determine the microclimate within the forest. Sustainability of the forest depends, among other things, on this self-induced microclimate; thus, when considering forest utilization types, major attention should be paid to changes in microclimate and their effect on growth and regrowth. Another climatic aspect that should be kept in mind when adapting the ecosystem for some kind of land use, are the consequences of rain water falling in excessive amounts. From a source of life water may become a transport medium carrying away valuable plant nutrients, soil particles and even complete soils. Unfortunately, for forest land-use planning purposes, no useful climatological classification is available. Existent classifications are too general, or too exclusively focused on agricultural crop production.

Marked differences in parent material, in landform and in its stability are related with differences in soils, and thus in forest types and in forest land-use possibilities. The given overview of major soil groups in the tropical rain forest belt can only be general and not complete, due to the endless variation in local environmental conditions. With each soil group description a short diagnosis of land-use possibilities is given, with special reference to their susceptibility to deterioration as a result of changing the vegetation cover. It appears that most tropical rain forest soils are not suited for any form of intensive land use; only a few are of higher productivity, but these soil types generally are already in culture for permanent crops.

In tropical forest areas environmental factors, such as climate, topography, geology, hydrology and soils, cannot be controlled very well by human action, apart from the triggering of degradation processes, which is relatively easy. Therefore, restrictions on land use, imposed by environmental conditions, must be known and should be respected. Hence, it is obvious that, if survey and mapping of environmental conditions is an important tool for land evaluation and land-use planning in general, it is virtually indispensable in tropical areas.

This is why it is important to carry out a systematic physiographic soil survey - a survey method relating soils to, among other factors, geomorphology, topography and hydrology. References for such survey systems are given. Soil survey can be done at very different scales, depending on the planning scale and on the purpose of soil maps. Characteristics in relation to the type of survey are given in two tables. Soil maps resulting from the above surveys can be directly linked with biotic data (vegetation structure, floristic and faunistic data) plotted on the same base. Such a resource inventory should be focused not only on production potentials, as is usually the case, but also on natural values which might need protection.

The main question to be answered is: what are the sustainable and relevant land-use alternatives for a given area? There may be production land-use potentials as well as conservation land-use potentials. Conservation or restoration of (parts of) the original ecosystem should always be one of the alternatives to be considered. Loss of qualities that are inherent to the primeval forest ecosystem should anyway be accounted for, whenever arriving at a recommended land use.

## 5. Planning systems

Coming now to the planning of tropical rain forest use, it is obvious that only those planning systems can be expected to be successful, in which full allowance is made for the essentials that have been stressed in the *demand* side papers by Luning, and Boerboom and Jonkers, as well as those in the *supply* side contributions by Oldeman, and van IJssel and Sombroek. The well-known system of land evaluation can meet this requisite, given its essential two-track character. This land-evaluation method has been outlined in the contribution by Van Goor, with special regard to the specific position of tropical rain forests*.

In the present context land evaluation is an approach to planning a sound utilization of tropical forest land, on the basis of suitability classification. For this land-use planning, the following two-track system is characteristic and essential (see Fig. 17):

- one track is dealing with the socio-economic,

* The method described by Van Goor has been derived from FAO Forestry Paper 48, Land Evaluation for Forestry (Rome, 1984) but adapted to specific conditions prevailing in tropical rain forests.

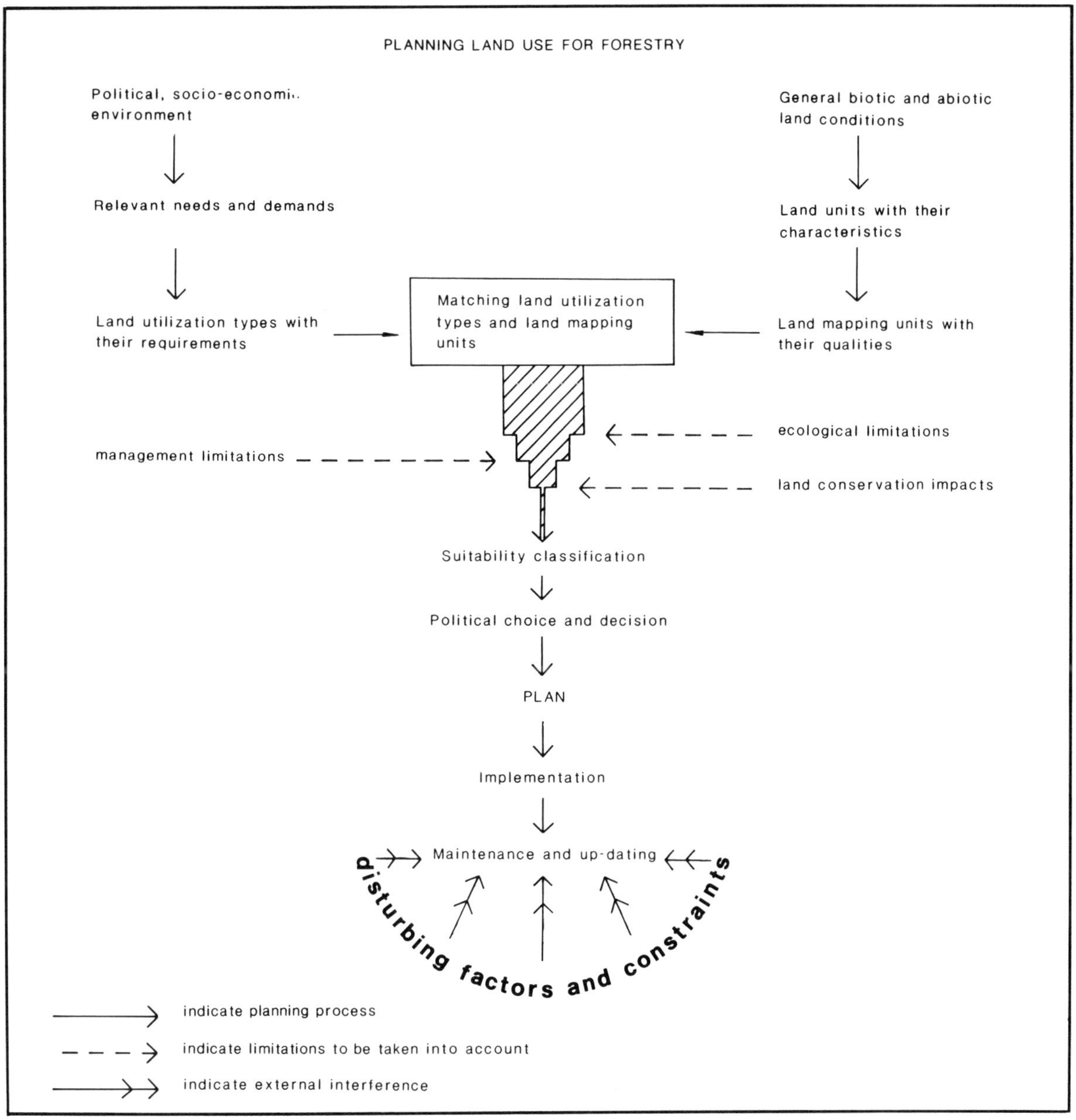


Fig. 17 Land evaluation for tropical rain forest land. Source: compiled by author.

cultural and political setting, identifying the needs of society concerning forest land and forest produce. This is the *demand* side, resulting in land-use requirements, described as land utilization types (LUT). Before defining and describing land utilization types it is, in order to avoid an unrealistic picture, most important that initial consultations are executed, comprising an inventory and analysis of so-called fundamental references related to the social, economic and physical situation of the area. In this way only relevant LUTs are selected and wishful thinking is prevented. Examples of well-elaborated LUTs can be found in the Suriname (Boxman et al.) and the Ivory Coast (Vooren) case studies;

- the other track deals with the physical and ecological properties of the forest land. This is the *supply* side, in which the land qualities are identified and described as land mapping units (LMU). For tropical rain forest already quite some knowlegde and experience about various land qualities are available. In the field of nature conservation, however, such knowledge is lagging behind. Since nature conservation in tropical countries is so badly needed, Van Goor pleads for a land quality study in this field, to be executed by nature conservancy organizations. In principle LMUs can be made on every scale. In tropical rain forest the basic LMU usually coincides with the forest mosaic as defined by Oldeman.

The above two-track approach is relevant for land-use planning on every scale, from the most generalized, national level up to the detailed, local level.

An important step in the process of land evaluation is the matching, in fact the confrontation of demand and supply. All relevant LUTs with their requirements are combined with all LMUs with their specific land qualities. Every combination is analysed according to the following items:

- suitability rating;
- possibilities of suitability improvement;
- forecast of the effects of suitability improvement;
- input-output relations;
- effects on adjoining land (e.g. catchment areas of river systems).

On the base of this analysis suitability ratings for each combination of LUT and LMU can be made, leading to suitability classification of each specific LMU for various types of land use. Classes run from very suitable to not suitable. Following this method it is possible to establish which land is most suitable for specific types of land use, on a fairly objective basis.

In order to make the results of land evaluation useful for decision makers, it is recommendable to translate these results into a number of proposals, considering socio-economic situations and political options. Various consequences of each proposal, e.g. ecological, financial and social, are made clear. For an example of the application of the land evaluation approach in tropical rain forest, reference is made to the case study of Kali Konto (Thalen).

For successful land-use planning with the help of the land evaluation approach it is essential to have a good team of experts in various disciplines co-operating in a strongly integrated programme. In practice this condition often appears to be a serious handicap (Otto). In situations where the pressure on the land is endangering natural resources - in many places in the world - only an integrated approach offers relief.

This is not enough, however. When such integrated planning is developed, adopted, and implemented, it is of paramount importance to maintain it. Systematic feedback of data and results is necessary. Lack of maintenance in tropical rain forest projects is a common phenomenon; see for instance the Rondônia case study (Groeneveld). Therefore plan maintenance should be given serious attention.

## 6. Constraints

In the introduction to this book mention already has been made of many fundamental constraints standing in the way of almost every promising attempt towards better management of tropical rain forest. In spite of all good advice that specialists may give about socio-economic needs, the ecosystem, the environment, and the planning, no lasting result may be expected without the elimination of such constraints. It appears that many failures are due to a weak public institutional infrastructure in tropical countries, as well as lack of proper legislation regarding land rights, land use, forest protection and exploitation. Also, the distribution of power and low degree of co-ordination between different ministries and institutions often do not favour successful forest management, whatever the quality of programmes and planning. However, such handicaps can be overcome, provided that the forces behind the process of deforestation can be brought under control.

In the final contribution presented by Otto, a comprehensive picture of these background forces is given. Basically, Otto says, these forces stem from poor economic and social conditions, weak national economic management and a tendency to pursue short-term benefits no matter what the long-term consequences are. But in particular it is neglect of rural areas and lack of concern for natural resources that create hunger, poverty, unemployment, and land degradation in rural areas and thus create the pressure upon the forest.

A prerequisite to combat hunger and poverty and to relieve the pressure on the forests therefore is to bring about a shift in priorities of national governments in favour of more rural development, including reafforestation and rehabilitation of devastated lands instead of depletion of natural resources. Such a shift against the prevailing *urban bias* certainly will run into stubborn resistance of the vested political, commercial and industrial interests in and around the cities.

It is a hopeful sign, however, that gradually governments and public opinion are becoming aware of the serious global impact of the current process of deforestation in tropical countries. Therefore the question of 'how to stop deforestation' is becoming an issue of frequent discussion on national and international level. In circles of international development co-operation, there is a growing willingness to spend more money and efforts on research, education, transfer of knowledge and financial aid in the forestry sector. But no infusion of money and know-how in the forestry sector, however large, can stop deforestation if, and as long as, the forces behind this process remain active.

Since forest policies are at the mercy of the game of political forces, in the foregoing observations forest policies have been placed in the wider context of national development strategy, rural development and management of natural resources. *It becomes clear that in the rural areas the long-term interests of agriculture and forestry run parallel. Therefore they should build an alliance for their joint survival.*

Author's address: Dr. C.F. van Beusekom, State Forest Service, P.O. Box 20020, 3502 LA Utrecht, The Netherlands.

# II. Case studies

# Rondônia - Brazil

by W.P. Groeneveld*

## 1. Introduction

Brazil is rapidly developing its part of the Amazon basin. Highways, complete new towns and hydroelectric power stations are being constructed. Various mining operations have started. Large forested areas have been converted into pastures for cattle ranching and land settlement schemes are carried out. The resulting rapid deforestation, its ecological effects and the threat to the future of what is left of the Amerindian tribes pre-occupies large groups both in and outside Brazil.

The developments in Rondônia, which forms an integral part of Brazilian Amazonia, are depicted below.

## 2. Setting

The western Brazilian state of Rondônia covers 243,050 km. It has climatic conditions and areas with soils more suitable for agriculture than most other parts of Amazonia. The monthly mean temperatures in Rondônia are between 21° and 27° C. Mean annual rainfall ranges between 1,800 mm in the south to 2,200 mm in the center and west of the state. Rondônia has a three-months dry season (June-August).

The soils of the Amazon basin have, generally speaking, good physical properties but are chemically very poor and thus infertile. Fortunately some quite extensive pockets of relatively fertile soils occur in the Amazon basin, some of them in the state of Rondônia.

Extensive soil and land capability surveys have been carried out in Brazil's part of the Amazon basin to detect suitable land for agriculture. In 1980, SUPLAN (National Secretary for Agricultural Planning) published the results of such a survey for Rondônia. This publication with maps at a scale of 1 : 1,000,000 is largely based on earlier surveys carried out by Radambrasil. It indicates the suitability of the soils in Rondônia for agricultural utilization on three management levels:

- low-input management level, with practically no input of capital, research findings, fertilizers and pesticides, and largely based on manual labour;
- medium-input management level, with modest input of capital, research findings, land conservation measures, fertilizers and pesticides and based on manual labour and animal traction: no mechanization;
- high-input management level, with high and intensive input of capital, research findings, etc. and based on mechanization.

The results of this survey such as the extent of land with a good or moderate suitability for crops and planted pasture as the main land utilization types (LUTs), at low, medium or high input management levels, are given in Table 8. For two LUTs included in this survey, natural pasture and silviculture, the land was only marginally suitable. As a whole, only 9,064 km or 3.7 per cent of the surface of Rondônia was found suitable for sustainable cultivation of annual crops.

## 3. Migration

According to the most recent demographic census, the population of Rondônia grew between 1970 and 1980 with the very high annual rate of 15.8 per cent. In 1980 it amounted to almost 500,000 inhabitants against 150,000 in 1970. Migration has been responsible for most of the demographic expansion.

* The author wishes to thank K.J. Beek, C.P. van Goor, P. Schmidt and W.G. Sombroek for their constructive criticism and useful suggestions.

Table 8 The extent of land (in km² and as percentage of total land area) with a good or moderate suitability for crops and planted pasture at low, medium or high management levels.

| Land utilization type | management level input | | | | | |
|---|---|---|---|---|---|---|
| | low | | medium | | high | |
| | suitability | | suitability | | suitability | |
| | good | moderate | good | moderate | good | moderate |
| crops | 24,409 $km^2$ 10% | 5,009 $km^2$ 2% | 27,442 $km^2$ 11% | 108,598 $km^2$ 45% | 26,924 $km^2$ 11% | 109,146 $km^2$ 45% |
| planted pasture | - | - | - | 5,051 $km^2$ 2% | - | - |

Source: SUPLAN, 1980.

The opening up in the middle of the 1960s of Rondônia by the highway BR 364, which links the capital, Porto Velho, with Cuiaba and the rest of Brazil, and the rapid spreading news that fertile land could be obtained cheap or even free, made Rondônia attractive for Brazil's landless. Besides, several factors caused rural workers to leave the south and the center west of Brazil, such as:

- continuing agricultural mechanization and consequently a decline in rural employment opportunities;
- sales of small holdings to large commercial farmers seeking to expand the production of export crops, particularly of soybeans;
- fragmentation of land holdings through inheritance in regions of earlier small holder settlements, such as northern Paraná and southern Matto Grosso;
- periodic frosts and other climatic hazards in southern coffee-growing regions;
- the growth of Brazil's population.

Most settlers came from rural areas. Accordingly, the principal previous occupation of the family heads had been agriculture. However, about 50 per cent of them were illiterate and of those who received a formal education, only about 2 per cent completed primary school.

When in the 1960s this migration-rush started, the government was not prepared to allocate land, to assign landownership titles, to build feeder roads or to provide agricultural extension services and credit. Serious land conflicts and a disorderly occupation were the result.

In 1970, the government agency INCRA (National Institute for Colonization and Land Reform), which has the jurisdiction over land within 150 km of an international boundary and over land located within 100 km of any federal road in Amazonia, was called in to regulate the occupation and to provide guidance to the migrants. To accomplish this, INCRA founded between 1970 and 1975 seven 'colonization' projects in Rondônia (Table 9). These seven colonization projects occupy, to a large extent, the fertile land occuring in the state.

The INCRA land settlement schemes all have essentially the same layout. The total project area is mapped and a gridlike pattern of roads, conforming to rectangular 100 ha parcels, is superimposed upon it. Each settler selected by INCRA receives such a parcel. In theory, feeder roads are built by INCRA, prior to the arrival of the settlers. In practice, however, INCRA has fallen far behind this goal. For instance, in the Ouro Preto project, roads give

Table 9 Area and capacity of INCRA settlement projects established between 1970 and 1975.

| Project | Year founded | Total area (ha) | No. of families |
|---|---|---|---|
| Ouro Preto | 1970 | 512,585 | 5,133 |
| Sidney Girão | 1971 | 76,300 | 500 |
| Ji-Paraná | 1972 | 479,737 | 4,756 |
| Paulo de Assis | 1973 | 293,560 | 2,974 |
| Padre Adolpho Rohl | 1975 | 456,366 | 4,341 |
| Burareiro | 1975 | 304,925 | 1,215 |
| Marechal Dutra | 1975 | 494,661 | 4,520 |
| Total | | 2,618,134 | 23,439 |

Source: derived from SUPLAN, 1980 and World Bank, 1980.

access to approximately 70 per cent of the project area during the dry season. During the rainy season, however, access drops to only about 10 per cent. As rice and corn are harvested during the rainy season, much of this produce is lost due to lack of access to proper storage facilities or markets.

The settler is allowed to clear 50 per cent of his parcel. The remaining 50 ha have to be set aside for nature conservation purposes. This measure, known as the 50-per cent-rule, is disobeyed by the majority of the settlers, mainly because its implementation cannot be controlled.

At the beginning of 1980, some 24,000 families had been settled in the seven colonization projects, implying that their capacity had been reached (see Table 9). As population forecasts for the 1980s assume migratory inflows even larger than those of the previous decade, new settlement programmes are set up even though fertile land is no longer available. INCRA intended to settle before 1986 another 22,000 families in Rondônia, mainly along the President Medici-Costa Marques Road (BR 429), which is now reaching completion. These settlement projects form a part of Polonoroeste, the overall development programme of this region.

The design of these new settlement projects differs from those set up earlier. The settlers in these new settlement projects will receive parcels of 45 ha, its size depending also on the site's suitability for agriculture. The settler is allowed to clear all the 45 ha of his parcel. The legally required forest reserves, equal to 50 per cent of the area of the parcels, have been set aside in blocks, rather than on the individual parcels as was the case in the past. Unauthorized deforestation is checked by IBDF (Brazilian Institute of Forestry Development).

A fair number of migrants settle outside the official INCRA colonization areas. They occupy a piece of public or private land, often on the fringe of an INCRA colonization project. When a squatter occupies less than 100 ha of public land, he has a legitimate claim to it if he has been present for more than 12 months, has cultivated the land using family labour, and has no other land in his name in Brazil. When he claims more than 100 ha and has the resources to cultivate all this land, he is permitted to make a preferential bid when the land is sold at public auction. The improvement he has made - deforestation is considered to be a land improvement - counts toward the price of the land. Other migrants take up residence on parcels of others - usually family - and work for the owner (tenancy or share-cropping) until INCRA provides them with their own parcel of land. The number of squatters in Rondônia is not known, but it is thought to be in the order of tens of thousands of families.

## 4. Polonoroeste (Brazil's integrated development programme for the northwest region)

In 1979 the government, wanting to regulate the future socio-economic development of the region served by the Cuiabá-Porto Velho Highway (BR 364), proposed the Polonoroeste programme. The programme was formally established in 1981. Central in the programme is the reconstruction and pavement of the Cuiabá-Porto Velho Highway, budgetted at approximately US $ 568 million. To maximize the socio-economic benefits of this great improvement of the regional transport system, parallel projects involving construction and consolidation of secondary and feeder roads, implementation and consolidation of settlement projects, execution of land tenure regulations, services in support of agricultural, forestry and agro-industrial activities, provision of social services and infrastructure to small rural communities, environmental protection and support of indigenous communities will be carried out. The main financier of the programme, with a budget of US $ 1,135 million, is the World Bank, who has committed US $ 443 million.

One of the major problems of the Polonoroeste programme is the imbalance in the progress of programme components. While road construction has been proceeding rapidly there has been little progress in implementing the measures intended to provide services to the settlers and to protect areas which are unsuitable for agricultural development. Neither biological nor Amerindian reserves have been established or protected, as should have been done according to the terms of the loan agreement with the World Bank.

## 5. Present-day dominant agricultural system

The present-day dominant agricultural system is very traditional. At the end of the rainy season (May/June) the forest is cleared. Of the 80-150 m $ha^{-1}$ of timber occurring, only a few valuable species, such as Mahogany (*Swietenia macrophylla*) Imburana (*Torresea acreana*), and Ipê (*Tabebuia serratifolia*), normally not more than 5 $m^3$ $ha^{-1}$, are sold. The remaining vegetation is left to dry till the end of the dry season (August), when it is set to firè. At the onset of the rainy season, upland rice is planted. Frequently grass seeds are mixed with the rice seeds, to establish pasture after the rice has been harvested. Where soil is fertile, the rice crop might be followed by other annual crops.

In most other parts of Amazonia, cattle ranching has become the main land-use form. The devastating ecological impacts of this system are not compensated by the meagre amount of beef it produces. In Rondônia, cattle ranching is not yet important. This is mainly due to INCRA's enforcement of government policy, that prohibits distribution of public land in parcels larger than 2,000 ha (Law No. 2597 art. 8 of 1955). Investors in large cattle ranches consequently have preferred other Amazonian states, where this law has not been enforced. Sometimes this law is circumvented by registering several contiguous parcels in the name of different family members (Fearnside, 1983) or by buying several adjoining parcels of settlers in INCRA's colonization projects.

Recently two tree crops, cacao and coffee, have been planted on a substantial scale on the more fertile soils. The cultivation of rubber and Guaraná (*Paullinia cupana*), a woody vine of which seeds are used to prepare a popular soft drink, is promoted. The cultivation of rubber has become possible now, because efficient methods of controlling the serious leaf disease caused by the fungus *Microcycles ulei* have been found. In contrast to the cultivation of annual crops and ranching practices, some fertilizers and lime are usually applied in tree crops.

## 6. Amerindian affairs and nature conservation

The massive immigration has led to rapid accelerating deforestation of the state of Rondônia and forms a threat to the future of both Amerindian and nature reserves. The indigenous population of Rondônia is estimated to be about 2,300, belonging to some fourteen different tribal groups (see Table 10).

Table 10 Population and size of Rondônia's Amerindian reserves.

| Name | Population | Area (ha) |
|---|---|---|
| Roosevelt | 191 | 233,100 |
| Ribeirão | 79 | 47,900 |
| Lage | 175 | 107,300 |
| Lourdes | 446 | 185,500 |
| Rio Guapore | 131 | 69,800 |
| Rio Negro Ocaia | 193 | 104,100 |
| Pacaas Novas | 463 | 279,900 |
| Sete Setembro | 165 | 247,900 |
| Karitiana | 80 | 89,700 |
| Kaxarda | 206 | n.a. |
| Kariruna | n.a. | 205,000 |
| Tubarões | 106 | 200,000 |
| Kaxarari | 109 | 83,000 |
| Uru-eu-wau-wau | n.a. | 878,000 |
| Total | 2,344 | 2,731,200 |

n.a. = not available.

Source: derived from SUPLAN, 1980 and World Bank 1980.

To guarantee their future, fourteen Indian reserves, with an area totalling about 2.7 million ha, have been created. However, many of these Amerindian reserves have been invaded by squatters. Besides, new projected roads, as shown on maps published by the Department of Roads and Highways of Rondônia (DER) and the Company for Agriculture and Cattle Ranching Development of Rondônia (CODARON), will bisect the Rio Branco, Roosevelt, Karitiana, Kariruna, Rio Negro Ocaia and Tubarões Indian Reserves (see Fearnside and Lima Ferreira, 1984).

The future of two of the three established nature reserves of Rondônia is obscure and discouraging. The Guapré Biological Reserve, created in 1982 with 600,000 ha, will be bisected by three planned roads. When this happens, the reserve will be substantially reduced due not only to the direct loss to road construction, but also to the rapid entry of squatters along these roads. The Jarú Biological Reserve was originally created in 1961 as a forest reserve with 1,085,000 ha and has since been reduced to 268,150 ha by the development of cacao plantations within its boundaries. What little remains is being destroyed by a number of squatters, carrying out clearing within its boundaries, and the planned construction of a road. The Pedras Negras Reserve, created in 1961 with 176,000 ha, has recently been rescinded completely. The only reserve, which future is not threatened, is the Cunião Ecological Reserve.

## REFERENCES


Fearnside, P.M. (1980). The effects of cattle pastures on soil fertility in the Brazilian Amazon: consequences for beef production sustainability. *Tropical Ecology* 21, 125-137.

Fearnside, P.M. (1983). Land use trends in the Brazilian Amazon as factors in accelerating deforestation. *Environmental Conservation* 10, 141-148.

Fearnside, P.M. and Lima Ferreira, G. de (1984). Roads in Rondônia: highway construction and the farce of unprotected reserves in Brazil's Amazonian forest. *Environmental Conservation* 11, 358-360.

Hecht, S.B. (1983). Cattle ranching in the eastern Amazon: environmental and social implications. In *The dilemma of Amazonian development,* ed. E.F. Moran. Boulder: Westview Press. Pp. 155-188.

Moran, E.F. (1981). *Developing the Amazon, the social and ecological consequences of government-directed colonization along Brazil's Transamazonian Highway.* Bloomington: Indiana University Press.

Poelhekke, F.G.M.N. (1984). Prikkeldraad in het oerwoud: de veeteelt in het proces van economische en sociale integratie van het Amazone-gebied in Brazilië. *Nijmeegse Geografische Cahiers* 25. Nijmegen: Katholieke Universiteit.

Smith, N.J.M. (1981). *Rain forest corridors: the Transamazon colonization scheme.* Berkeley: University of California Press.

SUPLAN (1980). *Aptidão agrícola das terras de Rondônia.* Ministério da Agricultura, Secretaria Nacional de Planejamento Agrícola. Brasília: BINAGRI.

World Bank (1980). The integrated development of Brazil's northwest frontier. Washington D.C.



Author's address: W.P. Groeneveld, Universidade Federal de Rondônia, Coordenação de Geografia, Av. Presidente Dutra 2965, Centro, 78.900 Porto Velho (Ro), Brasil.

# Forest land use in Suriname*

by O. Boxman
N.R. de Graaf
J. Hendrison
W.B.J. Jonkers
R.L.H. Poels
P. Schmidt
R. Tjon Lim Sang

## 1. Introduction

Suriname is the smallest independent country on the South American mainland and is 163,820 km$^2$ in area. Its population of approximately 370,000 is concentrated in the narrow coastal plain. The remaining 90 per cent of the land area is covered with largely untouched and mostly uninhabited tropical rain forest. Compared with other countries, only small areas have been deforested and the forest probably is not seriously threatened in the near future (see also the contribution of Luning, this volume). The economy is dominated by the aluminium industry, which accounts for 75 per cent of the country's export. There is a need not only to diversify the economy but also to develop employment opportunities to counter the high rate of unemployment. Development of the largely untapped forest resources may well contribute to the economic development of Suriname.

These forest resources are located mainly in two areas in the interior of Suriname. Firstly, there is the Forestry Belt, which co-incides partly with the sedimentary and very poor, acid soils of the Zanderij formation (Fig. 18). This is an area of about 1,200,000 ha which is accessible by almost 2,000 km of forest roads and by large rivers, navigable by barge. About 75 per cent of the forests here have been selectively felled. Transport of logs is controlled by the Suriname State Forest Service at strategic points along roads and rivers. Secondly, there is the forest area to the south of the Forestry Belt, which extends as far as the border with Brazil. These barely accessible forests are situated mainly on residual and poor, acid soils.

These forest resources can be developed and used in various ways. Some of those forest land-use systems practised in or with potential for use in Suriname are discussed. Special attention is given to the forest land-use system based on natural regeneration, which was developed by Project LH/UvS 01 (see also Boxman et al., 1985).

## 2. Nature conservation

The Foundation for Nature Conservation in Suriname (STINASU) manages eight nature reserves with a total area of 600,000 ha. Three reserves were established along the coast mainly to protect wildlife (sea-turtles and birds); the other five were established in the interior to protect both wildlife and vegetation. Four easily accessible reserves have simple accommodation for visitors and are frequented by tourists from Suriname and from abroad. This type of land use helps to preserve the original situation reasonably well.

## 3. Shifting cultivation

In Suriname, about 10,000 Amerindians and about 30,000 Bush Negroes subsist on slash-and-burn agriculture. This type of land use is characterized by cutting and burning the vegetation and planting crops, such as manioc, rice, maize, pineapple and taro, in the fertile ash. After two to three years, a field is abandoned and left fallow for a period of ten to fifteen years. However, because of increasing population pressure, the limited area of accessible land and the introduction of the chain-saw, the period of fallow has been reduced, thus jeopardizing the sustainable character of the system.

* Based mainly on the work of Project LH/UvS 01 (MAB Project 949). Reports on this project can be obtained from Project LH/UvS 01, c/o Department of Silviculture, Agricultural University Wageningen, P.O. Box 342, 6700 AH Wageningen, The Netherlands.

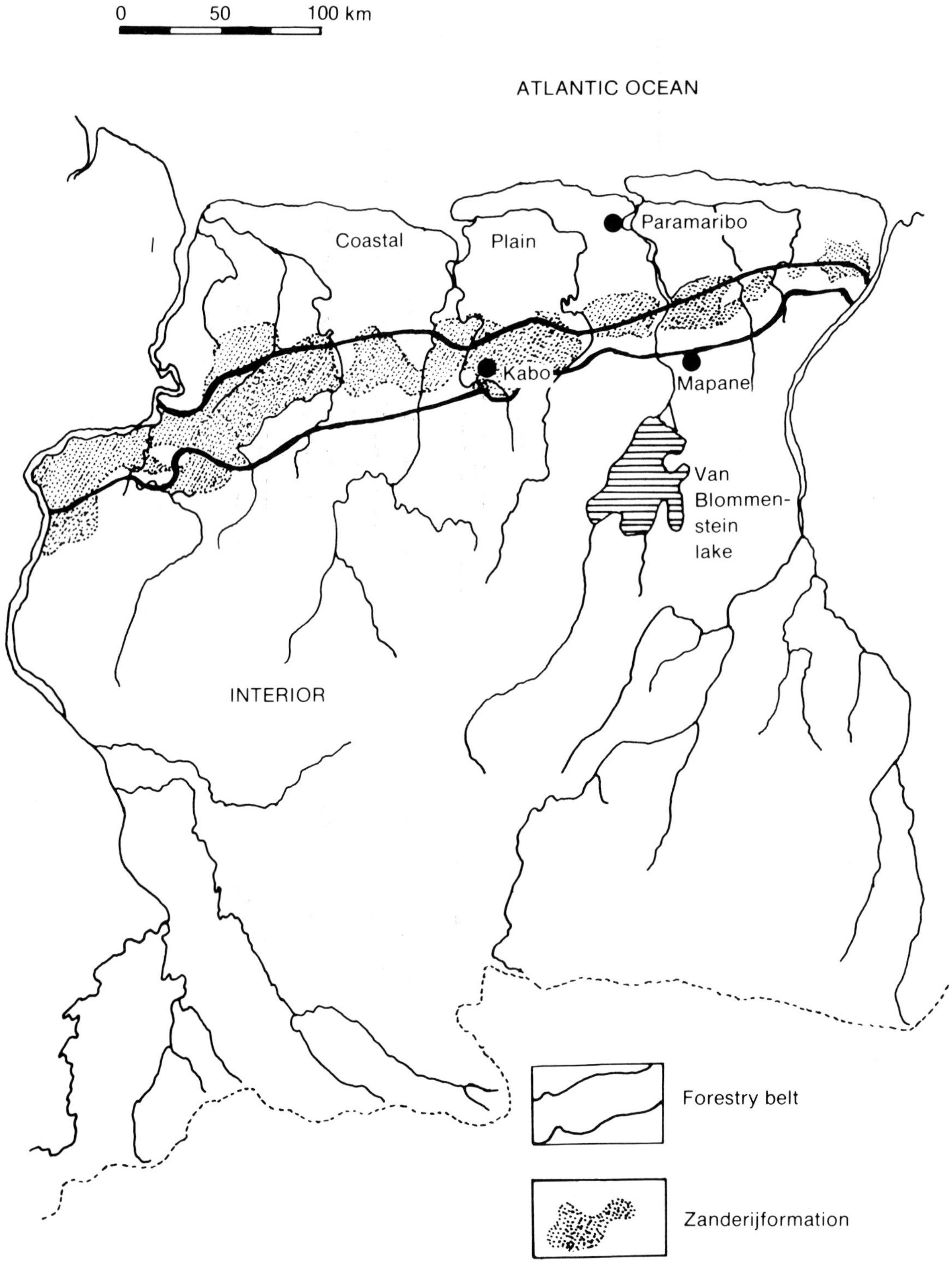


Fig. 18 Map of Suriname showing location of the Forestry Belt.

## 4. Permanent agriculture

Perennial crops: with 6,000 ha of oil palm, Suriname has become self-sufficient in vegetable oil and is likely to be able to export palm oil shortly. However, as yet not all the long-term ecological and economic consequences of this type of cultivation have become apparent. There is no large-scale production of other perennial crops in the interior of Suriname.

Annual crops: there is no permanent cultivation of annual crops in the interior of Suriname; these crops are grown almost exclusively under shifting cultivation. More than six years of research by Project LH/UvS 02, 'The Permanent Cultivation of Rainfed Annual Crops on the Loamy Soils of the Zanderij Formation', has indicated that mechanized cultivation of annual crops on these soils poses many ecological problems and has little economic prospect. Under economic conditions prevailing in the early 1980s, mechanized cultivation of groundnuts is feasible, but high investments are necessary. More detailed information is provided in the final report of Project LH/UvS 02 (Janssen et al., in preparation).

## 5. Animal husbandry

This type of land use occurs on such a small scale in the interior of Suriname, that it does not warrant discussion here.

## 6. Mining and hydro-electricity

Open-cast mining of bauxite has been concentrated in the coastal area, but there are plans for mining in the interior. In the 1960s, a large artificial lake for the generation of hydro-electricity was established in the interior and there are plans for a second lake. As both types of land use inevitably begin with complete destruction of the vegetation, all parts of this vegetation, particularly the stems, should be used in preference to damaging other areas.

## 7. Forest plantations

Since the 1950s, efforts have been made to develop a silvicultural system for the rain forests of Suriname. Initially, artificial regeneration seemed to be preferable to natural regeneration. During the 1960s and 1970s, before rising oil and labour costs made clearing and weeding too expensive, about 9,000 ha of forest plantations, mainly of *Pinus caribaea* were established. The original production aim of pulpwood for the paper industry was abandoned after a few years. Now there is a limited local market for preserved stems of thinnings for telephone poles and furniture.

To establish pine plantations, the original tropical rain forest was removed mechanically and burned. This clearing technique has severe consequences for the productivity of the site, as is illustrated in Figure 19. Because of the extremely low level of soil fertility, growth in the plantations depends largely on the nutrients supplied by the dead phytomass left from the original forest, which under the conditions prevailing after clearing, are quickly reduced (Fig. 20). This phenomenon holds little promise for further development, especially in future rotations.

## 8. Forestry based on natural regeneration

Early investigations on natural regeneration by the Suriname State Forest Service demonstrated that reduction of competition in a stand results in a substantial increase in the growth of the remaining desirable species (Boerboom, 1965; Schulz, 1967). This line of research was continued by researchers from the Agricultural University, Wageningen, The Netherlands, working at the Centre for Agricultural Research in Suriname (CELOS). However, an operational system was not developed until the 1970s. This system was tested and developed further within the framework of the joint project of the Agricultural University, Wageningen and the Anton de Kom University of Suriname (Project LH/UvS 01, MAB Project 949), entitled 'Human Interference in the Tropical Rain Forest Ecosystem', which was stationed at CELOS. As a result of the project research, a polycyclic system for sustained timber production in the tropical rain forests has been formulated. This system is referred to as the CELOS Silvicultural System. In addition, a system for improved logg-

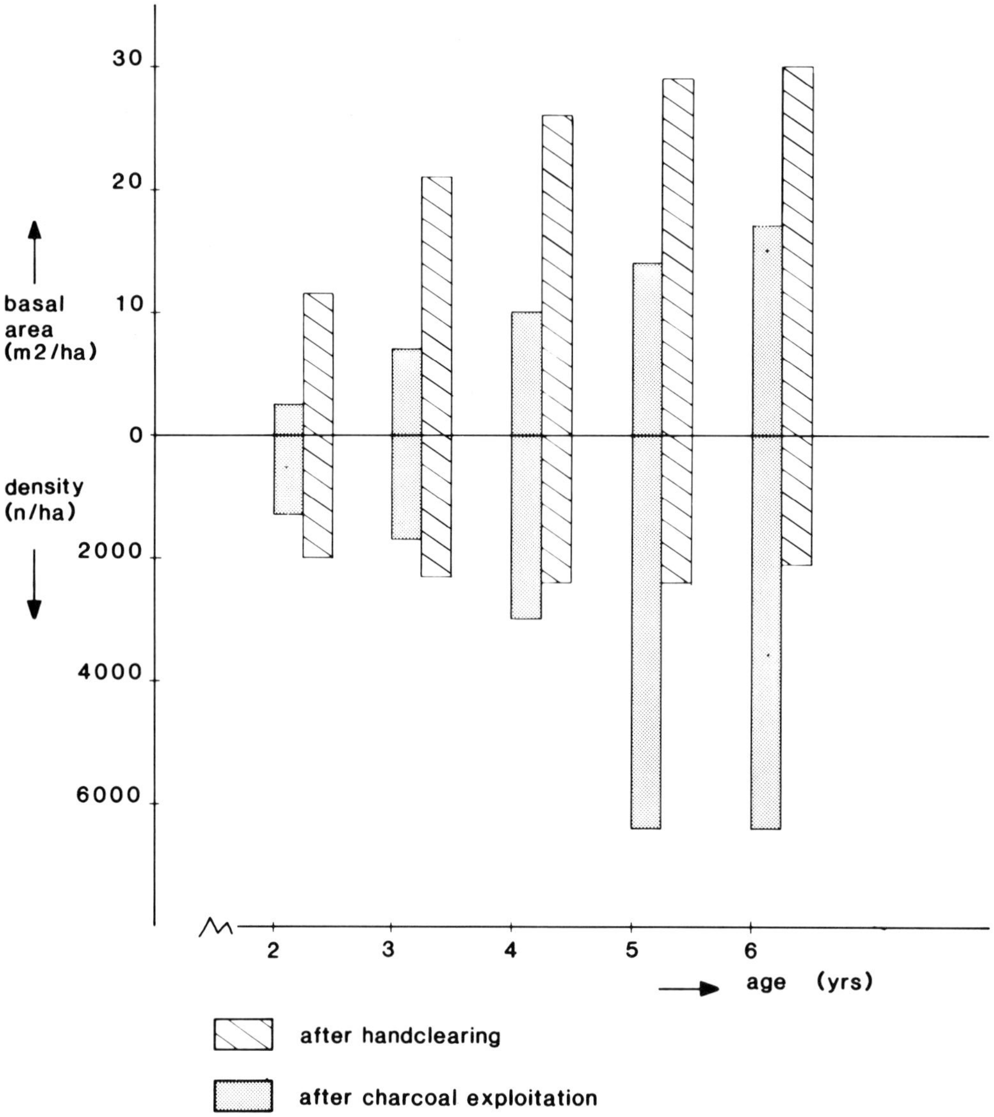


Fig. 19 Effects of clearing techniques on development of secondary vegetation. Hand clearing: felled trees were left *in situ*, no burning; charcoal exploitation: felled trees concentrated by crawler tractors, most of the wood used for charcoal (source: Boxman et al., 1985).

ing, the CELOS Harvesting System, has been developed

*CELOS Harvesting System*

The starting point of any silvicultural system based on natural regeneration should be a logged forest stand with enough good quality trees of commercial species to secure future yields. Therefore, logging damage should be kept at an acceptable level.

In Suriname, logging is organized rather haphazardly. There is no planning in advance and organized communication between concessionaire, feller and skidder operator is very limited. The consequences are that:

- although the concessionaire gives some basic instructions regarding species and sizes to be felled, the feller selects the trees mainly according to his own preference;

- some felled timber is damaged by fungi and insects before the skidder arrives, long after felling has taken place;
- the skidder operator spends more time and causes more damage than necessary searching for logs, the location of which is unknown to him;
- the possibility of extracting two logs in one trip is easily overlooked, thus resulting in two trips instead of one:
- good quality logs are easily overlooked and left to rot in the forest;
- often obstacles in the terrain which hinder extraction, such as creeks, are not avoided.

These logging operations are inefficient and wasteful, causing much unnecessary damage. The CELOS Harvesting System, which aims to reduce both aspects, includes:

- mapping of characteristics of the terrain and

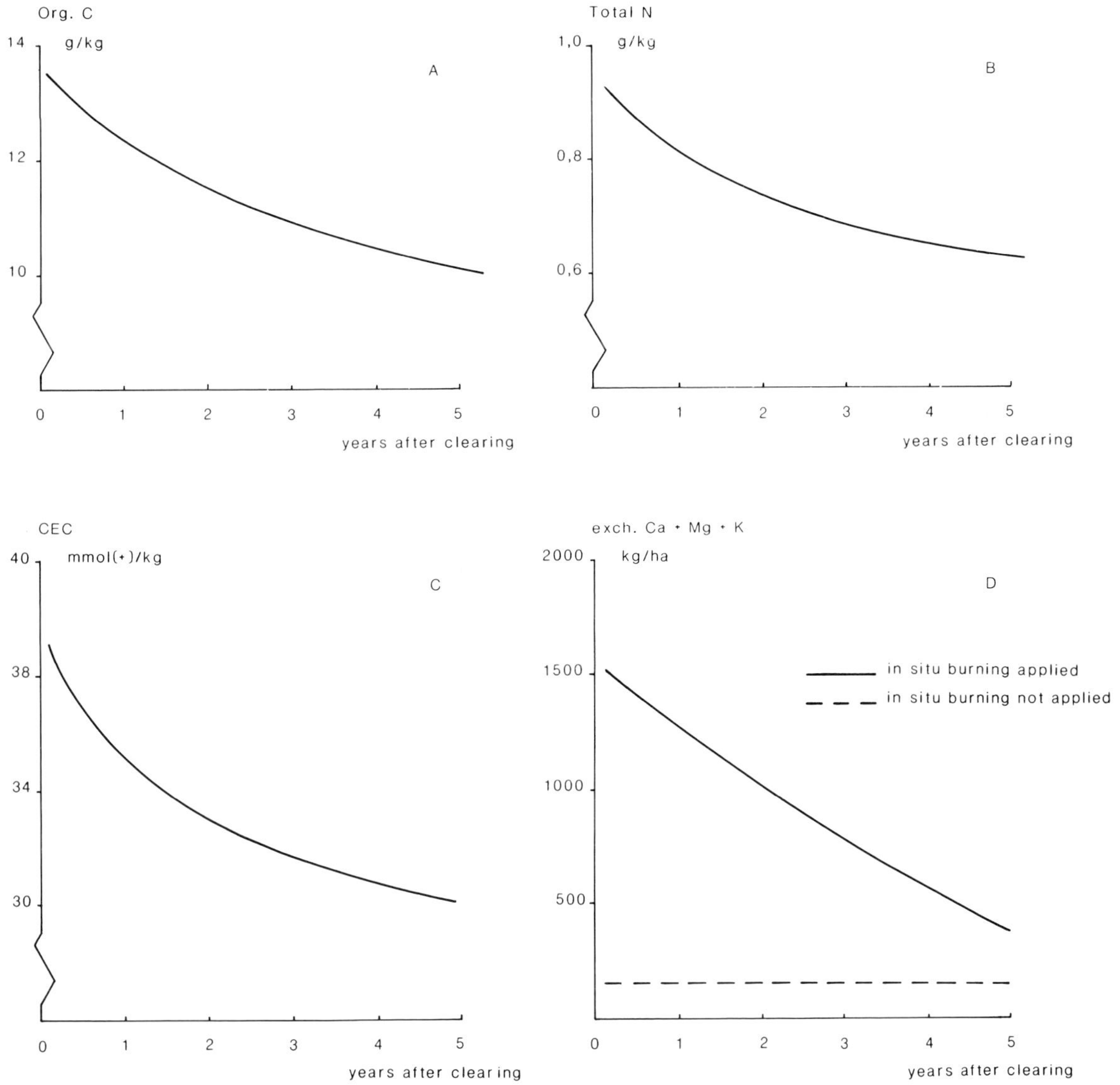


Fig. 20 Deterioration of soil properties such as organic matter content (A), total nitrogen (B), cation exchange capacity (C), and the sum of total exchangeable calcium, magnesium and potassium (D) after mechanical clearing for tree plantation, resulting in the total removal of the original vegetation (source: Boxman et al., 1987).

trees to be felled;

- planning and opening-up of skid trails prior to felling;
- directional felling to facilitate skidding;
- winch extraction from stump to skid trail;
- registration of the log flow from stump to terminal.

With this system, skidding cost has been reduced by 10 to 20 per cent and skidding damage by about 50 per cent (Fig. 21), thus creating better conditions for subsequent silvicultural treatment. In the CELOS Harvesting System little attention has been given to reducing felling damage. Probably, restriction and regulation of the volume harvested is the most effective in this respect. Some reduction may also be achieved by cutting lianas several years in advance of logging.

*CELOS Silvicultural System*

The principal aim of the CELOS Silvicultural System is to stimulate growth of medium-sized and large trees of commercial value in selectively logged forests, preferably by the CELOS Harvesting System, so that the next harvest of quality timber can be achieved in 20 to 25 years. The second aim is to promote recruitment and growth of smaller trees of commercial species, even seedlings and

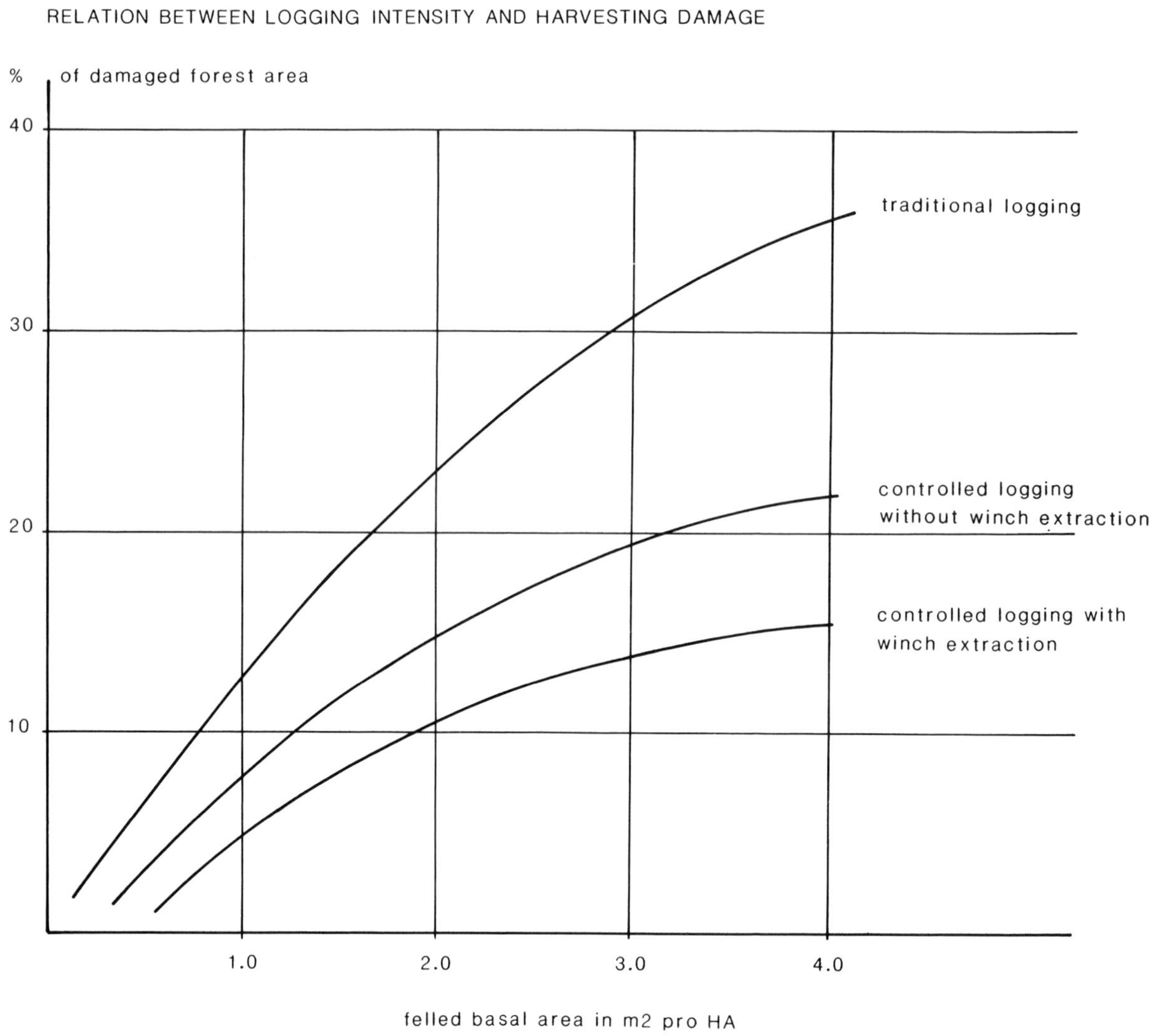


Fig. 21 Impact of logging techniques on harvesting damage in relation to logging intensity (source: Boxman et al., 1985).

saplings, to secure future harvests. These objectives are achieved by killing large and medium-sized trees of no commercial value and lianas, thus reducing competition for the remaining commercial trees of similar dimensions. Moreover, the treatment has also a fertilizing effect on the remaining vegetation, that is the nutrients stored in the trees and lianas killed by the treatment become available gradually to the remaining vegetation. Small trees of both commercial and non-commercial species also benefit from the treatment.

The CELOS Silvicultural System, as it was formulated at the end of the 1970s (De Graaf, 1982), included three silvicultural treatments. The first, called refinement or refining, is scheduled one or two years after logging. It was proposed to kill by poison-girdling all non-commercial trees above a diameter limit of 20 cm at breast height or above the buttresses, and to cut all lianas. However, the results of research carried out by Project LH/UvS 01 suggest that not all these trees should be poison-girdled and that the diameter limit for non-commercial trees standing more than 10 m away from a commercial tree should be raised.
In these experiments, the mean annual diameter growth was found to increase from 4 mm to about 10 mm during a period of approximately eight years and the mortality to increase from about 1.5 to 2 per cent. Indications of the changes in the forests as the result of logging and refinement are given in Figures 22 and 23.

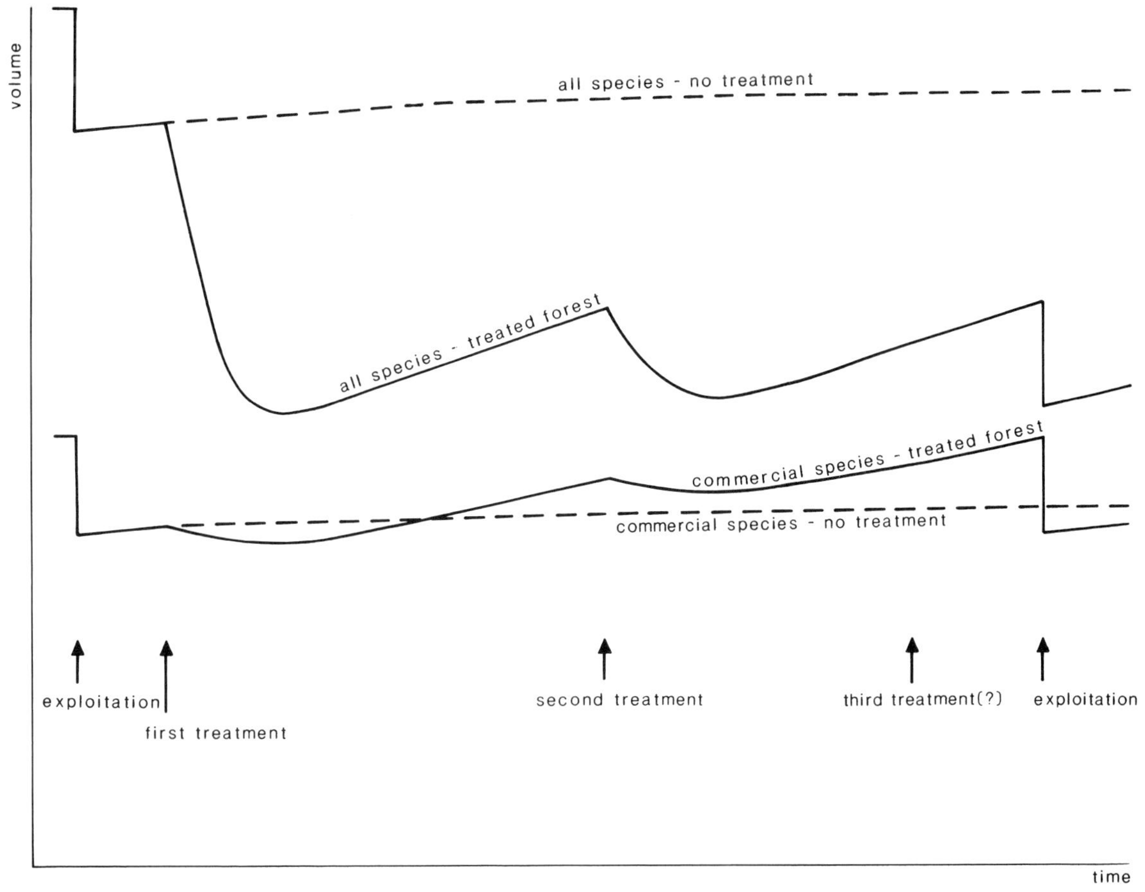


Fig. 22 Changes in standing volume after logging and silvicultural treatment (source: Boxman et al., 1985).

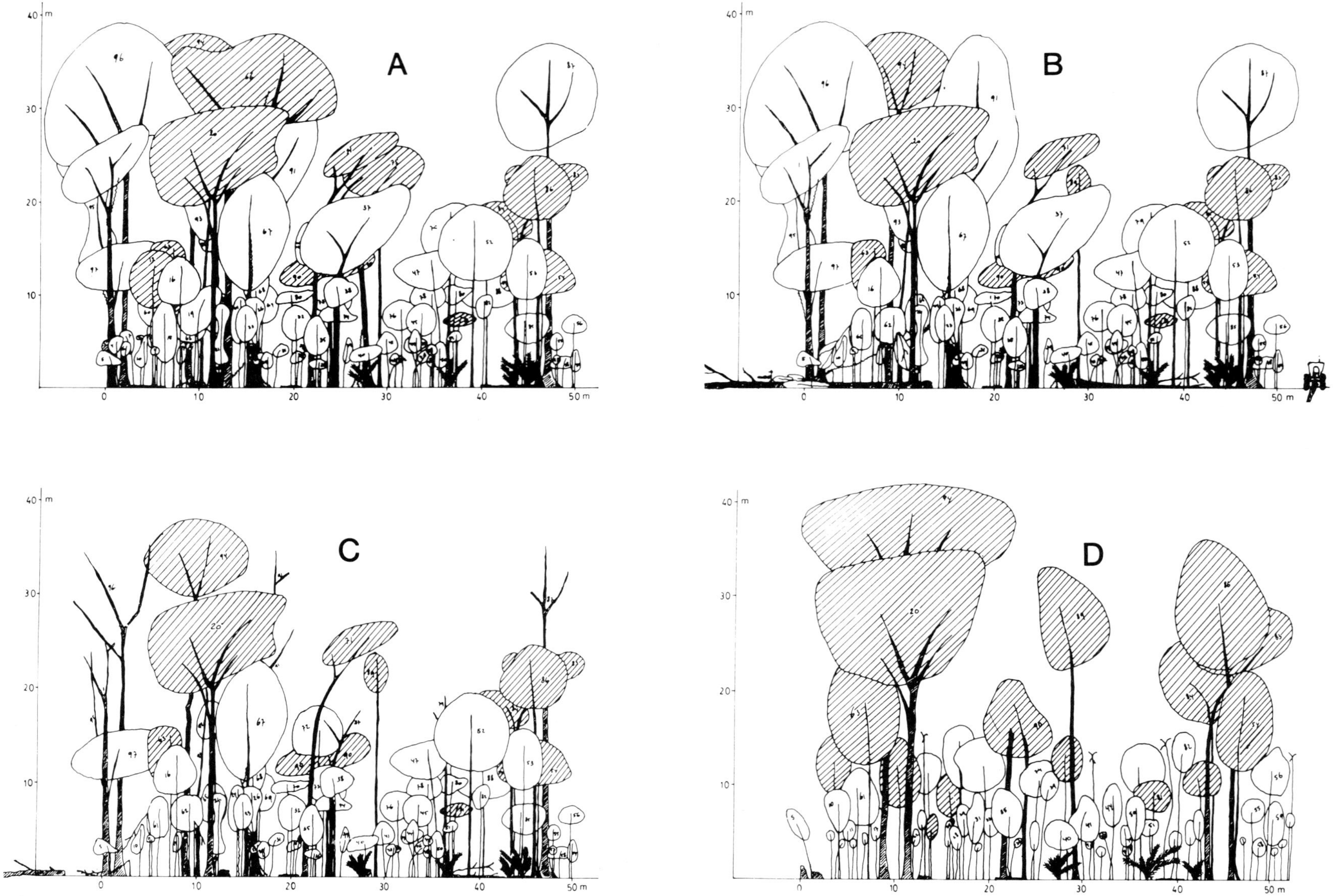


Fig. 23 Visual impression of forest structure before logging (A), after logging (B), after refinement (C), and before second logging (D). Commercial trees are hatched (source: Boxman et al., 1985).

The rate of increment of the medium-sized and large commercial trees should be kept at an economically acceptable level. To maintain this rate, a second treatment, analogous but not as drastic as the first, is prescribed. In small-scale experiments, this second treatment resulted in increment rates comparable with those after the first treatment. A third treatment is proposed a few years before the second harvest. It is thought to consist mainly of cutting lianas, aiming both to stimulate growth and to reduce felling damage. However, the need for a third treatment should be confirmed by experiment.

For refinement of 200 ha an input of 2.8 man-days per ha and of 17 litres of a 2.5 per cent solution of 2,4,5-T solution in diesel oil was required. The cost of line cutting, overheads and some minor expenses have to be added to this. The second and third treatment are likely to cost less.

*Effects on phytomass and nutrient cycling*

Logging and silvicultural treatments have a number of side-effects (see Jonkers and Schmidt, 1984), of which the most crucial seems to be the potential loss of considerable amounts of nutrients from the ecosystem. The rain forest in the study area can be characterized as luxuriant vegetation growing on very poor, acid soils. The living phytomass of about 500 t $ha^{-1}$ acts as the main store for the nutrients. An almost closed nutrient cycle is maintained, in which the mineral soil plays only a minor role. Nutrients in the dead phytomass (fallen leaves, branches, dead stems) are taken up directly by the living vegetation through roots penetrating the litter and mycorrhiza. Only a minor part of the nutrients reaches the soil and can be washed out. In managed stands, a sufficient amount of living phytomass and a closed nutrient cycle should be maintained.

Logging and refinement reduce the amount of living phytomass considerably. A relatively small anount is removed from the ecosystem as logs (about 15 t $ha^{-1}$ phytomass with about 43 kg $ha^{-1}$ nitrogen and about 3 kg $ha^{-1}$ phosphorus, see Jonkers and Schmidt, 1984), but considerably more is killed as a consequence of the first refinement (about 190 t $ha^{-1}$ phytomass). The nutrients in this vast amount of dead and slowly decaying phytomass are released over a number of years, and can be taken up by the reduced but vigorously growing remaining vegetation or can be leached out and thus lost to the ecosystem. Comparison of the nutrient cycle in undisturbed forest one year before exploitation and in logged and refined forest in the second year after refinement (Fig. 24) indicates, that these interferences have resulted at most in a very slight increase in leaching of nutrients. It would seem that logging according to the CELOS Harvesting System, followed by a refinement according to the CELOS Silvicultural System does not lead to serious chemical impoverishment of the ecosystem.

## 9. Conclusions

Of the various types of land use in the interior of Suriname, it may be concluded that:

- open-cast mining and artificial lakes lead to complete destruction of the original vegetation and are of very local importance only;
- shifting cultivation is of local importance, but transgression of traditional regulation of soil fertility may endanger sustained productivity;
- forestry based on artificial regeneration, and large-scale production of annual crops are both ecologically and economically problematic;
- agriculture based on perennial crops, such as oil-palm, is of local importance only;
- nature reserves, which protect the original vegetation relatively well, are of local importance;
- for large-scale development of the forest land in the interior of Suriname, only forestry based on natural regeneration, of which the CELOS Silvicultural System is an example, is suitable.

Overall results of research, carried out by the Suriname State Forest Service, CELOS, and Project LH/UvS 01, indicate, that the CELOS Silvicultural System is economically feasible and ecologically acceptable, especially if preceded by harvesting according to the CELOS Harvesting System.

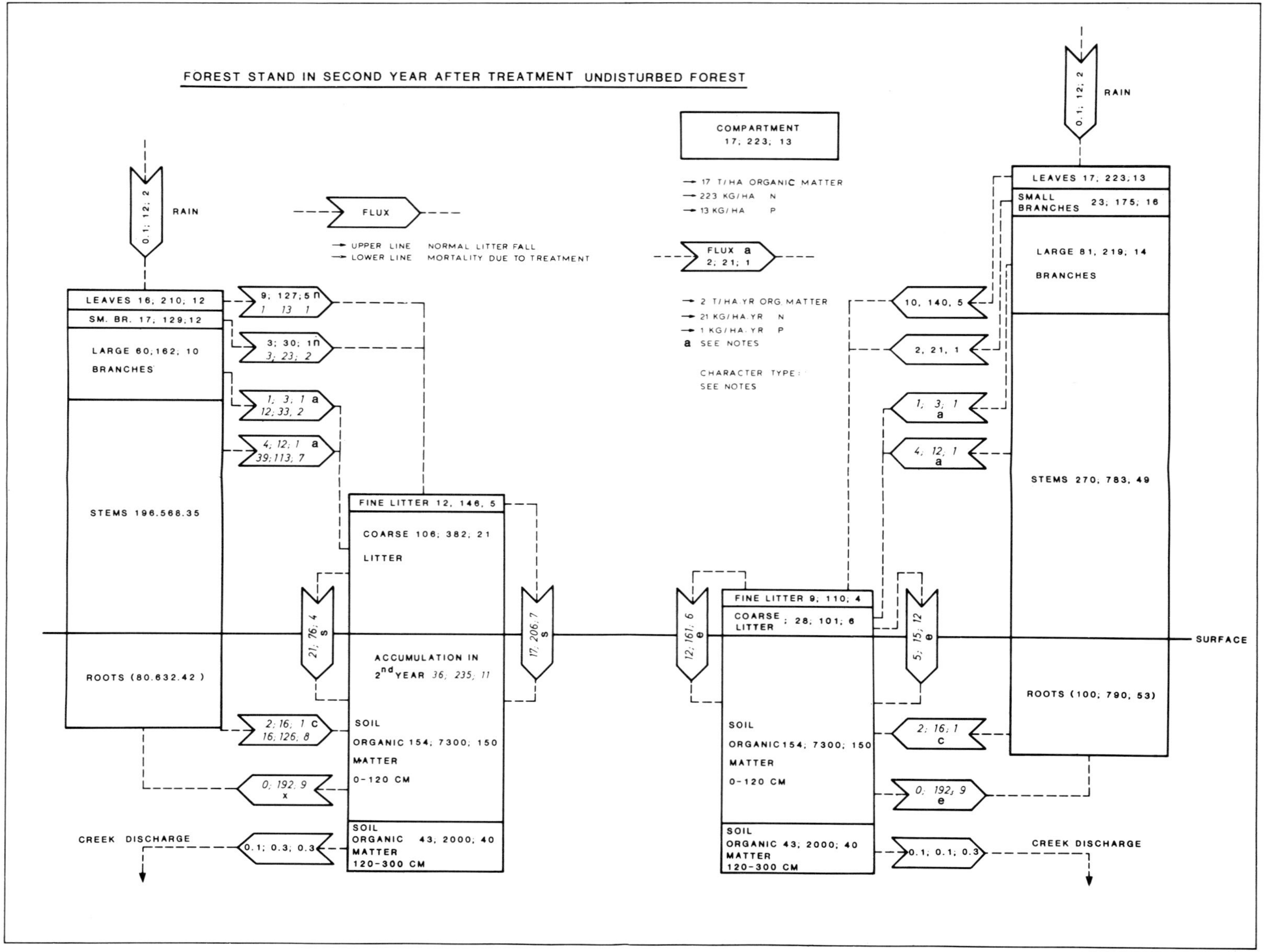
FOREST STAND IN SECOND YEAR AFTER TREATMENT
UNDISTURBED FOREST
RAIN
0.1; 12; 2
FLUX
UPPER LINE NORMAL LITTER FALL
LOWER LINE MORTALITY DUE TO TREATMENT
COMPARTMENT
17; 223; 13
17 T/HA ORGANIC MATTER
223 KG/HA N
13 KG/HA P
FLUX a
2; 21; 1
2 T/HA.YR ORG.MATTER
21 KG/HA.YR N
1 KG/HA.YR P
a SEE NOTES
CHARACTER TYPE:
SEE NOTES
LEAVES 16; 210; 12
SM. BR. 17; 129;12
LARGE 60;162; 10
BRANCHES
STEMS 196.568.35
ROOTS (80.632.42 )
9; 127;5 n
1 13 1
3; 30; 1n
3; 23; 2
1; 3; 1 a
12; 33; 2
4; 12; 1 a
39; 113; 7
FINE LITTER 12, 146, 5
COARSE 106; 382; 21
LITTER
21; 76; 4
s
17; 206; 7
s
ACCUMULATION IN
2nd YEAR 36; 235; 11
SOIL
ORGANIC 154; 7300; 150
MATTER
0-120 CM
2; 16; 1 c
16; 126; 8
0; 192; 9
x
SOIL
ORGANIC 43; 2000; 40
MATTER
120-300 CM
0.1; 0.3; 0.3
CREEK DISCHARGE
LEAVES 17; 223;13
SMALL
BRANCHES 23; 175; 16
LARGE 81, 219; 14
BRANCHES
STEMS 270; 783, 49
ROOTS (100; 790; 53)
10, 140, 5
2, 21, 1
1; 3; 1
a
4; 12; 1
a
FINE LITTER 9; 110; 4
COARSE
LITTER ; 28; 101; 6
12; 161; 6
e
5; 15; 12
e
SOIL
ORGANIC 154; 7300; 150
MATTER
0-120 CM
2; 16; 1
c
0; 192; 9
e
SOIL
ORGANIC 43; 2000; 40
MATTER
120-300 CM
0.1; 0.1; 0.3
CREEK DISCHARGE
SURFACE

Fig. 24 Phytomass and two nutrients stored in major compartments and moving through major pathways of the tropical rain forest ecosystem before and during the second year after treatment (provisional data).
Notes: numbers in roman: measured data, numbers in italics: calculated data, numbers in brackets: estimated data.

a Based on mortality rate of 1.5% (undisturbed forest) or 2% (disturbed forest).
c See a, excluding turnover of rootlets.
e Assuming steady state.
i Including standing dead trees.
n Partly due to normal litterfall, partly due to treatment.
s Assuming same decomposition rate as in undisturbed forest.
x Assuming no changes in nutrient uptake in first two years after treatment.

Source: Boxman et al., 1985.

## REFERENCES

Boerboom, J.H.A. (1965). De natuurlijke regeneratie van het Surinaamse mesofytische bos na uitkap. Wageningen: Department of Tropical Silviculture, Agricultural University.

Boxman, O., Graaf, N.R. de, Hendrison, J., Jonkers, W.B.J., Poels, R.L.H., Schmidt, P. and Tjon Lim Sang, R. (1985). Towards sustained timber production from tropical rain forests in Suriname. *Netherlands Journal of Agricultural Science* 33, 125-132.

Graaf, N.R. de (1982). Sustained timber production in the tropical rain forest of Suriname. In *Proceedings of the Joint Workshop on Management of the Low Fertility Acid Soils of the American Humid Tropics,* ed. J.F. Wienk and H.A. de Wit. San Jose, Costa Rica. Pp. 175-189.

Graaf, N.R. de (in press). *A silvicultural system for natural regeneration of tropical rain forest in Suriname* (D. Sc. Thesis) Wageningen: Agricultural University.

Janssen, B.H., et al. (in preparation). Final report of the project The Permanent Cultivation of Rainfed Annual Crops on Loamy Soils of the Zanderij Formation.

Jonkers, W.B.J. and Schmidt, P. (1984). Ecology and timber production in tropical rain forest in Suriname. *Interciencia* 9, 290-298.

Schulz, J.P. (1967). La regeneracion natural de la selva mesofitica tropical de Surinam despues de su aprovechamiento. *Boletin* 23. Mérida: Institute Forestal Latino-Americano de Investigacion y Capacitacion.

Authors' addresses: O. Boxman, Department of Soil Science and Plant Nutrition; Dr. N.R. de Graaf, W.B.J. Jonkers and Dr. P. Schmidt, Department of Silviculture and Forest Ecology; J. Hendrison, Department of Forest Technique and Forest Products; R.L.H. Poels, Department of Soil Science and Geology; R. Tjon Lim Sang, Department of Vegetation Science, Plant Ecology and Weed Science. All, Agricultural University Wageningen, The Netherlands.

# Development versus forest conservation: avoiding a conflict in the Taï region (Ivory Coast)

by A.P. Vooren


## Abstract

The southwestern Ivory Coast is a scene of rapid development. In less than a 20-year time-span, a change occurred from a thinly populated forest area towards an area loaded with potential conflicts between different competing land uses. Scientific research and detailed land-use planning can still demonstrate that the needs of development are compatible with the needs of nature conservation in the region.


## 1. The problems

*History*

Until the mid 1960s the southwestern Ivory Coast (Fig. 25) was largely uninhabited, with 120,000 inhabitants on 37,000 km$^2$ (Lena, 1984). Vast, mainly virgin rain forests occupied the central part of the region. Only small populations lived closely along the two main rivers Sassandra and Cavally, along the sparse roads and on the coastal belt.

*Development*

In 1965, the Ivory Coast government decided to develop the southwest region in order to counterbalance the rapid development of the eastern and central coastal regions. 'L'Autorité pour l'Aménagement de la Région Sud-Ouest (ARSO)' was set up as a state developing agency. The development strategy consisted of three phases:

- immediate (timber) exploitation of the forests in order to make the port of San Pédro profitable;
- creation of major agro-industrial projects to provide employment and trade after the timber harvest;
- setting up viable industries to ensure the region's economic development (Dosso et al., 1981).

Massive investments were made in such projects as the San Pédro port and town, the San Pédro-Soubré-Man road, agro-industrial complexes of rubber, oil palm, coconut, paper and pulpwood, and the Buyo hydro-electric dam in the Sassandra river.

*Stimulated migration*

Government policy was tending to link rural migration to the development of the south west. Reception centres were set up in the region for Baoulé immigrants from the Lake Kossou district, a hydro-electric impoundment reservoir. A government-stimulated westward spread of the speculative farming of coffee and cacao further led a good many Baoulé peasants of the central parts of the country to migrate to the west rather than regenerating their old plantations when yield fell off (UNESCO, 1977).

*'Spontaneous' migration*

Forest enterprises, public work projects and state-owned agri-business plantations in the region were incentives for the spontaneous immigration of large numbers of people from the savanna regions of the centre and the north of the country, from Mali, Guinea and many Mossi from Upper-Volta. This north-south movement accelerated with bad yields in the savanna countries due to insufficient rainfall after 1966. Timber extraction and other industries employing paid labour served as a staging-post for the immigrants and enabled them to save up the small amount of capital required to start their own small-scale plantations.

*Pioneer fronts*

This spontaneous population movement, by people who arrived to discover a forest region rich in potential and practically uninhabited, produced local pioneer fronts along the fringes of the Taï National Park (see Lena, 1984). In 1971, the population of the Bakwé Canton (approximately 3,300 km$^2$) of the Sub-Prefecture of Soubré totalled 3,484; by 1975 it had grown to 11,956 and in early 1977 it was estimated at around 15,000 (UNESCO, 1977). The primary characteristics of these pioneer fronts are the intensity of the forest clearing and the

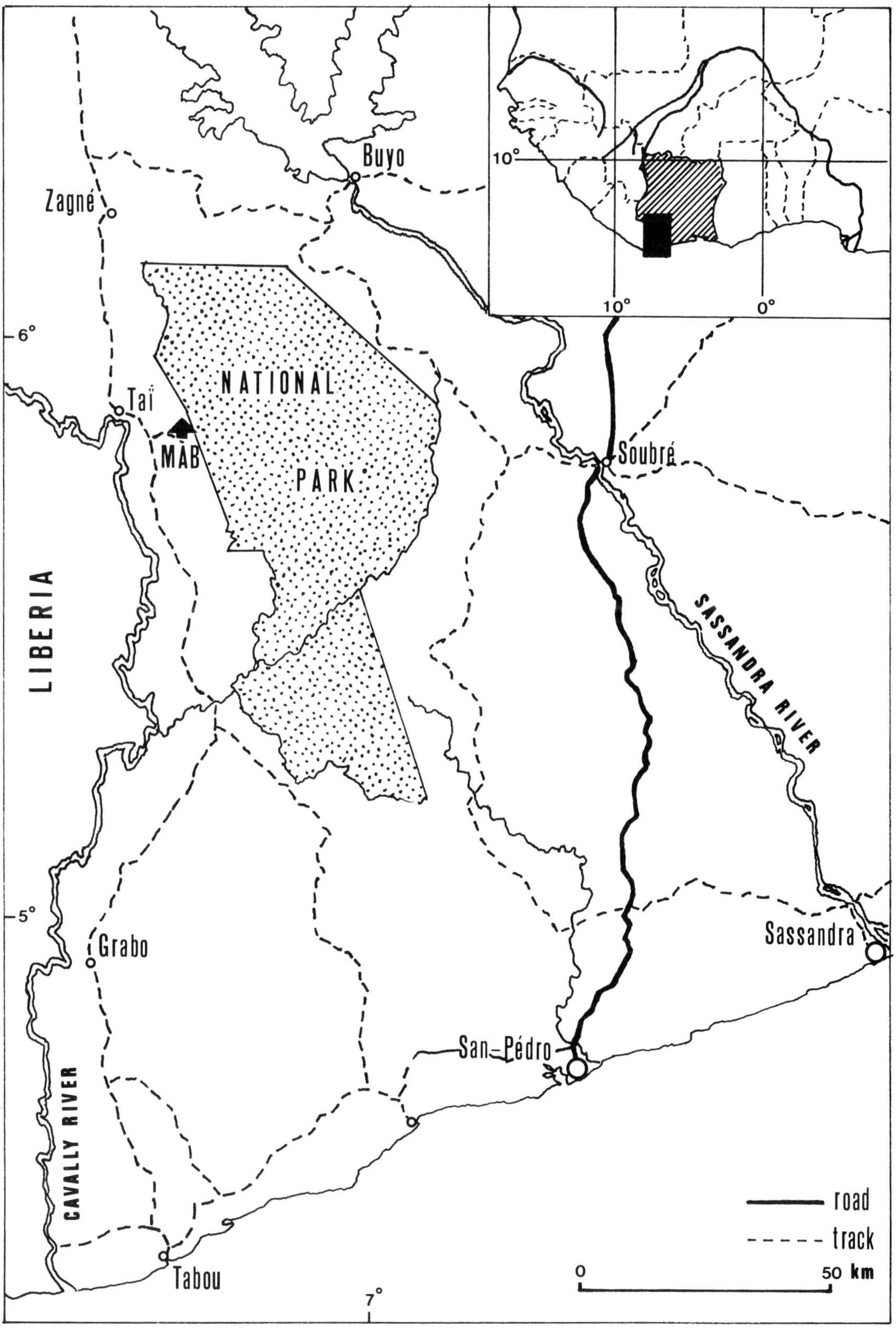


Fig. 25 Southwest Ivory Coast.

density of land settlement. A favourable factor for settlement was the presence and location of forest tracks left by timber extraction activities. A very dense tree-like network of tracks, following interfluvial ridges and hilltops, connects up those areas best suited for coffee and cacao growing (UNESCO, 1977). Human settlement follows this network of tracks which stretches to the borders of the National Park and sometimes crosses them.

*National Park*

The centre of the southwest region is still dominated by a vast tract of rain forest. This former 'Taï Forest Reserve', established in 1926, is the last extensive tract of rain forest remaining in West Africa with an estimated 200,000 hectares of untouched forest (Bousquet, 1978). In 1972 it received the status of National Park with by law fixed objectives of nature conservation, scientific research and education. Attempts have been made to promote touristic activities in the southern part (FGU Kronberg, 1979). An actual remaining 330,000 hectares with a protection zone of 47,600 hectares figures on the list of UNESCO Biosphere Reserves since 1978. The forest has a rich flora with over 150 endemic species and a considerable fauna, including populations of pigmy hippopotamus, chimpanzee and elephant (see Bousquet, 1978).

*Land-use planning*

The ARSO land-use map (Fig. 26), which assigned land to different categories of users, is based on a 1 : 250,000 soil map of the region (DRC, 1967a). The areas lying between the projected large agro-industrial complexes had to be divided into more detailed land-use schemes, amongst the small land users: native cultivators, immigrant planters, village plantations, various types of family agriculture with rice, cacao, coffee, etc. This aspect of small-scale land use is the most difficult to plan and has been rather neglected in the past (UNESCO, 1977). It actually appears to be the one most urgently in need of organization. Anarchic land occupation in areas not designated for future small-scale use, now a sporadic event, will be difficult to alter once it becomes a mass process. Land uses without direct economic interest or effective management, e.g. the National Park, are most vulnerable to uncontrolled land occupation.

## 2. Research programmes

In 1973 the Ivory Coast government started a research project in order to guide and to help shape the desired economic development of the southwest region (Lorougnon Guédé, 1976). The general objective of the Taï Forest Project is to improve the scientific basis for management of forest ecosystems. The project, executed by a multidisciplinary and international team of researchers within the framework of the MAB-UNESCO 1 'Rain Forest Projects', since 1975 gathered extensive data and analysed natural and man-made ecosystems on a local level. The synthesis of this work has recently been published as a MAB technical note (Guillaumet et al., 1984). Future work should further extend these results to a regional level (Guillaumet and Couturier, 1984). Specific attention has to be paid in future work to small-scale land-use systems in order to dissolve the increasing human pressure on the untouched forest and agro-industrial plantation areas. Direct guidelines for sound management of small-scale agricultural systems and forest estates should be developed and linked to detailed land-use schemes, as highlighted in the Dutch **Tropenbos** research programme. These aspects are of the utmost importance for a future balanced development of the region.

Agricultural University Wageningen has contributed since 1977 in a modest way to the Taï Forest Project with research activities on floristic, silvicultural, and agricultural items. Research work on the forest potential for selective logging operations started in 1981. Some preliminary results of this work will be discussed in the following section of this paper.

## 3. Buffer-zone forest potential

*Research objectives*

The conflicting situation of a strict natural reserve near the centre of the southwest Ivory Coast and increasing human pressure from its surroundings makes it urgent to establish a contact zone in which conservation and development objectives gradually intermingle in compatible land uses. A system of different co-existing buffer-zones as land-use belts

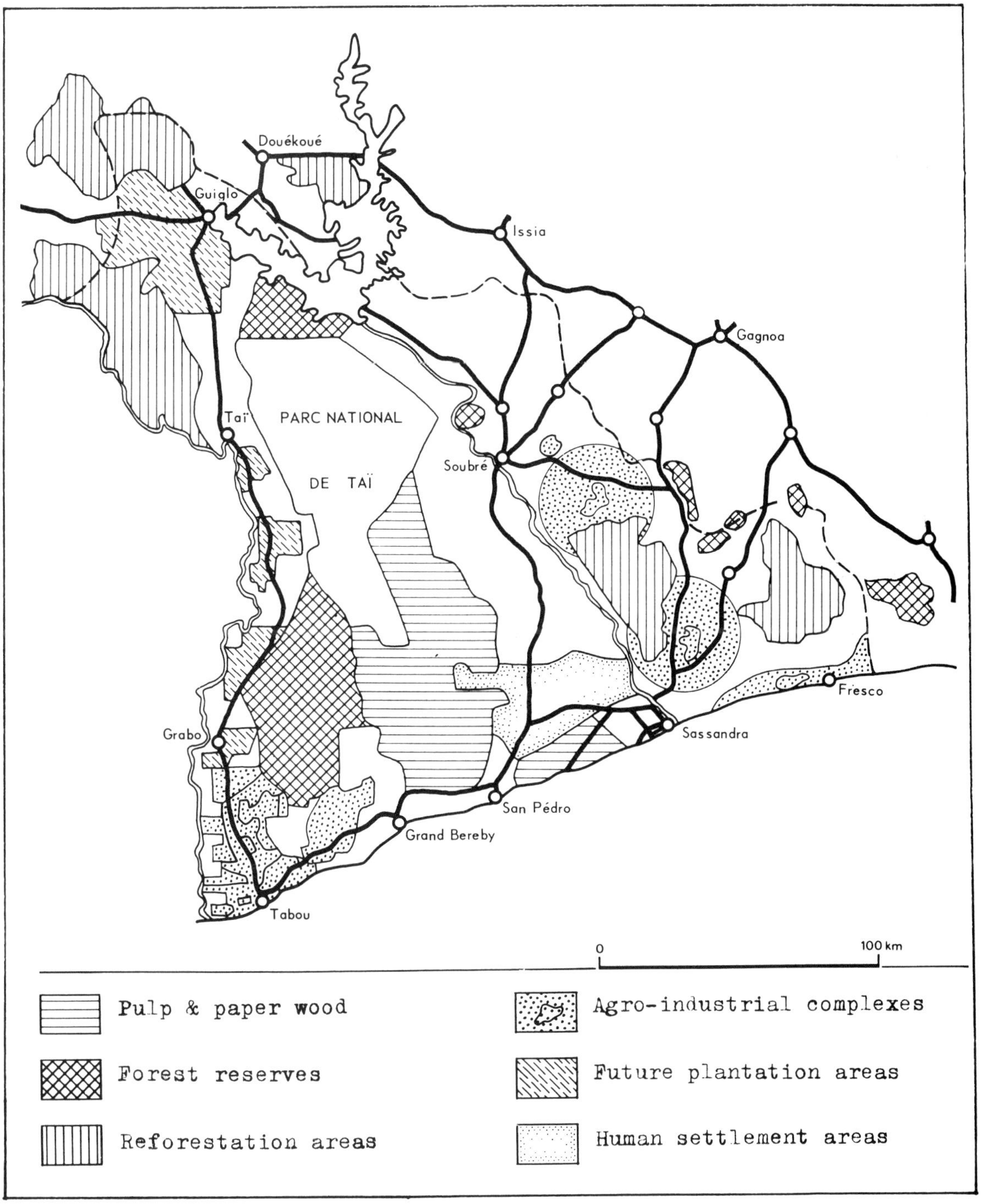


Fig. 26 ARSO Land-use planning (1977) (source: Guillaumet et al., 1984).

with decreasing human activity and increasing similarity with a forest ecosystem should surround the untouched core of the Biosphere Reserve (see Synnott and Kemp, 1976; di Castri and Loope, 1977). The vegetation belt touching the natural forest (buffer-1) has predominantly a protection function. Notwithstanding this priority, a sustained production system will be a guarantee for its conservation in the long run (see Leslie, 1977; Okali, 1982).

A timber production objective project for the area is considered useful to a future first-quality timber supply (see Kio, 1983). The Taï forest area is rich in high-value timber species (DRC, 1967b). With a still increasing demand for timber on the international, as well as the national markets (Wadsworth, 1983), a forced shift to less appreciated timber species occurs. Famous hardwood timbers such as Acajou, Makoré, Sipo, Aboudikro, Tiama, Dibétou, with a wood quality which can not be produced in plantations, are rapidly disappearing and will be a scarce commodity in the future: they do not regenerate well in overexploited forests (Arnaud and Sournia, 1980). Such valuable species, producing veneer and saw-logs, are expected to rise steeply in price in the next 25 years as world demand outstrips supply (Guppy, 1983). In a near future they can constitute the economic backbone of a timber extraction system aiming at conservation of sustained-yield semi-natural forests. Cautious exploitation of small quantities of highly valuable timber, in a frequency dictated by forest growth and mortality, i.e. imitating natural forest gap formation in size and frequency, is the concept at the base of a sustained timber yield for land-use systems in a protection zone.

Guidelines for a future buffer-zone 1 management system were set by earlier research outcomes of the Taï Forest Project:

- permanent surveillance of a protection zone is costly but indispensable as a 'life-insurance' for the area (Bousquet, 1978; FGU Kronberg, 1979);
- clear-cutting practices or gap-creating activities which outmeasure or outnumber natural forest gaps create pools of fast-growing, agressive secondary species (Guillaumet et al., 1978; Vooren, 1979), capable of invading the nearby core of natural forest vegetation;
- present timber extraction operations leave a multitude of forest tracks, opening up the forest to unguided tourism, game hunting (poaching), gold prospecting and human settlement (FGU Kronberg, 1979). UNESCO (1977) emphasized this last aspect: 'Without forest track(s), there would probably be no pioneer front(s)';
- regular aerial surveys or aerial photo covers have been recommended for research objectives and for surveillance tasks (UNESCO, 1977; Bousquet, 1978).

Out of the conceptional framework arose a first draft for a future management system (Oldeman and Vooren, 1980). Aerial logging methods were retained in this concept as a yarding system answering to all the requirements, recommendations and restrictions listed above. In combination with aerial detection of exploitable trees, a future 'ripe-fruit-picking' timber-yield system as a highly selective large-scale logging operation was hypothesized.

*Preliminary results*

The first research phase was concentrated on the assessment of the tree and forest potentials for such sustained wood production. The main research item was the definition of criteria to establish a 'harvest-point' for forest trees. From an ecological point of view a sufficient seed production per individual (i.e. optimalization of the number of seed years) to assure a regeneration stock is of crucial importance for the perpetuity of the species. Cutting trees too early means a loss of regeneration potential, whereas postponed harvesting implicates a loss of wood quality.

The difficulty of interpreting the chronological code of growth-rings in the wet tropics and, hence, of using age in the assessment of growth rates and productivity of trees (see Mariaux, 1981) stressed the need of other production related criteria (Smith, 1963). Tree architecture and its changes with energy availability and age (see Hallé et al., 1978; Oldeman, 1978; Hallé and Ng, 1981) appeared to be a promising new criterion. Chronologic series of architectural phase changes in the crowns of the tree species *Piptadeniastrum africanum* (Mimosaceae) and *Pycnanthus angolensis* (Myristicaceae) were established in the Taï Forest. The emphasis was laid on the phase changes which indicate the start of senescence. A species-related, stereotypical mortality pattern appeared to exist in these two tree species. In *Piptadeniastrum*, for instance, the sequential loss of main axis and an overall growing interspace between sub-crowns and crownlets indicate a definite and final loss of vigour in aging individuals. Aerial photographs at large-scales taken from an ultralight aircraft (see Vooren and Offermans, 1985) visualized these phenomena. Their analysis will lead to conclusions about a possible future use of remote sensing techniques to detect exploitable trees in the rain-forest canopy.

A next research phase will include wood property studies which will set criteria to establish a tree harvest point, acceptable from the view-points of wood technology and forest ecology.

A second research item focused on forest dynamics with an emphasis on the rate, distribution and frequency of chablis (tree falls). Natural forests are perpetually producing living systems, although the net forest production (difference between production and loss of organic matter) seems to oscillate around a near zero level in mature stands (e.g. Foggie, 1957; Bormann and Likens, 1979). This means that in a mature, steady-state forest, where no net biomass changes occur, the mean annual fall of dead wood would be approximately equal to wood production (Whittaker and Woodwell, 1971). The bulk of the wood mass is formed by the stems and branches of large trees. A rough estimate of the annual wood production therefore can be obtained by measuring the annual accumulation of dead wood on the forest floor. Only fallen trees and branches with a diameter over 30 cm were measured on a 10 hectare plot of untouched forest in the Taï National Park. Preliminary results indicate an annual amount of approximately 2 $m^3$ $ha^{-1}$ of fallen dead wood. With a mean wood density (dry weight/green volume) of 650 kg $m^{-3}$ (Huttel and Bernhard-Reversat, 1975) an annual production of 1.3 t $ha^{-1}$ is obtained in this forest.

The forest potential for sustained production seems promising. However, the quota of annually produced marketable stem-wood will be low. Moreover, future research work has to demonstrate that technical problems in the development of an operational aerial detection and yarding system can be overcome.

## REFERENCES


Arnaud, J.C. and Sournia, G. (1980). Les forêts de Côte d'Ivoire. *Annales Université Abidjan* (Serie G) 9, 6-93.

Bormann, F.H. and Likens, G.E. (1979). *Patterns and process in a forested ecosystem.* New York: Springer Verlag.

Bousquet, B. (1978). Un parc de forêt dense en Afrique: le Parc National de Taï (Côte d'Ivoire). *Bois et Forêts des Tropiques* 180, 23-37.

Castri, F. di and Loope, L.P. (1977). Biosphere reserves: theory and practice. *Nature and Resources* 13, 2-8.

Dosso, H., Guillaumet, J.L. and Hadley, M. (1981). The Taï Project: land use problems in a tropical rain forest. *Ambio* 10, 120-125.

DRC (1967a). *Étude des sols de la région Sud-Ouest.* Rapport au gouvernement de la République de Côte d'Ivoire. New York: Development and Resources Corporation.

DRC (1967b). *Ressources forestières de la région Sud-Ouest.* Rapport au gouvernement de la République de Côte d'Ivoire. New York: Development and Resources Corporation.

FGU Kronberg (1979). *État actuel des Parcs Nationaux de la Comoé et de Taï, ainsi que de la Réserve d'Azagny et propositions visant à leur développement aux fins de promotion du tourisme* (Tome 3: Parc National de Taï. FGU Kronberg Consulting and Engineering.

Foggie, A. (1957). Forestry problems in the closed forest zone of Ghana. *Journal of the West African Science Association* 3, 131-147.

Guillaumet, J.L., Alexandre, D.Y., Kahn, F. and Namur, Ch. de (1978). Observations sur les premiers stades de la reconstitution de la forêt dense humide (Sud-Ouest de la Côte d'Ivoire). *Cahiers ORSTOM, serie Biologie,* 13, 189-270.

Guillaumet, J.L., Couturier, G. and Dosso, H. (1984). Recherche et aménagement en milieu forestier tropical humide: le Projet Taï de Côte d'Ivoire. *Notes Techniques du MAB* 15.

Guillaumet, J.L. and Couturier, G. (1984). Critiques et perspectives. In *Notes Techniques du MAB* 15, 225-232.

Guppy, N. (1983). The case for an Organization of Timber Exporting Countries (OTEC). In *Tropical rain forests: ecology and management,* ed. S.L. Sutton, et al. Oxford: Blackwell Scientific Publications. Pp. 459-463.

Hallé, F., Oldeman, R.A.A. and Tomlinson, P.B. (1978). *Tropical trees and forests. An architectural analysis.* Berlin: Springer Verlag.

Hallé, F., and Ng, F.S.P. (1981). Crown construction in mature dipterocarp trees. *Malayan Forester* 44, 222-233.

Huttel, Ch. and Bernhard-Reversat, F. (1975). Recherches sur l'écosystème de la forêt subéquatoriale de basse Côte d'Ivoire. V. Biomasse végétale, productivité primaire et cycle de la matière organique. *Terre et la Vie* 29, 203-228.

Kio, P.R.O. (1983). Management potential of the tropical high forest with special reference to Nigeria. In *Tropical rain forests: ecology and management,* ed. S.L. Sutton et al. Oxford: Blackwell Scientific Publications. Pp. 445-455.

Lena, Ph. (1984). Le développement des activités humaines. *Notes Techniques du MAB* 15, 59-112.

Leslie, A. (1977). Where contradictory theory and practice co-exist. *Unasylva* 29(115), 2-17.

Lorougnon Guédé, J. (1976). Le Projet de la forêt de Taï en Côte d'Ivoire. I. Recherche et développement écologiques. *Nature et Resources* 12(2), 2-3.

Mariaux, A. (1981). Past efforts in measuring age and annual growth in tropical trees. In Age and growth rate of tropical trees, ed. F.H. Bormann and G. Berlyn. *Yale University Bulletin* 94, 20-30.

Okali, D.U.U. (1982). Africa: research to conserve the environment. *Unasylva* 34(136), 2-7.

Oldeman, R.A.A. (1978). Architecture and energy exchange of dicotyledonous trees in the forest. In *Tropical trees as living systems,* ed. P.B. Tomlinson and M.H. Zimmermann. Cambridge: Cambridge University Press. Pp. 535-560.

Oldeman, R.A.A. and Vooren, A.P. (1980). Sylviculture durable et coupes sélectives en basse Côte d'Ivoire. Wageningen: Agricultural University.

Smith, J.H.G. (1963). Analysis of crown development can establish biological and economic limits to growth of trees and stands. *Commonwealth Forestry Review* 42, 27-33.

Synnott, T.J. and Kemp, R.H. (1976). Choosing the best silvicultural system. *Unasylva* 28(112/113), 74-79.

UNESCO (1977). Human settlements and socio-cultural environment. 4. Taï Project (Report no. SS-77/WS/15). Paris.

Vooren, A.P. (1979). La voûte forestière et sa régéneration (Thèse). Wageningen: Agricultural University.

Vooren, A.P. and Offermans, D.M.J. (1985). An ultralight aircraft for low-cost, large-scale stereoscopic-aerial photographs. *Biotropica* 17, 84-88.

Wadsworth, F.H. (1983). Production of usable wood from tropical forests. In Tropical rain forest ecosystems, structure and function. In *Ecosystems of the world* 14A, ed. F.B. Goley. Amsterdam: Elsevier Scientific Publications. Pp. 279-288.

Whittaker, R.H. and Woodwell, G.M. (1971). Measurement of net primary production of forests. In *Productivity of forest ecosystems,* ed. P. Duvignaud. Paris: UNESCO. Pp. 159-175.

Author's address: A.P. Vooren, Agricultural University, Department of Silviculture and Forest Ecology, P.O. Box 342, 6700 AH Wageningen, The Netherlands.

# Planning for rational use of tropical forest land - the case of the Kali Konto upper watershed, Java, Indonesia

by D.C.P. Thalen

## 1. Introduction

*Background*
In 1978 and 1979 teams of Dutch experts visited Indonesia, in response to a request from the Indonesian Government 'for technical co-operation to evolve a plan for forestry as a base for rural community development in one of the catchment areas of the Brantas river basin (East Java)'. The second mission resulted in the Project Kali Konto 'Forestry for rural communities'. In September 1979 the project was officially started, aimed at the following broader objective:

A planning and management model has to be drawn up for a study area on Java as an example for all watersheds in densely populated areas of Indonesia. It should stress on the following priorities:

- improving living conditions of the local people, encouraging self-reliance and maintaining and increasing their standard of living;
- creating sound and stable ecological systems;
- creating a forest system based upon multi-purpose management fitting in the national forest policy.

To meet these broader objectives the following project objective was given:

To draw up a master plan for forestry and agro-forestry for the upper watershed of the Kali Konto in such a way that a proper balance is achieved and can be maintained between the functions of the forest and the needs of the population.

*Approach and execution*
The project has been executed as a joint effort of the Government of Indonesia (originally Perum Perhutani of the Directorate General of Forestry in the Ministry of Agriculture, now in the new structure, the Directorate General of Reforestation and Land Rehabilitation RRL of the Ministry of Forestry) and the Government of The Netherlands (Directorate General of International Co-operation).

The first phase included an inventory of the project area, in particular the forest land, but also incorporating an analysis of the land-use patterns in the cultivated village lands in the lower reaches of the catchment area. A socio-economic inventory was started and the history of land use in the upper watershed was studied. The preliminary results of this inventory can be found in the Inception Report (PKK, 1982a).

It was soon realized that in the planning procedure the man-land relations in the entire upper watershed had to be incorporated. It was then decided to produce three documents as a basis for the masterplan:

- a land evaluation of the forest land;
- a study of the actual and potential land use of the (cultivated) village land;
- a study of the socio-economic situation.

This was later supplemented by a survey of the soils and soil conditions carried out by the Universitas Brawijaya in Malang. Moreover, in the first and second phases of the project agro-forestry trials were done on a pilot scale.

In the present report the emphasis is on the land evaluation study of the forest land.

*Present status, documentation*
In 1985 the second phase of the project was completed with the presentation of the General Watershed Plan (PKK, 1985). In 1986 the third phase has started with implementation, training and (at a limited scale) supplementary studies as the key issues.

The results of the Kali Konto project have been laid down in a number of reports and a few published papers, included in the list of references attached to this paper (PKK, 1982a, b; 1984a, b; 1985). More detailed information on the land evaluation of the forest land can be found in RIN (1985) and Thalen and Smiet (1984, 1985). The data presented in this paper and parts of the explanatory text have been taken from these sources.

## 2. Study area

*Land and land use in the Kali Konto upper watershed*

The area of approximately 223 $km^2$ covered by the Kali Konto Project is situated in the Kabupaten Malang in East Java, some 90 km south of Surabaya, 20 km north-west of Malang, and comprises the upper watershed of the river Kali Konto, a tributary of the Brantas which drains most of East Java. This upland plateau is surrounded by steep mountain slopes ranging in altitude from 620 m to 2,800 m above sea-level. The project boundaries are determined by the crests of the mountain ridges.

The area has a seasonally distributed rainfall with June to September as the driest months (on average less than 100 mm rainfall monthly) and November to April as the wet months (more than 200 mm), the other months having an intermediate precipitation. Due to the topographical variation climatic conditions show considerable variation, so far poorly documented. The general pattern is that slopes with a northern and eastern aspect are drier than the slopes oriented towards the other directions. Stowage rainfall occurs under the influence of southeastern winds in the dry season. The higher parts of the area have a less pronounced dry season with rainfall more equally distributed over the year. Temperature decreases proportionally with altitude, some 0.6°C per 100 m rise.

The geological formations in the project area are typical for inland Java, comprising several volcanic complexes of recent geological origin. Of the four complexes (Kelud, Kawa and Butak, Dorowati/Andjasmoro, and Luksongo), the Kelud is still active. More than ten major eruptions have been recorded in the past 200 years, the last one in 1966. Geomorphologically, five major land-form groups can be distinguished, viz.:

- valleys;
- intervolcanic plateaux;
- foothill slope areas;
- hilly areas;
- volcanic mountain areas.

Hydrological data on the area are scarce. A study is proposed. Three rivers, Kali Pinjal (catchment 43 $km^2$), Kali Konto (catchment 137 $km^2$), and Kali Kwayangan (catchment 52 $km^2$) feed an artificial storage lake, which came into existence in 1970 after completion of the Selorejo dam. A total of 131 wells and 43 tributaries were counted but no recent discharge figures are available. In the Kali Konto the flow can increase from about 2 $m^3 sec^{-1}$ to 100 $m^3 sec^{-1}$ in a few hours only. Sedimentation in the Selorejo reservoir is fast, and estimated 250,000 $m^3$ annually. It has been calculated that in the village lands of the project area an average 3 mm of top soil erodes away annually.

The soils of the area, clearly associated with the volcanic nature of this region, are mainly andosols and cambisols. Soil depth varies from a few centimeters on the upper mountain ridges to deposits of hundreds of meters in the Kali Konto valley. In some areas the soils are highly susceptible to erosion. Gully erosion, sheet erosion, and landslides occur widely, especially in the agricultural area and on disturbed steep slopes in the forest lands (PKK, 1984b).

About 92,000 people live in the project area, about equally distributed over the two subdistricts Pujon and Ngantang. Agriculture and animal husbandry are the main means of subsistence, practised on the 34 per cent of privately owned land (see Table 11 and PKK, 1984a). The remaining 66 per cent is the state forest land discussed below and managed by Perum Perhutani. The village lands are located mainly on the relatively flat and accessible plains and valleys along the rivers. The forest land is situated higher on the surrounding mountain slopes, which are relatively steep and inaccessible.

*The forest land and its utilization*

General

Intensive field surveys supplemented by information derived from aerial photo interpretation enabled the project staff to analyse the forest land vegetation in all its complexity. This complexity is the result of centuries-long developmental history and is further determined by such natural factors as altitude, topography, (micro-)climate, and volcanic eruptions. In the last hundred years human influence became another significant factor influencing vegetation structure and composition. In the second half of the last century large stretches of natural forest were cleared and turned into coffee plantations, which were again abandoned when infectious diseases affected the crop early this century. The abandoned coffee gardens were replanted with the aim to restore the protective functions of the forest. Although the forest land was managed as a protection forest throughout this century, management could not prevent utilization of the forest through illegal cutting of timber, fuelwood and fodder.

The present state of the forest reflects above all the impact of past and current utilization. An initial division of the forest land can be made on a purely functional basis: the distinction between *natural forest* with primarily protection functions (12,975 ha) and *plantation forest* with primarily a production function (2,465 ha). By plotting a 20 per cent crown cover line on an orthophotomosaic the natural forest area was again divided into scrub (with a crown cover of less than 20 per cent) and montane high forest (with a crown cover of more than 20 per cent). This division was based on the vegetation physiognomy as visible on aerial photos.

### The natural forest

Natural forest data were processed along two main lines. In the first place the data of 936 sample plots yielded mensuration data (basal area, volume), vegetation types and ecological species groups, distinguished and classified by a computer programme. And in the second place, the data for 13 forest transects provided information on vegetation structure and structural processes. In combination these data facilitated a qualitative ecological assessment of the natural forest, not just describing the actual situation, but also appraising the qualities and potentials for different types of utilization. Aerial photo interpretation and field data from various parts of the forest land permitted the delineation of vegetation types on a vegetation map and a quantitative description of the vegetation. The following floristic types were distinguished:

- Casuarina forest:
  The *Casuarina junghuhniana* forest is essentially a fire climax vegetation developed through centuries of dry-season fires.
- Engelhardia forest:
  This forest is dominated by *Engelhardia spicata*, which locally occurs in pure stands. Essentially the Engelhardia forest is a transi-

Table 11 Areas under the major land use types in the village land of the Kali Konto Project area.

| Major land use | Area (ha) | Percentage of area of village land | Percentage of area of project area |
|---|---|---|---|
| dry-land agriculture | 4,540 | 57.6 | 19.5 |
| irrigated agriculture | 1,794 | 22.7 | 7.7 |
| village area and home yards | 1,268 | 16.1 | 5.4 |
| miscellaneous | 284 | 3.6 | 1.2 |
| total village land | 7,886 | 100.0 | 33.8 |

Source: Thalen, 1987.

tion vegetation between Casuarina forest and the Fago-Myrtaceous forest.

- Fago-Myrtaceous forest:
  This forest type is characterized by tree species of the Fagaceae (e.g. *Lithocarpus* spp.) and the Myrtaceae (e.g. *Eugenia* spp.). It probably represents the natural climax vegetation for most of the project area. Twenty to thirty tree species commonly occur in forests of this type, but dominance of certain species sometimes occurs and several subtypes of the Fago-Myrtaceous forest can be recognized.
- Euphorbi-Urticaceous forest:
  Species of Euphorbiaceae and Urticaceae dominate in this forest type. The structure ranges from closed dense to open light forest and scrub with isolated trees of large dimensions (usually *Ficus* spp.). The type is the result of prolonged exposure to exploitation. The shrubs *Eupatorium inulifolium* and *Lantana camara* form extensive thickets.

Large differences in forest structure occur in the forest land. Near the official forest boundary, trees are often absent or occur in isolated stands. Further away from the boundary the forest is open and light and gradually becomes more dense at high altitudes and in inaccessible places far away from the village land. Many gaps occur in the forest, ranging in size from a few hundred square metres to several hectares.

Throughout the area, evidence was found of past and recent utilization of the forest by man, such as saw-pits and tree stumps with traces of cutting or sawing. Especially species with good-quality timber had been cut. Past and current human utilization appeared to be the determining factor for the great structural variations encountered in the forest land. In the Kali Konto project area, this long-term and large-scale exposure to human utilization of the forest land is leading to accelerated degradation of the forest vegetation. This degradation process was quantitatively described in terms of a reduction in basal area, volume and canopy closure. Various stages of degradation, indicated by the letter A to E, could be clearly recognized from the transect sample data. To some extent, degradation stages and vegetation types overlap. The Euphorbi-Urticaceous forest, for example, always falls within the most degraded stage E, because the original Fago-Myrtaceous forest has been degraded to such a degree that the species composition has drastically altered, resulting in a totally different vegetation

Table 12 Areas of forest land under different vegetation types and by stage of degradation.

| Vegetation type | Stage of degradation | Area (ha) | Percentage of total forest land | Remarks |
|---|---|---|---|---|
| Plantations | – | 2,465 | 16.0 | – |
| Euphorbi-Urticaceous | E | 6,328 | 41.0 | scrub |
| Casuarina | F | 1,026 | 6.7 | montane high forest (6,647 ha) |
| Engelhardia | G | 51 | 0.3 | |
| Fago-Myrtaceous | D | 2,939 | 19.0 | |
| ,, | C | 1,683 | 10.9 | |
| ,, | B | 603 | 3.9 | |
| ,, | A | 312 | 2.0 | |
| Elphin | – | 33 | 0.2 | |
| Total | | 15,440 | 100.0 | |

Source: Thalen, 1987.

type. Stages B, C and D also reflect stages of Fago-Myrtaceous forest degradation, but here the degradation process has not yet altered species composition, although it has significantly changed the forest structure and relative species abundance. Table 12 summarizes the findings.

The general state of the natural forest ca ben illustrated by a few figures on volume data. Although some parts of the forest land carry good forest with a total wood volume of 600 $m^3$ $ha^{-1}$, the average volume for the montane high forest (6,647 ha) is only 230 $m^3$ $ha^{-1}$ (864 plots) and the average total volume in the scrub area (6,328 ha) is as low as 87 $m^3$ $ha^{-1}$ (72 plots). Allowing for increment, the net rate of volume reduction appears to be so high (between 4 and 7 $m^3$ $ha^{-1}y^{-1}$, in total approximately 40,000 $m^3$ annually), that it may be feared that the average volume of the montane high forest will be less than 100 $m^3$ $ha^{-1}$ in about 25 years. This means that if present trends persist, the entire natural forest area will have been turned into scrub by the end of the century.

The plantations

Plantations in the Kali Konto area were laid out on land that was formerly planted with coffee. Some abandoned plantations developed into scrub. The present plantation area of 2,465 ha is spread out across the entire forest land and consists of numerous lots ranging in size from a few hundred square metres to a few hundred hectares of adjacent plantations. Most of the plantation lots are situated along the forest boundary on relatively accessible, gently sloping grounds. The plantation lots are very heterogeneous, differing in size, species composition, age, and basal area ratio. Mixtures of tree species can be found on the same ground, for example *Eucalyptus*, *Pinus* and *Calliandra*. The oldest plantation is more than 40 years old, but most plantations are much younger. Table 13 gives the areas covered by the seven most important species.

Low basal areas were recorded in many plantations, especially for *Agathis loranthifolia*, but also for *Eucalyptus* spp. and *Swietenia* spp. Improvement of nursing, planting and tending techniques together with the prevention of non-prescribed cutting, can certainly lead to increases in basal area ratios and, ultimately, in yield. Furthermore, a large part of the forest land has the potential to support forest plantations and current utilization is far below its capacity. One of the results of the study

Table 13 Areas of important plantation species in the forest land.

| Species | Local name | Area | |
|---|---|---|---|
| | | ha | % |
| *Pinus merkusii* | pinus | 747 | 30 |
| *Agathis loranthifolia* | damar | 285 | 12 |
| *Swietenia* spp. | mahoni | 258 | 10 |
| *Eucalyptus* spp. | eucalyptus | 219 | 9 |
| *Maesopsis eminii* | maesopsis | 192 | 8 |
| *Anthocephalus cadamba* | jabon | 123 | 5 |
| *Calliandra calothyrsus* | calliandra | 514 | 21 |
| others* | | 127 | 5 |
| Total | | 2,465 | 100 |

* *Trema orientalis, Michelia velutina, Acacia decurrens.*

Source: Thalen, 1987.

was the identification and localization of areas suitable for different types of plantations.

In general, projections for product output (see Table 14) show a continued discrepancy between the need for fuelwood and light timber (respectively 120,000 $m^3$ and 20,000 $m^3$ annually) and the yields from the plantation area (respectively 21,290 $m^3$ and 7,540 $m^3$ annually for the next 5 years).

## 3. Planning for improved land use: the land evaluation

*Procedure*
The land evaluation procedure, applied to forestry, has been discussed in detail elsewhere, e.g. Laban (1981) and FAO (1984) and by Van Goor in this volume. The reader is referred to these sources. The standard method was followed after 155 land mapping units had been identified and 13 land utilization types described (see below).

*Land mapping units (LMUs)*
The 155 LMUs were delineated mainly on the basis of terrain characteristics. An initial division of the forest land yielded five major landscape types, which were later subdivided according to landforms as follows (number of hectares given between parentheses):

Valleys:
  Colluvial valleys (472) and Lahar valleys (222); 16 LMUs in all.

Intervolcanic plateaux:
  Upper plateaux (59), middle plateaux (48), lower plateaux (163), deep valleys with steep sides (653) and dissected plateaux remnants (568); 20 LMUs in all.

Foothill slope areas:
  Gently sloping (249), undulating (510) and moderately steep (449); 28 LMUs in all.

Hilly areas:
  Moderately steep (2,007), steep (181), very steep (4,092), extremely steep (837), old cone remnants (78) and hill spurs (298); 53 LMUs in all.

Volcanic mountain areas:
  Moderately steep (264), steep (448), very steep (510), extremely steep (2,351) and extremely steep with landslides (981); 38 LMUs in all.

Each of the LMUs was described in detail, giving information on: location, major landscape, landform, soil type, elevation, slope-class distribution, total area, vegetation (in detail), erosion hazard (in four classes) and external and internal accessibility (for access by foot and by vehicle separately).

Table 14 Projections of total yields of forest plantations by 5-year period based on current stocking and management (2,465 ha). Source: Thalen, 1987.

| Product | 1983-1987 | 1988-1992 | 1993-1997 | 1998-2002 | 2003-2007 | Total 25-year |
|---|---|---|---|---|---|---|
| | | | cubic meters | | | |
| Fuelwood | 106,471 | 84,302 | 81,616 | 89,425 | 85,290 | 447,104 |
| Poles | 8,726 | 6,619 | 6,134 | 4,281 | 6,801 | 32,561 |
| Light saw-timber* | 37,713 | 48,577 | 41,029 | 9,832 | 30,068 | 167,225 |
| Heavy saw-timber/ veneer* | 561 | 0 | 0 | 6,447 | 6,321 | 13,329 |
| Pulpwood | 31,766 | 23,126 | 47,719 | 73,246 | 89,553 | 265,404 |
| Total | 185,237 | 162,624 | 176,498 | 183,231 | 218,033 | 925,623 |

* Including fuelwood or pulpwood obtained by sawing light and heavy saw-timber (40–50% of total $m^3$ delivered at the saw-mill).

*Land utilization types (LUTs)*
Relevant types of land use for the Kali Konto forest land study area are LUTs, related to forestry only. Thirteen (Appendix 3) were described in detail. Some of these were subdivided according to different technology levels. The LUTs can be distinguished on the basis of their objectives: conservation, production, or a combination of these two, with recreation as a separate category, but also on the basis of the technology level required, or on the input of labour. Only relevant land-use options were taken into consideration.

*The criteria*
The following criteria were used in the matching procedure:

External accessibility by foot or vehicle, determined directly by aerial photo interpretation and from field information, mainly on the basis of distance and slopes, footpaths and roads.

Vegetation, taking into account the degradation stages, the presence of plantation forest, etc. The following assumptions were made:
- wherever the present vegetation is plantation forest, this implies 'not suitable' for any of the natural forest LUTs (nrs. 1 – 5);
- the present vegetation is not relevant as a quality for any of the plantation LUTs (nrs. 6 – 12).

Slope class as the integrating land characteristic for two qualities, i.e. internal accessibility and erosion hazard. Two land qualities were disregarded, i.e. soil fertility and moisture availability, because:
- they were considered relatively irrelevant compared with the qualities already incorporated, being rather uniform for the forest land area and not limiting for the forest LUTs considered;
- no detailed information on these qualities was available.

After the requirements of each LUT had been checked against the qualities of the LMU, a final suitability rating $S_1$, $S_2$, $S_3$, or NS could be assigned to each slope class within the LMU. Where several vegetation degradation stages occurred within one LMU it was assumed that the most degraded stages occurred on the least steep slopes. Compared with the natural forest vegetation types, plantation forest was assumed to occur in the most accessible parts of a LMU.

*Results*
The number of hectares in each suitability class added for all LMUs per LUT results in an overall picture showing the hectarage of the study area assigned to each of the four suitability classes (Table 15). The major conclusions that could be derived from this table in combination with the suitability maps were as follows:

Of the total forest land area of 15,440 ha, 54 per cent (8,385 ha) is suitable ($S_1$ or $S_2$) for forest plantations in one form or another. A comparison of suitability maps with the vegetation map showed that virtually the entire present scrub area is suitable for plantation forest.

The scope for exploitation of remaining natural forest (LUTs 4 and 5) is very limited. Only some 10 per cent (1,523 ha) of the total forest land area can be regarded suitable ($S_1$or $S_2$).

The areas suitable ($S_1$ and $S_2$) for the natural forest 'conservation' (LUTs 1, 2, and 3) are not suitable ($S_3$ and NS) for any of the 'exploitation' LUTs. The two types of LUTs (conservation *vs* exploitation) have contradicting requirements, e.g. as related to slope and external accessibility.

*Management models and quantified policy options*
In the present study the LUTs were 'translated' in one or more management models, specifying quantitatively produce, labour input, and proceeds with projections over a range of years, assuming sound silvicultural practices (e.g. no illegal exploitation). It will be clear that calculations could only be carried out for those aspects that allow quantification in terms of money or otherwise. For the calculation systems applied, standards were set for the inputs and outputs used and for the assumptions regarding labour, specifications of products, cost factors in relation to slope angle, costs of forest activities, etc.

For some utilization types more than one management model was quantified. This is based on the assumption that for these types several relevant

Table 15 Suitability ratings for 155 land mapping units covering the total forest land area of 15,440 ha. Figures are the numbers of ha in each suitability class.

| Land utilization type | Technology* | Suitability class** | | | |
|---|---|---|---|---|---|
| | | $S_1$ | $S_2$ | $S_3$ | NS |
| Strict protection forest | trad. | 313 | 592 | 1,506 | 13,029 |
| Natural water-conservation forest | trad. | 934 | 4,211 | 1,073 | 9,222 |
| Natural soil-conservation forest | trad. | 2,371 | 6,415 | 2,564 | 4,090 |
| Natural production-forest under extensive management | a. trad. | 867 | 656 | 1,418 | 12,499 |
| | b. semi-trad. | 408 | 479 | 610 | 13,943 |
| | c. advanced | 39 | 0 | 0 | 15,401 |
| Natural production-forest under intensive management | a. trad. | 469 | 194 | 431 | 14,346 |
| | b. semi-trad. | 269 | 200 | 194 | 14,777 |
| | c. semi-adv. | 0 | 0 | 0 | 15,440 |
| | d. advanced | 0 | 0 | 0 | 15,440 |
| Timber and veneer plantations | a. trad. | 5,598 | 2,787 | 3,119 | 3,936 |
| | b. semi-trad. | 2,593 | 2,341 | 2,485 | 8,021 |
| | c. semi-adv. | 1,749 | 1,383 | 0 | 12,308 |
| Pulpwood plantations | a. semi-trad. | 2,593 | 2,341 | 2,485 | 8,021 |
| | b. semi-adv. | 1,749 | 1,383 | 0 | 12,308 |
| Fuelwood plantations | trad. | 5,598 | 2,787 | 3,119 | 3,936 |
| Bamboo plantations | trad. | 5,082 | 2,541 | 2,619 | 5,198 |
| Village fuel and timber plantations | trad. | 5,598 | 2,787 | 3,119 | 3,936 |
| Agroforestry plantations | trad. | 2,646 | 2,447 | 2,548 | 7,799 |
| Soil conservation plantations | trad. | 1,287 | 5,903 | 5,759 | 2,500 |
| Recreation forest | trad. | 1,813 | 1,630 | 1,123 | 10,874 |

* Technology can be traditional, semi-traditional, semi-advanced or advanced.

** Suitability classes: $S_1$ highly suitable; $S_2$ suitable; $S_3$ marginally suitable; NS not suitable.

Source: Thalen, 1987.

technologies and/or rotation periods can be distinguished.

LUT requirements vary greatly per slope class, influencing the proceeds and labour input. The proceeds and labour input were therefore calculated separately for three slope classes. Details on the calculations related to the management models can be found in RIN (1985). With the area suitable for particular LUTs and a quantification of these LUTs through the management models (in terms of produce, labour input and proceeds), the quantitative picture of certain land-use policy options can be worked out. Such 'policy options' are land-use alternatives for the area as a whole defined through a combination of the relevant most suitable LUTs and in our study quantified through the management models of these LUTs.

In the Kali Konto study several policy options have been worked out:

- *present land use*, a combination of LUTs and management models simulating as closely as possible the present use pattern, be it under sound silvicultural management;
- three *extreme policy options*, conservation orientated, financial return orientated, and population orientated;
- three *integrated policy options*, using elements from each of the extreme options mentioned above.

It must be emphasized that as far as financial analysis is involved, such analysis only could take into account the direct quantifiable costs and benefits. The indirect costs and benefits, e.g. related to the protective functions of forest which are difficult or impossible to quantify but nevertheless of great importance, had to be left out in this study.

The results, shown in Table 16, clearly demonstrate that the potential of the forest land leaves enough flexibility for the decision makers to choose an acceptable compromise, meeting at the same time the demands of the local population in terms of fuelwood and timber, the requirements for proper conservation of soil and water and leaving intact the yet remaining natural montane high forest.

## 4. Concluding remarks

The basic data, procedure and results presented above in a summarized description have only been part of the input in the General Watershed Plan for the upper watershed of the Kali Konto. Other inputs, related to the situation of the village lands and the socio-economic conditions were also used (see 1). The forest lands study as presented above was in a later phase further refined and a clear picture of alternatives was offered to Perum Perhutani. A choice was made and reforestation and other forest land management measures will be part of the third phase of the Kali Konto project (PKK, 1985).

The material presented clearly shows the scope for the general methodological approach that was followed. In a modified and adapted form as dictated by the conditions (and as already shown in the General Watershed Plan) it seems a suitable tool for rational forest land-use planning in a variety of situations. This has been recognized by the Indonesian government and is reflected in the important training component of the third phase.

Table 16 Summary of the produce, labour input and direct benefits for various land-use policy options.

| Policy options | LUTs* | Annual production ($10^3$ $m^3$ $yr^{-1}$) | | | | | Labour input | Direct benefits, |
|---|---|---|---|---|---|---|---|---|
| | | fuel-wood | poles | pulp-wood | light timber | heavy timber | (man-year) | NPW** $10^6$ Rp $yr^{-1}$ |
| *Present land use* | 2,3,6,7,8 | 20.5 | 3.8 | 12.8 | 13.4 | 0.0 | 462 | − 21.4 |
| *Extreme use* | | | | | | | | |
| Conservation orientated | 2,3,6a | 25.3 | 18.6 | 0.0 | 52.6 | 24.0 | 975 | + 21.5 |
| Financial return | 4a,5b, 6a,7a | 29.8 | 15.4 | 42.8 | 61.3 | 2.9 | 1,647 | + 543.5 |
| Population orientated | 2,3,6, 8,11 | 181.9 | 7.3 | 0.0 | 25.9 | 0.0 | 2,668 | − 16.9 |
| *Integrated use* | | | | | | | | |
| Fuelwood and timber | 2,3,6a, 8,11 | 110.3 | 5.5 | 4.8 | 32.7 | 0.0 | 1,665 | + 172.5 |
| Heavy timber | 2,3,6a, 8,11 | 85.3 | 11.9 | 0.0 | 37.8 | 10.7 | 1,454 | + 270.0 |
| Pulpwood | 2,3,6a, 7a,8 | 98.8 | 6.4 | 29.4 | 22.2 | 3.6 | 1,446 | + 133.7 |

* See Table 15. Although LUTs may be the same for certain policy options, the management models used to calculate the quantitative data may differ.

** NPW = Net Present Worth in rupiahs (Rp), US $ 1.00 equals appr. Rp 1,100.

Source: Thalen, 1987.

**REFERENCES**


FAO (1984). Land evaluation for forestry. *Forestry Paper* 48.

Laban, P., ed. (1981). Proceedings of the Workshop Land Evaluation for Forestry. *ILRI Publication* 28.

PKK (1982a). The Kali Konto upper watershed in East Java: the state of the forest land and its meaning for the rural population under the prevailing socio-economic conditions (Project Kali Konto, Inception Report). Malang.

PKK (1982b). *Manual Servei Vegetasi* 1-5. Malang.

PKK (1984a). Evaluation of village land, Kali Konto upper watershed, East Java (Project Kali Konto Report). Malang.

PKK (1984b). Soils and soil conditions, Kali Konto upper watershed, East Java (Project Kali Konto, Final Document). Malang.

PKK (1985). General Watershed Plan for the Kali Konto upper watershed (Project Kali Konto, Final Report 2nd phase). Malang.

RIN (1985). Evaluation of Forest Land, Kali Konto upper Watershed, East Java, 1-4 + maps. Leersum: Research Institute for Nature Management.

Thalen, D.C.P. and Smiet, A.C. (1984). Evaluation of forest land for watershed management in East Java, Indonesia. In *Annual Report 1983*. Leersum: Research Institute for Nature Management. Pp. 87-108.

Thalen, D.C.P. and Smiet, A.C. (1985). Quantified land use policy options in forest land evaluation for watershed management. *Netherlands Journal of Agricultural Science* 33, 89-103.



Author's address: Dr. D. C. P. Thalen, Research Institute for Nature Management, P.O. Box 46, 3956 ZR Leersum, The Netherlands.

# Appendix 3. Description of land utilization types Kali Konto project

## A. LUT: strict protection forest

*Objective*
Conservation of natural montane high forest as a gene pool and for scientific and educational purposes. Especially remnants of relatively undisturbed montane high forest have high values in these aspects.

*Produce*
Main benefits are conservation of species and facilities for scientific training, research and education. Additional produce/benefits: medicinal plants, soil and water conservation.

*Requirements*
Physical

Relatively undisturbed vegetation types with sufficient area (human interference on basal area <5 $m^2$ $ha^{-1}$. Location of vegetation type. Minimum area 50-100 ha per vegetation type. Description of vegetation type (basal area of trees, composition of flora and fauna, diameter distribution of tree species, regeneration of tree species, etc.). Food/water-shelter for fauna components. Guaranteed stable ground water and climate.

Non-physical

Labour input is low. Capital investment per ha is low and restricted to establishment of permanent observation plots to monitor vegetation development. Aerial photographs may provide additional information. Fire protection (Casuarina forest) may need investment in communication, training and handtools. Technology required is traditional. Management level is medium. Management measures are protection against disturbing, fire and poaching, establishment of permanent observation plots, regular surveying, monitoring vegetation development (preferable with recent aerial photographs), training and education.

## B. LUT: natural water conservation forest

*Objective*
Establishment and maintenance of a continuous supply of water, which can be relied upon for both agricultural and household purposes. It is probable that further reduction of the montane high forests will result in water shortage during the dry season. Locally there is already water shortage in the upper watershed.

*Produce*
Main produce is a continuous supply of good quality water to villages and agricultural land without damage to land and roads. Additional produce/benefits: soil conservation, fuelwood and timber.

*Requirements*
Physical

Balanced distribution of forest per subwatershed, preferably consisting of native deciduous trees. Minimum total forest area is the existing area of natural forest (the impression was gained that supply of water during the dry season is becoming critical). Information per subwatershed about shortage (dry season) or excess of water (rainy season). Data on outflow of water in $m^3$ $ha^{-1}$ of forest per subwatershed at the forest boundary.

Non-physical

Labour input is low. Capital investment per ha is moderate and mainly restricted to rainfall and flow recorders and the establishment of permanent observation plots. Aerial photographs may provide additional information. Required technology can be semi-traditional (hand recording of rainfall and flow), semi-advanced (mechanical recording), or advanced (fully automatic recording and data transmission, flood-control dams). Management level is medium. Management requires experience in water conservation and monitoring forest development (permanent observation plots). Management measures to be taken: preservation of crown cover and root systems, prevent soil erosion, prevent surface run-off, prevent fire (Casuarina forest), protect against overcutting, monitor the vegetation development (aerial photographs will give additional information), monitor rainfall in the forest area, monitor outflow of water at the forest boundary.

## C. LUT: natural production forest: extensive* management

*Objective*
Production of saw-timber and additional fuelwood/charcoal (not exceeding the average annual increment). The physiognomy of natural forest must be conserved. Generally only small-scale operations with a (semi-)traditional technology. In the absence of other acceptable alternatives the local need for timber and fuelwood/charcoal may require the harvest of at the most the average annual increment of these forests.

*Produce*
Main produce is timber, fuelwood and charcoal at a low production level (2-5 $m^3$ $ha^{-1}$ $y^{-1}$). Additional produce and benefits are water and soil conservation, raw material for small-scale local industries, bark for medicinal use (quinine).

*Requirements*
Physical

Information about values of basal area, expected basal area increment, optimal basal area. Species composition and expected natural development. Natural regeneration of trees per species. Diameter distribution and stocking of trees for dominant and desired species. Volume of desirable species per ha. Total volume per ha. Total number of trees per ha. Increment levels in $m^3$ $ha^{-1}$ $y^{-1}$. Estimated allowable cut in $m^3$ $ha^{-1}$ per product group (fuelwood/charcoal/timber) per forest unit $>5$ ha. Forest units $>$ 5 ha. Slope classes 0-15-50-70-100%. Accessibility to nearest village within 2 to 3 hours walking distance.

Non-physical

Labour input is low. Capital investment is low to moderate, mainly restricted to harvesting equipment, portable saws and communication equipment. Technology is (semi-)traditional. Management level is low to medium. Management measures to be taken: monitor forest development (vegetation surveys, permanent observation plots, aerial photographs), prevent non-prescribed cutting and fire, plan silvicultural treatment (individual trees to be harvested, natural regeneration, enrichment planting), develop knowledge on harvesting and conservation methods (chain-saw, portable saw-mill, charcoal making), train personnel.

## D. LUT: fuelwood plantations

*Objective*
Optimum production ($m^3$ $ha^{-1}$ $y^{-1}$) of fuelwood under sustained-yield principles at the lowest possible costs. Establishment and management on basis of a sustained yield of a substantial amount of fuelwood plantations will improve in the short term the fuelwood situation in the project area. In consequence of this, illegal cutting of fuelwood in other plantations could be prevented as much as possible. The employment input of fuelwood plantations is considerably higher compared to the LUTs for other forest plantations.

*Produce*
Species: *Acacia decurrens*, *Calliandra calothyrsus*, *Eucalyptus* spp. A large amount of fuelwood must be collected for household consumption (cooking

* The terms extensive and intensive management are in this context related to the amount of produce, irrespective of the available capital, manpower, etc.

and heating during cold nights). The amount of fuelwood needed for industrial purposes is comparatively small (brick and tile manufacturing). Especially species which are easy to handle (straight poles in small dimensions) and with a high caloric value are suitable. In particular during the dry season a substantial amount of fodder can be collected from fuelwood plantations. The first year after establishment in *Calliandra* plantations a medium production level (10-15 $m^3$ $ha^{-1}$ $y^{-1}$) is possible. Afterwards a very high production level (25-35 $m^3$ $ha^{-1}y^{-1}$) can be reached. The caloric value of *Calliandra* is 4,500-4,750 kcal per kg; the specific gravity amounts to 0.51-0.78. *Calliandra* grows very quickly; its dense foliage provides a good ground cover. Its extensive and deep root system binds soil, thereby making this species particularly suitable for erosion control on slopes and for rejuvenating degraded soils. By its nitrogen fixation and litter production *Calliandra* improves soil quality and productivity. Because of this, farmers in East Java sometimes rotate agricultural crops with *Calliandra* plantations. Livestock relish the leaves and the plant is a good fodder crop. In Indonesia annual yields of 7-10 tons of dry fodder per ha have been recorded. The seeds of *Calliandra* are palatable. In Indonesia *Calliandra* is planted in strips on state forest land to protect the forest against fire (as well as illegal wood-cutting). Most fuelwood species are suitable for the production of charcoal. In production of charcoal half the wood's energy is wasted. On the other hand charcoal is easier and cheaper to transport and gives a steady and concentrated heat and smokeless burning.

*Requirements*

Physical

Further data on yield should be collected. Possible on slopes up to 70%. In case of yearly clear cutting preferably not on steeper slopes. *Calliandra* can even grow on less fertile and compacted soils. On Java *Calliandra* grows on altitudes between 150 and 1,500 meters above sealevel. Preferably on areas located near villages.

Non-physical

During establishment, especially on slopes, a medium total labour input for site preparation and planting will be required. Once established a medium labour input per ha is needed for harvesting operations and some replanting. Average labour input is medium. Labour can be done by both adult males and females and by older children. Labour income will be proportionally low (500-750 Rp $day^{-1}$). Almost no capital input is required. Average cost level is medium to high. The technology is traditional. Management level can be low or medium. Plantations are easily established by direct seeding or cuttings (usually at the beginning of the wet season). Spacing 2 x 2 m. After one year's growth *Calliandra* can be cut at about 50 cm above the ground. On erodable areas more extensive harvesting operations (instead of clear cutting) or clear cutting in strips could be considered.

## E. LUT: agro-forestry plantations

*Objective*

Establishment and cultivation on a sustained basis of forest plantations with short to medium rotations (10-25 years) together with temporary or permanent crop husbandry and/or fuelwood or bamboo plantations. In agro-forestry an integrated approach is used combining forestry and agriculture for the production of multipurpose woody products and agricultural crops and a better soil protection (compared to most agricultural systems). Agro-forestry can be a suitable system for replanting part of the scrub area and for changing intensive agricultural systems on highly erodable areas into more sustainable land uses.

*Produce*

Depending on the applied agro-forestry system (see under non-physical requirements) and the species used, several product groups can be distinguished: saw-timber, fuelwood (including charcoal) and bamboo at medium to high production levels, together with agricultural crops and fodder. Additional benefits are employment (higher than in pure forest LUTs) and soil conservation/improvement. With respect to soil conservation trees are important for making more nutrients available to agricultural crops, protection of the soil against erosion and improving the physical condition of soils.

Four groups of advantages of agro-forestry over agricultural monocultures can be distinguished:

- ecological advantages: through the several vegetation layers a more efficient use is made of the natural resources. The protective function of the trees decreases the hazards of environmental degradation;
- economic advantages: total production per land unit can be increased by the ecological efficiency of the system. In relation to pure forest plantations, the costs for tree management can be lower;
- socio-economic advantages: labour input is more even throughout the year. By production of various products the risks under unfavourable conditions will be lower. The dependency on the local market situation is lower, because various products are produced and the production can be directed towards self-suffiency and/or marketing;
- psychological advantages: in areas where traditional production methods are non-optimal or non-sustainable, agro-forestry systems can be applied with relatively small changes. For example, when shifting cultivation is applied with too-short fallow periods or when intensive agricultural systems are used on highly erodable areas.

However, depending on the agro-forestry system applied also several constraints or limiting factors can be distinguished:

- ecological constraints: the more intensive form of land use might, especially on marginal soils, cause disturbances in the mineral cycle. Between the various species there can be a strong competition for radiation, moisture and/or nutrients;
- economic constraints: in case of establishment of agro-forestry systems, substantial investment costs might be needed. In areas with a high population pressure, the private land-holding might be too small as viable production unit;
- socio-economic constraints: agro-forestry is a rather complex form of land use; both agricultural and forestry knowledge will be needed, together with knowledge on management planning and the interaction between the forest plantations and the agricultural crops. Compared to pure agricultural systems part of the yields will only be obtained after some time; furthermore, total agricultural yields will be somewhat lower compared to pure agricultural systems. This can cause insufficient management of the trees or worse;
- organizational and scientific constraints: the various phases of preparation and execution of agro-forestry projects need to be well organized and should be combined with sufficient education of the local population and proper forms of their active involvement. Furthermore, there is still a lack of knowledge and few experiences on the establishment and management of specific agro-forestry systems under various conditions.

*Requirements*

Physical

For data required on forest species see fuelwood plantation and other LUTs not described here. For agricultural crops data are required on production level, ground cover throughout the year, use of agricultural waste for fodder, root systems and resprouting capacities. Knowledge is required on competition for radiation, moisture and nutrients between agricultural crops and tree species. On soils with at least a moderate fertility which are not too susceptible to erosion. Possible on slopes up to 30%; for areas with slopes from 15-35% terracing will be required. For steeper slopes (up to 50%) only forest plantations (possibly as part of agro-forestry systems with strips or blocks) or the permanent mixed agro-forestry system (see under non-physical requirements) with shade tolerant agricultural species and a final stocking of the forest stands, depending on site class and species, of at least 75-150 trees per ha. On locations easy to reach for the local population the intensive management requires a good accessibility throughout the year. Depending on the system the minimum area required varies between 0.25 and 1.50 ha.

Non-physical

During establishment the total labour input is medium; when land improvement is necessary (terracing) labour input is high. Capital investment is low. Once established, agro-forestry systems require a medium labour input and a low to moderate capital investment. Depending on ownership starting capital should at least partly be furnished or loaned by the forest authorities. Establishment, maintenance and exploitation of the agricultural crops should be done by the plotholders, together with establishment (partly) and maintenance of the forest plantations. Establishment (partly) and exploitation of the forest plantations should be done by forest service employees. Supervision (intensive) and training in forestry, crop husbandry and soil protection should be done by the forest authorities. A high technical knowledge on different agro-forestry systems is necessary. For the participants a reasonable level of technical knowledge on establishment and maintenance of forest plantations and agricultural cropping is required, together with knowledge on soil conservation and land improvement. For soil conservation activities and exploitation of forest plantations adult males are required. The income position of the participants will be relatively high. The technology can be traditional or semi-traditional (site preparation and exploitation). The management level is medium or high. Surveying (choosing the best location for different species), planning (agro-forestry system to be executed) and execution are intensive. Rotations depend on the system and the tree species chosen. Intensive surveillance is needed to apply the proper cultivation and soil conservation methods.

In general the following agro-forestry systems can be distinguished:

| Trees and agricultural crops | Crop husbandry permanent | temporary |
|---|---|---|
| mixed intimately | a | b |
| divided in strips or bloks | c | d |

*a.* *Permanent intimate mix of forest trees with agricultural crops*
Stocking and crown cover of the tree layer is adapted to the needs of the agricultural species. Stocking of the final forest stand may be reduced to 50-100 trees per ha. Agricultural species must be shade tolerant; tree species with deep root systems and not too dense crowns are suitable. Agricultural crops are allowed for at least one rotation of the forest stand, e.g. maize under *Albizia* spp. On areas not very susceptible to erosion; on slopes $< 15\%$: if steeper, soil conservation measures are required.

*b.* *Temporary intimate mix of forest trees with agricultural crops*
Agricultural crops are allowed during the establishment phase of the forest stand. In general the forest stand is not adapted to the agricultural crops; only the planting distance of the trees can be somewhat wider. Agricultural cropping period up to the closure of the tree canopy; on areas susceptible to erosion preferably a shorter cropping period, e.g. the 'Tumpangsari' system. Depending on slope length and length of cropping period, on slopes up to 30%.

*c.* *Permanent strips or blocks of agricultural crops in forest*
Size of agricultural areas between 0.01 and 0.25 ha. Layout in strips or blocks (checker board). Depending on size and shape of the agricultural areas the influence of the forest stand is limited to intense. Strips preferably along contour lines, e.g. maize in strips between forest plantations. On slopes up to 30%. In case of many larger agricultural areas terracing can be considered. Blocks/strips under permanent forest cover also on steeper slopes (up to 50%).

*d.* *Temporary strips or blocks of agricultural crops in forest*
As c, but in areas more susceptible to erosion, e.g. very long slopes up to 50%, if terraced, e.g. 'Komplangan' or the 'MAMA-system'.

## F. Other LUTs

Other land utilization types, not described here, are:

- natural soil conservation forest;
- natural production forest, intensive management;
- timber and veneer plantation forest;
- pulpwood plantation forest;
- bamboo plantation;
- village fuel and timber plantation;
- soil conservation plantations;
- recreation forest.

* Source Thalen, 1987.